Margaret Fell, Letters, and the Making of Quakerism

Intensely persecuted during the English Interregnum, early Quakers left a detailed record of the suffering they endured for their faith. *Margaret Fell, Letters, and the Making of Quakerism* is the first book to connect the suffering experience with the communication network that drew the faithful together to create a new religious community. This study explores the ways in which early Quaker leaders, particularly Margaret Fell, helped shape a stable organization that allowed for the transition from movement to church to occur. Fell's role was essential to this process because she developed and maintained the epistolary exchange that was the basis of the early religious community. Her efforts allowed for others to travel and spread the faith while she served as nucleus of the community's communication network by determining how and where to share news. Memories of the early years of Quakerism were based on the letters Fell preserved. Marjon Ames analyzes not only how Fell's efforts shaped the inchoate faith, but also how subsequent generations memorialized their founding members.

Marjon Ames teaches at Appalachian State University, USA.

Material Readings in Early Modern Culture

Series editors: James Daybell, Plymouth University, UK, and Adam Smyth, Balliol College, University of Oxford, UK

The series provides a forum for studies that consider the material forms of texts as part of an investigation into the culture of early modern England. The editors invite proposals of a multi- or interdisciplinary nature and particularly welcome proposals that combine archival research with an attention to theoretical models that might illuminate the reading, writing, and making of texts, as well as projects that take innovative approaches to the study of material texts, both in terms of the kinds of primary materials under investigation and in terms of methodologies. What are the questions that have yet to be asked about writing in its various possible embodied forms? Are there varieties of materiality that are critically neglected? How does form mediate and negotiate content? In what ways do the physical features of texts inform how they are read, interpreted, and situated?

Recent in this series:

The Age of Thomas Nashe
Text, Bodies and Trespasses of Authorship in Early Modern England
Edited by Stephen Guy-Bray, Joan Pong Linton, and Steve Mentz

Ovidian Bibliofictions and the Tudor Book
Metamorphosing Classical Heroines in Late Medieval and Renaissance England
Lindsay Ann Reid

Manuscript Miscellanies in Early Modern England
Edited by Joshua Eckhardt and Daniel Starza Smith

Tottel's *Songes* and *Sonettes* in Context
Edited by Stephen Hamrick

The Elizabethan Top Ten
Defining Print Popularity in Early Modern England
Edited by Andy Kesson and Emma Smith

Margaret Fell, Letters, and the Making of Quakerism
Marjon Ames

Margaret Fell, Letters, and the Making of Quakerism

Marjon Ames

LONDON AND NEW YORK

First published 2017 by Routledge

2 Park Square, Milton Park, Abingdon, Oxfordshire OX14 4RN
52 Vanderbilt Avenue, New York, NY 10017

Routledge is an imprint of the Taylor & Francis Group, an informa business

First issued in paperback 2019

Copyright © 2017 Marjon Ames

The right of Marjon Ames to be identified as author of this work has been asserted by her in accordance with sections 77 and 78 of the Copyright, Designs and Patents Act 1988.

All rights reserved. No part of this book may be reprinted or reproduced or utilised in any form or by any electronic, mechanical, or other means, now known or hereafter invented, including photocopying and recording, or in any information storage or retrieval system, without permission in writing from the publishers.

Notice:
Product or corporate names may be trademarks or registered trademarks, and are used only for identification and explanation without intent to infringe.

British Library Cataloguing in Publication Data
A catalogue record for this book is available from the British Library

Library of Congress Cataloging-in-Publication Data

Names: Ames, Marjon, author.
Title: Margaret Fell, letters, and the making of Quakerism / by Marjon Ames.
Description: New York: Routledge, 2016. | Series: Material readings in early modern culture | Includes bibliographical references and index.
Identifiers: LCCN 2016015664
Subjects: LCSH: Fell, Margaret, 1614–1702. | Letter writing—Religious aspects—Christianity. | Society of Friends—History.
Classification: LCC BX7795.F425 A44 2016 | DDC 289.6092—dc23
LC record available at https://lccn.loc.gov/2016015664

ISBN: 978-1-4094-6698-7 (hbk)
ISBN: 978-0-367-34669-0 (pbk)

Typeset in Sabon
by codeMantra

Contents

	Acknowledgments	vii
	Introduction	1
1	The making of Quakerism	8
2	The Quaker letter network	42
3	Margaret Fell reexamined	73
4	Apostolic epistolary influences	93
5	Suffering, prison, and the law in the Quaker tradition	128
6	The afterlife of the movement	151
	Conclusion	178
	Bibliography	181
	Index	191

Acknowledgments

Over the past decade this work has transitioned from thesis to book with the help of many people along the way. First, I must thank my dissertation advisor, Joe Ward, who has provided invaluable guidance over the years, and I cannot thank him enough. Also, thanks to the members of my graduate committee, Jeffrey Watt, Sheila Skemp, and Ivo Kamps, for their helpful criticism throughout the revision process. This project would not have been possible without the remarkable staff at the Friends House Library in London. Working with unpublished letters can be a daunting prospect at best, and the Friends House staff, particularly Josef Keith, whose knowledge of Quaker manuscript sources is unparalleled, provided me with the most amazing archival experience a historian could ask for. I am grateful to the University of Mississippi Graduate School for dissertation and travel fellowships, the Making Publics Project at McGill University funded by Social Sciences and Humanities Research Council of Canada Major Collaborative Research Initiatives, the Andrew W. Mellon Foundation Paleography Seminar at the Folger Shakespeare Library, the Appalachian State University History Department and Belk Library Special Collections for their support during my time as a Rhinehart Postdoctoral Fellow, the Delta State University Women's Studies Forum, and the North Carolina Wesleyan College Teaching and Learning Center's research grant support. I'd also like to thank all of my friends and colleagues who have read drafts, participated in conference panels, and patiently helped me wade through this process. There are far too many people to mention here by name, but I would be seriously remiss if I did not thank Caroline Boswell, Michelle DiMeo, and Sarah Waurechen for all of their help as we navigated through the seventeenth century in our respective studies. This project ultimately found its home with the incredible scholars involved with the Material Readings in Early Modern Culture Series and the Women's Early Modern Letters Online Project. Portions of this text may be found in "Quaker correspondence: religious identity and communication networks in the interregnum Atlantic world" in *Women and Epistolary Agency in Early Modern Culture, 1450–1690*, edited by James Daybell and Andrew Gordon (Routledge, 2016). I am particularly grateful to James Daybell, Adam Smyth, and Erika Gaffney for their support in embracing this project. Most of all I'd like to thank my family for their love and support. Paul and Oscar—this is for you.

Introduction

The Quakers were one of many religious sects to emerge during the English Interregnum, but only one of a few to survive the Restoration. The problem with the traditional Quaker narrative is that it is teleological—it operates with the knowledge of what the church became, that it survived the tumultuous English Interregnum and successfully morphed into a quietist, pacifist religion that while small in size has persisted through the modern centuries. However, during the 1650s when Quakerism came into being, it was not a church, it was an amorphous movement of like-minded people that in the beginning had about as much chance of succeeding as the sects with Harry Potter-esque names like the Muggletonians, Grindletonians, and Fifth Monarchists. The 1650s were chock-full of charismatic, messianic figures who won over hearts or conversely enraged strangers wherever they went. The Quakers were no different. They had the Valiant Sixty or First Publishers of Truth—itinerant ministers who traveled the English countryside and beyond in an effort to spread their message of the inner light, with George Fox, a wild-eyed, unwashed apprentice at the forefront.[1] What the people who would become Quakers had that their contemporaries did not was someone to organize and maintain a communicative structure that enabled their ministers to evangelize. Margaret Fell fulfilled that function for the Quakers.

Fell's role in early Quakerism started with her hospitality to nonconformist missionaries in Lancashire. It continued when she started the process of receiving, copying, and sending off letters to members of the emergent faith, thus allowing the process of sharing experiences and ideas to flourish in the first phase of the church. Margaret Fell's role in Quakerism has always been described as supporter and nurturer, but never as innovator. In the context of the Interregnum, as difficult as it is to pin down, the people called Quakers were bound together by Margaret Fell's efforts to organize the group. George Fox may or may not deserve the title of founder of Quakerism, but undoubtedly his role was contingent on Fell's organization. Therefore he owes his status in the faith to her, rather than she owing her notoriety to him.

Much scholarly attention has focused on the rift between James Nayler and George Fox as the key moment in the creation of a Quaker church, with Fox at the helm.[2] Furthermore, many have discussed Margaret Fell's role as an important supporter and friend to Fox's camp and cause. That argument obfuscates the far more important point of how the Quaker community grew so that a fracture between key itinerants could lead to the creation of a church. I contend that attention should also focus on the time Fox and Nayler were still friends, co-religionists with the same goal for their brethren, when their ideas were unformed, and they both (along with many others) depended on the support of Margaret Fell. Only then can we assess the meaning of the schism and subsequent period when Fox dominated the group.

The stability of the letter network that Fell created and its subsequent organization allowed the Quakers to flourish in the later seventeenth century when their contemporary sectarians did not. This differs from earlier arguments about the Quakers' transition from Interregnum sect to Restoration religion. In *The Experience of Defeat*, Christopher Hill argues that the godly revolution failed once the Restoration occurred. Radical sects that sought to establish a new church and state in the aftermath of the Civil War had their hopes dashed. Most groups did not survive the 1650s because they did not adapt to the changed circumstances of the restored king and Church of England and were able to flourish only in a period of crisis, such as the Interregnum. However, unlike the Fifth Monarchists, Muggletonians, or Grindletonians, the Quakers adapted to their new environment. Hill identifies the Quakers as one of several religious groups altered by the return of Charles II, stating:

> The Society of Friends was something very different after the restoration from the loose body of Quakers that had existed before. Imposing the peace principle meant organizing, distinguishing, purging. ... Reliance on everyone's inner light had to be controlled by a new emphasis on 'the sense of the meeting.' Organization meant exclusion, which necessitated machinery.[3]

According to Hill, by the end of the Interregnum, a transformation within the Quaker sect became apparent, or rather the group shifted away from a dynamic network that emphasized wild expressions of faith, toward a stable institutionalized religious organization more interested in practical matters that allowed for the church to move forward. Hill notes that prior to the Restoration, the Quakers' *raison d'être* was "absence of central control."[4] After 1660, Fox was clearly the leader, and their original purpose fell away. Hill attributes this change, in part, to the deaths of so many of the early leaders during the Interregnum or shortly after the Restoration, thus allowing Fox to consolidate power under himself.[5]

While there is much to agree with in Hill's thesis, this current book argues that Fox's position of authority started to develop as early as 1656 with Nayler's fall and that Fell claims a much larger place than Hill's interpretation allows. We cannot underestimate the importance of this event, or Fox's clever use of factionalism to his benefit. Furthermore, Hill largely leaves Fell out of his narrative. This Quaker watershed would not have been possible without her efforts. Fox would never have become the "founder of Quakerism" if Fell had not established the foundation for his work. From 1652 forward, Quakers communicated in such a way that all principle players—not just Fox, Fell, and Nayler—were aware of their brethren's successes and failures in their efforts to convert godly folk to their fold. They knew about one another's movements and the suffering they endured. From at least 1653, Fell encouraged Fox to regulate how information flowed throughout the community by censoring those who appeared out of line with the group's greater message and providing some oversight of future itinerancy. This process was only partially successful in the middle years of 1652–1656, but when Nayler threatened the success of the movement at large, Fox was able to consolidate authority. The largely untold story is Fell's role in making that happen.

Prior to Fell's involvement, the Quakers looked like a lot of other sects of the era—they included small bands of itinerant preachers and their followers. Dissidents from the north of England wandered around the countryside seeking out congregations of like-minded reformers. The reception was cold in the beginning (even more so than it would be later, although it was never terribly warm), and the early seeking sort of Quakers did not have much success in the first years of the Interregnum. As described in Chapter 1, the early members came to Quakerism from a variety of reform-minded communities. Furthermore, they lacked a central space, both spiritually and physically, that enabled them to grow and thrive. Fell provided that space with the use of her home and the creation of an environment where ideas could be shared and the faith fostered.

The formation of the Quaker church is indicative of a process that certain types of new religious groups experience, that is, transforming over time in order to successfully weather external pressures and internal group dynamics. Success in this context is defined in the most basic of ways—survival. Scholarship in the field of the sociology of religion echoes the idea of a process seen with the early Quakers. David Horrell's work examines how the structure of religious groups changes when they evolve from loose networks of people to stable churches: "Identity salience hierarchies may change over time, as individuals, when they age and mature, become more or less committed to particular identities."[6] This is made evident when religious groups transition from itinerant to resident ministries; Horrell claims that a religious group's itinerant phase is naturally followed by the more stable period of institutional development. He further states that this transition "is inextricably connected with the development of more socially conservative patterns of ethical instruction."[7] Ben Pink Dandelion, a sociologist of Quakerism, also articulates this process in the development of the Quaker faith as it progressed from a "personal religion in which there are no organizational constraints on belief-subscription," to an "institutional religion," which is "defined by the organization." Dandelion states that Quaker orthodoxy represents the institutional form of the faith, whereas heretical beliefs would thereby be demonstrated by emergent personal beliefs.[8]

Hill reiterates Horrell's point when he summarizes the Quakerism of the Restoration as "a preaching ministry" with "regular meeting times and places, a hierarchical structure of meetings, greater emphasis on sin and discipline, financial organization." This "resident" form of ministry became increasingly stable as Quakers "dropped exuberances like interrupting church services and going naked as a sign."[9] Fell's efforts to organize the early membership allowed for this transition to occur. In the case of the Quakers, their growth from the Interregnum to the Restoration resulted in a shift from traveling ministries to the establishment and maintenance of regular meetings because they already had an infrastructure in place.

Therefore, it is inappropriate to discuss groups like the early Quakers as if they were a fully formed church, or were understood as such, during the Interregnum. During the early 1650s, there was no sense of stability within the Quaker community. Since there was no single leader, the Quaker faith was not based on the ideas of an individual. Their beliefs, like their egalitarian structure, were mutable and subject to change based on the incorporation of new people and ideas. The abundance of radical religious groups and a fluid current amongst them, allowing people to float between religious communities, demonstrates the desire for spiritual answers but also the absence of any sort of structure that could prevent them from exploring their options. Groups like the Quakers proliferated particularly in the Interregnum because the breakdown of religious uniformity generated their creation. People like Fox, Nayler, and Fell came together, in part, out of a desire to discover "truth," but their story also suggests that they sought out a system of controlling the chaos around themselves. For those who became Quakers, the structure of the letter network, orchestrated by Fell, allowed them to forge an identity and curb the chaos around them. They could have attempted to maintain the loose association of the early movement, but those who survived the Nayler Affair used it as a catalyst for transitioning into an institutionalized church.

In actuality, the Quakers signify a society in transition, and it is their religious formation that tells us this, not their often difficult to decipher political beliefs. Social associations changed in this period because the ways that people related to one another changed. The political uncertainty of civil war and revolution allowed this to occur in England, but that is not the story unto itself. Rather, that merely tells of the political circumstances, not their results. Studying the Quaker's transition from a loose association or movement to an established religious organization tells us more than their story, or even Margaret Fell's role in developing the Quaker church; it tells a story of the Interregnum, and thereby the early modern period, as well as the process by which heterodox religious communities become orthodox churches.

Introduction 5

The purpose of this book is to examine the rise of Quakerism as a process of becoming—first a Seeker-esque loose association, then a burgeoning religious movement that eventually established a church structure—and finally to look at what it became from the long view of the eighteenth century. Fell is at the heart of these transitions, and so a study of this nature must begin by reviewing how she has been discussed in scholarship thus far. But that is not all. In addition to reconsidering Fell's role in Quakerism, this book provides a revised narrative to help explain the beginnings of the religious community. This will be done through examination of the letter network, which contrasts Quakers from the larger religious milieu of Interregnum England. Fell was integral to these processes; therefore it is only logical to begin with her. Only after reassessing her role can we talk about the development of the faith and what that meant to the wider religious world.

This book attempts to do just that. Chapter 1, "The making of Quakerism," describes the radical, sectarian foundations of the Quaker faith and explores the narrative process of the sect's evolution into a religion. The chapter begins by exploring Seekerism as a spiritual conundrum and how communication networks existed amongst religious ramblers even prior to the foundation of a relatively stable sect. This chapter also focuses on the development of the Quaker faith as an outgrowth of the Seeker presence in central and northern England. The chapter argues that the process culminated with the end of one type of Seekerism, resulting in the creation of an inchoate Quaker movement centered at Margaret Fell's home at Swarthmoor Hall.[10] The source material for this chapter comes almost entirely from the letters written during the 1650s, in particular the 407 letters from the Friends House in London that focus on suffering and imprisonment.

Chapter 2, "The Quaker Letter Network," explains the mechanics of the letter network, the people involved, and the network's change over time. This includes a reexamination of the relationships of the earliest members of the faith and how they arrived at Quakerism. Swarthmoor Hall, transitioned in this period from a salon-type environment for radicalism to the clearinghouse of letters amongst leaders and itinerants in the movement. This chapter also discusses the struggle for power between Fox's (backed by Fell) and Nayler's camps. Because Fell organized and maintained the letter network, she and Fox controlled communication within the movement and were therefore able to sway support to their side. I therefore argue that Fox's authoritative position is largely due to Fell's efforts, and he would not have been successful without her. With a clear power in place, the sect transformed into a church.

Chapter 3, "Margaret Fell reexamined" considers the different ways that Margaret Fell has been discussed in Quaker scholarship. Most works tend to fall into camps of either seeing her as a traditional, maternal figure or as a proto-feminist. This chapter argues that while elements of both of these claims are true, they ultimately miss her true significance by ignoring her greatest contribution as architect of the letter network. This chapter attempts to complicate the two most common tropes about Fell and instead claims that she was neither entirely submissive nor revolutionary, but rather a keenly practical sectarian with the mission of promoting her faith.

Chapters 4 and 5 explore thematic problems that defined the first generation of Quakerism. Chapter 4, "Apostolic epistolary influences," focuses on the early Christian example of correspondence between distant communities of like-minded faithful. Within the burgeoning Quaker community, Fell served the same function that Paul did for the Apostolic Christians. By comparing Quaker letters, particularly those written by Fell, to Paul's epistles and other Biblical passages, we can see how the earliest members of the group saw themselves as the realization of the Apostolic mission. Similarly, letters united both the first Christians and the earliest Quakers, as can be seen in the Biblical language used by Fell, Fox, and others in an attempt to link themselves to what they believed to be a revival of primitive Christianity.

Chapter 5, "Suffering, prison, and the law in the Quaker tradition," focuses on meanings of suffering that were particular to this religious movement. Suffering was a key feature of the early Quaker identity and helped shape their concept of martyrdom. While suffering came in many forms, the most common was imprisonment. Letters written to and by prisoners comprised the majority of correspondence for the movement. In an effort to establish their place in the sect and to earn respect from fellow members of the faith, Quakers courted suffering experiences in many instances in the record—either to promote the actions of the group or to elevate themselves amongst their brethren. It certainly worked for Fox. The letters that Fell preserved were a record of suffering in this period and provided the basis of subsequent memories of the early years.

Finally, Chapter 6, "The afterlife of the movement," discusses how the first generation of Quakerism was remembered by subsequent generations. The main source for this section is the eighteenth-century martyrology written by Joseph Besse, *A Collection of the Sufferings of the People Call'd Quakers*. In this work, the narrative established by Fell's preservation of the historical record through the maintenance of the letter network is solidified, and the first generation's leadership under Fox is promoted. Subsequent historiography was based on Besse's findings, and thus the institutionalization of a church history was made.

By reexamining Fell's role in the religious movement we have a fuller picture of how the Quaker faith not only developed, but also thrived in the mid-seventeenth century. This approach also allows for a new assessment of other leading figures in the Quaker movement vis-à-vis their relationships to Fell. The letters that Quakers wrote to one another provide an important and thus far under-examined insight into how they viewed themselves, as well as how they perceived themselves in relation to foundational Christian communities. Suffering was the key to their self-perception, and Fell was instrumental in developing the idea that Quakers were essentially martyrs for their faith.

Notes

1. The best explanation of the term "The Valiant Sixty" comes from William Braithwaite who suggested that the 60 were once 70 in reference to the number of Jesus' disciples described in the Gospel of Luke 10:1–24. Braithwaite describes the "First Publishers of Truth" as the group of "the itinerating Friends with the gift of ministry who spread the Quaker message." William C. Braithwaite, *The Beginnings of Quakerism* (Cambridge: Cambridge University Press, 1912), 26.
2. The historiography of the Nayler Affair is extensive. A small sample includes, but is not limited to: William C. Braithwaite, *The Beginnings of Quakerism*; William G. Bittle, "Religious Toleration and the Trial of James Naylor," *Quaker History* 73, no. 1 (1984); Christopher Hill, *The World Turned Upside Down: Radical Ideas during the English Revolution* (New York: Penguin Books, 1972); Rosemary Anne Moore, *The Light in Their Consciences: the Early Quakers in Britain, 1646–1666* (University Park: Pennsylvania State University Press, 2000); Geoffrey Nuttall, *James Nayler: a fresh approach* (London: Friends' Historical Society, 1954); and Patricia Crawford, *Women and Religion in England, 1500–1720* (London and New York: Routledge, 1993). The Nayler Affair is further explored in subsequent chapters.
3. Christopher Hill, *The Experience of Defeat: Milton and Some Contemporaries* (New York: Viking Penguin, 1984), 165.
4. Ibid.
5. "James Parnell had died in prison in 1656, at the age of 19, and John Camm in 1657. Lilburne also died (on parole from prison) in that year, aged only 42; if he had survived he might have been expected to exercise a powerful influence. Nayler died in 1660, aged 42, and Thomas Aldam in the same year; George Fox the Younger in 1661; Burrough and Richard Hubberthorne in 1662, aged 28 and 34 respectively; William Ames in the same year. John Audland died in 1664, aged 34, Samuel Fisher in 1665, Richard Farnsworth in 1666 (aged about 33?), Francis Howgill in 1669. Apart from Fox, only George Whitehead and William Dewsbury of the original leaders lived on, and neither of them was of the caliber of Lilburne, Nayler, Burrough, Hubberthorne, Fisher or Howgill." Hill, *The Experience of Defeat*, 166.
6. David Horrell, "Leadership Patterns and the Development of Ideology in Early Christianity" *Sociology of Religion* 58, no. 4 (Winter 1997): 339.
7. Ibid.
8. Ben Pink Dandelion, *A Sociological Analysis of the Theology of Quakers: The Silent Revolution* (Lewiston: Edwin Mellen Press, 1996), 21. Dandelion provides a useful chart on page 25 that explains the part that orthodoxy and heterodoxy play in the creation of new orthodox beliefs.
9. Hill, *The Experience of Defeat*, 165.
10. Margaret Fell's residence is spelled "Swarthmoor" whereas the manuscript collection maintained at the Friends' House in London is spelled "Swarthmore." Both spellings can be found throughout this text depending on the context in which each is used.

1 The making of Quakerism

The story of early Quakerism has been told many times. The definitive modern narrative work, William Braithwaite's monumental *The Beginnings of Quakerism*, is largely based on George Fox's journal, early suffering records like *The Great Book of Sufferings*, and Joseph Besse's *A Collection of the Sufferings of the People Call'd Quakers*.[1] Braithwaite's work also utilized, to a limited extent, letters written in the early period of the religious sect. Braithwaite's text was originally published in 1912 and reprinted in 1955, and while it is the most comprehensive narrative study to date, it is limited because of its focus on the "heroic period of Quaker history" by essentially providing "a Quakerly version of the late nineteenth-century style."[2] Braithwaite's tome overemphasizes the originality of Quaker beliefs, accepting the theory "that Quakerism derived not from Puritanism as much as from continental Anabaptism," a claim that is dismissive of England's seventeenth-century cultural milieu. Sydney James has stated that Braithwaite's work confined "attention too strictly to the Quakers" and "needed the sustaining power of a comprehensive understanding of English history, which [Braithwaite] did not give them."[3] Essentially, as a denominational study written by a sympathetic Quaker author, Braithwaite's work was not critical of his brethren's sources and therefore did not call Fox's or others' assertions into question. Thus, when Fox claimed originality and supremacy of the religious movement, Braithwaite reiterated this idea. In contrast, an examination of letters, rather than merely focusing on Fox's journal or other documents that provide a retrospective retelling of the early years, may give us new insights into the development of this religious community. Furthermore, by shifting the focus to letters, Margaret Fell's place in the development of the community becomes more centrally located and thereby provides new insights into this otherwise Fox-centric story.

This chapter attempts to provide an additional, rather than an alternative, narrative of the Quakers' development in the Interregnum. A few caveats need to be noted. First, the letter record is incomplete. This study examined over 400 letters from the Friends House Library in London, as well as Margaret Fell's published letters in Elsa F. Glines's *Undaunted Zeal*.[4] It is important to note that there are other extant letters that may modify the narrative if all could be included. These letters were selected because they were written in the 1650s and focus on the importance of suffering, particularly imprisonment, to the Quaker experience. Yet even if every extant manuscript source from this period had been used, no narrative is ever complete, particularly when retelling the story of a distant time with numerous sources that have either been lost or intentionally excluded from the historical record. As Jane Couchman and Ann Crabb state, even the letters that have been preserved over time indicate "there is often evidence of a wider correspondence no longer extant."[5] The second caveat is that this book argues that the letter network came into being coincident with Margaret Fell's involvement, so any narrative must rely on other types of sources for the period prior to 1652 before she was "convinced."[6] This means that the traditional narrative as told by Fox and subsequently Braithwaite is given greater weight for the years prior to Fell's involvement in the religious community.

This chapter attempts to enhance the traditional narrative by supplementing Braithwaite's account with additional information. To be clear, this study would not have been possible without the tremendous works of previous scholars. We will explore how nascent Quakers of various backgrounds came together to create a dynamic, malleable faith. The cornerstone of this emergent religion was the communication network that held itinerants together. Their letters will be the basis of the remainder of this chapter. While other scholars have used these letters in the past, they have not been used this extensively or as the main sources for recreating the early Quaker narrative. By telling their story using a myriad of Quaker voices, we can restore agency to those who were shaping the faith as it developed. At the same time, not all agency is given equal weight because the process of selecting and maintaining records gave Margaret Fell the power to determine the letters that best told the narrative that she and George Fox favored, which ultimately became the orthodox history of the Quakers' early years.

As the remainder of the chapter will challenge assumptions about the traditional narrative, an overview of what occurred is appropriate. In the early 1650s, numerous religious communities emerged in the uncensored, unregulated English countryside. George Fox, James Nayler, and numerous other early Quakers were amongst those who set out to preach the truth as they understood it. The origins of what became the Quaker faith started in the English Midlands and North sometime prior to the summer of 1652. The community did not coalesce, however, until Fox arrived at Margaret Fell's home, Swarthmoor Hall in Lancashire. From June of 1652 forward, Swarthmoor, and by extension Fell, became the center of the faith as traveling ministers would stop at her home for respite or write to her so that their news of the movement landed at a stable base, where messages could be transcribed, recorded, and sent on to others throughout the emergent Quaker community. Quaker itinerants experienced persecution during their travels in the subsequent years, most often being jailed in foreign communities. As the movement grew, some Quakers such as Fox gained notoriety for their brash appearance and blasphemy charges. The most infamous episode occurred in 1656 when James Nayler emulated Christ's entry into Jerusalem by riding a donkey as women bowed before him. It was, however, not the first schism nor the first time that another Quaker appeared to challenge Fox's authority. Yet this moment signaled the most challenging crisis within the Quaker fold because it garnered national attention, including Nayler's trial by Parliament. As a result, the Quaker ranks turned inward and began to admonish outward displays of faith like those shown by Nayler. Fox emerged as the sole leader of the community, in no small part due to Margaret Fell's efforts to promote him through the records she kept of Quaker movements back at Swarthmoor Hall. The ways that these first few years of the faith were remembered in Fell's preserved letters, Fox's journal, and subsequent historical accounts have become the basis of the traditional narrative that the rest of this chapter seeks to complicate.

Quaker beginnings and expansion through 1652

All of the early adherents to what became the Quaker faith could reasonably be described as Seekers in the most basic sense. Whether they flitted between congregations or sectarian belief systems or whether they undertook a more individualized journey, they all were waiting for a more meaningful answer than their hometown Puritan congregations offered. Braithwaite states that "the channel along which many of the Baptist influences which affected Quakerism probably came" originates with the first group Fox convinced.[7] The first group is perhaps also the most significant: the "Shattered Baptists" of Nottinghamshire. At some point prior to 1647, the congregation dissolved or shattered into different factions, one of which included the first convinced Quaker, the revered and influential preacher, Elizabeth Hooton of Skegby near Mansfield. These Seekers assumed the name Children of Light, both for the message of inner light that they embraced and because of the Biblical passages "Ye are all the children of light" (Thessalonians 5:5) and "walk as children of light" (Ephesians 5:8). Unsurprisingly, groups other than these proto-Quakers used this name, particularly those with similar theological traditions.[8]

But this is problematic in our effort to determine when and how Quakerism began. Because Fox said that the Children of Light were an early manifestation of Quakerism, historians have accepted this as fact—but in actuality, there were many other changes, adjustments, and schisms that happened along the way that made the Quaker faith what it was.[9] This version of events relies on the memories of an elderly Fox who had a particular stake in telling the story a certain way. Therefore, the Children of Light, or whatever they were before 1652, should be seen as a separate, less successful sect in the Seeker milieu rather than as an early stage of Quakerism. It would be ridiculous to separate the two completely—one obviously contributed to the other—but they were not one and the same as Fox, Braithwaite, and the Quaker narrative tradition would like for us to believe.

Fox's journal states that the Quaker faith was firmly established throughout the mid-1640s. This is irreconcilable with the Children of Light's emergence in 1648 and Braithwaite's subsequent claim that he sought to make this a "universal rather than sectarian" movement on the eve of 1649.[10] Fox traveled throughout Nottinghamshire in 1649, trademarking the Quaker way of interrupting sermons and speaking as an outsider in churchyards and markets, and, in return, being beaten with "hands, Bibles, and sticks," as well as being put in stocks and stoned out of town.[11] Although he and other itinerants frequently interrupted sermons, Fox states: "I regarded the priests less, and looked more after the Dissenting people," thus indicating that he knew where his bread was buttered.[12] This came to a head while preaching in Derby—Fox was one of the first to be tried under the Blasphemy Act of 1650 and brought before Justice Bennett and Colonel Nathan Barton on October 30, 1650. This illustrious meeting is apocryphally described as the moment when Bennett coined the term Quaker after Fox bid him "to quake and tremble at the name of the Lord."[13] Fox was sentenced to six months in jail, but he would not allow his family to provide surety of his good behavior, so the sentence was extended to a year, thereby temporarily hindering his missionary efforts.[14]

Afterwards, Fox went to Westmoreland, where the Preston Patrick Chapel meeting opened up to his message.[15] Fox was aware of Swarthmoor Hall as a home that welcomed preachers of all backgrounds. His journey led to the meeting with Fell at Swarthmoor Hall in June 1652, which may be described as the moment that Quakerism began. From the summer of 1652 forward, Quaker ministers began to flock to Fell's home with increasing frequency, signaling the beginning of her significance to the movement.

Little is known of Margaret Fell's early life other than that she was born Margaret Askew in 1614 in Dalton-in-Furness, Lancashire, near Ulverston. Her father was "a well-established gentleman landowner of sufficient stature," and as one of his two daughters, she inherited money and property at the time of his death.[16] This no doubt improved her marriage prospects, and in 1632 she married barrister, future judge, and Member of Parliament, Thomas Fell of Swarthmoor Hall. In her younger life, Margaret received an exceptional education by seventeenth-century standards, particularly for living in a remote northern English province. This may have contributed to Thomas Fell's trust that his wife was capable of managing their estate during his long absences as an itinerant justice. The household included eight children, numerous servants, and an uncommonly high number of visitors, such as George Fox and the future Quakers.

Fox first went there on June 20, but both Judge Thomas Fell and Margaret Fell were gone when he arrived. Ulverston minister William Lampitt, who took Fox to be a Ranter, argued with him at the house.[17] When Margaret Fell returned home, she had a long talk with Fox and was disappointed to hear about his disagreement with Lampitt. The next day, Lampitt gave a lecture at the Ulverston church, and when Fox finally arrived, the congregation was singing before a sermon, something he took to be unforgivably papist, and he said as much. Hearing Fox's denunciation of her minister and fellow congregants, Fell began to weep. This episode, which is of course only recorded by those who promote the Quaker perspective, has no shortage of dramatic flourishes. The Puritan magistrate John Sawrey, who was in attendance and was offended by the outsider's intrusion, ordered that Fox be taken away. For the first of many times, Fell interceded on Fox's behalf and said, "Let him along, why may he not speak as well as any other?"[18] Encouraged by her words, Fox stayed at Swarthmoor that night and preached to Fell's household servants, including Thomas Salthouse and Will Caton, both of whom became part of the Quaker inner circle, traveling extensively and writing numerous important theological tracts for the movement.

Over the next few weeks, Fox and other key leaders of this emerging Seeking/Children of Light/Quaker faith visited Swarthmoor and the surrounding area frequently. Fell was apparently comforted by their words, but was anxious that her husband may have been angered by her hospitality toward the Quakers, who were shunned by leaders of her community. Upon crossing the sandy shores from Lancaster, the judge was met by "a party of captains and magistrates, all in a great state of anger" who told him that Quakers had bewitched his family. Braithwaite states that Judge Fell returned home "greatly offended" and angry with his wife but was pacified by other Quaker ministers, James Nayler and Richard Farnsworth, who explained what had happened over the previous month. Building on their momentum, Fox arrived back at Swarthmoor that night and also spoke with Thomas Fell. Lampitt came back to the house the next day in the hopes that he could rid his community of the quaking Seekers; however, after Thomas Fell listened to the minister, he decided that while Fox, Nayler, the others, and now his wife could not persuade him, he allowed his family and household to convert to the new faith. The judge's consent was hugely significant to both the movement and individual Quakers' lives when they had trouble with the law throughout the remainder of the Interregnum. He interceded on their behalf, particularly on Fox's part, numerous times, and may have prevented extreme punishments being exacted during the 1650s. Therefore, the convincement of Fell and the majority of Swarthmoor Hall was arguably the most significant moment in the early movement. It also signals Fell's autonomy as both an anomaly for the time and essential for future Quaker developments.

As early as July 1652, Fell's home had become the ground zero of Quaker communication. Fox made repeated trips to Swarthmoor, and as a result Quakers from throughout the north wrote to him there to apprise him and Fell of the state of the religious movement. While it is not possible to recreate an exact order of events because the dating of these letters is imprecise, we know that Thomas Aldam and other prisoners in York Castle wrote to

Fox several times throughout the month. In one such example, Aldam and Elizabeth Hooton note that "Judge Fell's daughters" visited the prisoners and brought news from Swarthmoor.[19] Hooton had been jailed for speaking in a church service, and several other women were imprisoned, although they were not all mentioned by name—Jane Vallance, Thomas Aldam's wife, and Timothy Westobie Brunt's wife are noted. This missive is followed by another in the same month that notes that Jane Holmes's efforts were positive in Wakefield, and other Quakers had spread the message to Leeds and throughout Yorkshire even though "heathens" tried to deter their efforts, including "a terrible woman" who brought things to the prisoners but spoke contrary to the truth.[20] New prisoners arrived, including Mary Fisher who was jailed for speaking in church in Selby. Aldam warned against certain visitors coming to the prison: "I shovld desire thou wovld speake to jvdge fell wife and tell her it were better her daughters were at home with her, th[i]s place is mighty prophane and little good example."[21]

These letters taken together demonstrate that the Quaker message had convinced members of the Swarthmoor household very quickly. Fox and Braithwaite suggest as much, but the evidence they provide comes from a description of the meeting at the house, rather than substantive proof that Fell's children were compelled to visit prisoners over 100 miles from their home under what is described as potentially dangerous circumstances. Despite their efforts, we can also determine that in 1652 Margaret Fell was still perceived as a secondary figure to her husband, who never became Quaker, because she is referred to as Judge Fell's wife, rather than by her own name. Finally, we see that women played a large role in the early movement. Of the 14 people specifically mentioned in these two letters, 10 are women.

Yet Margaret Fell's role as the key disseminator of information was established by November of 1652. James Nayler wrote to her from the Appleby Gaol with news of Francis Howgill's confrontation with a minister. But more importantly, he sent a "paper" that he asks her to distribute amongst friends. Perhaps he asked Fell rather than Fox because Nayler could not locate Fox, but more likely, Fell's stationary position increased her value in the community—while others traveled, she stayed home, thereby allowing itinerants and prisoners alike to be sure that their messages would be received and that they could trust her to pass their news along. Nayler further stressed Fell's importance when he wrote to Fox in the same month asking that he be "remembered" to "MF & family." Nayler later wrote to Fox that he wished to be remembered to "Jvdge Fell and his wife" and that the paper enclosed in this letter should be copied so that it "may be sent into Fvrnass," Barrow-in-Furness being the peninsula where Swarthmoor Hall is located.[22] Likewise, when Thomas Aldam wrote generally to "Friends" (possibly the first use of this term), he states that his wife, Ann, wished to be remembered by whomever received the letter. The fact that it ended up in Fell's possession at Swarthmoor suggests that there was an expectation that it would circulate amongst the faithful. And in a final example from this period, Richard Farnsworth wrote to Fell on December 2, 1652, that he had circulated her previous letter, noting that he received it the last time he saw Nayler and Fox. Farnsworth further asked Fell to circulate books that he had printed so that "friends made soe bovld th[a]t they goe and reeds th[e]m in the steeplehouse yarthes after they haue done and in the markets on the crosse on the market."[23] And in a display of trust, Farnsworth asked that she forward an enclosed letter intended for Nayler.

Also in November there is evidence of discord within the community. Once again Thomas Aldam wrote that Richard Farnsworth had felt compelled to speak to Jane Holmes because she had been acting too proud, "declareing to her th[a]t the wilde natvre was elated in her, aboue the seed of god bvt shee called him lyer."[24] Despite Aldam's previous praise of Holmes's work in Maulton, she was chastised and, mysteriously, the division that he referenced between Farnsworth and Holmes was attributed to her having contracted a fever in prison—presumably leading to strange talk on her part that may have motivated a schism within the prison community. Thomas Aldam wrote to Fox from York in 1652 that "we are in good health all bvt my sister Jane Holmes, and shee hath a verye sore feavor."[25] The majority of those mentioned thus far sided with the future leaders of the Quaker sect—William Dewsbury, Farnsworth, Aldam, Elizabeth Hooton (who had been jailed for reproving a minister in Rotterdam), and Mary Fisher (who interrupted a Selby minister)—who were all of one mind against the ill (potentially mentally ill) Holmes. Here we see the "strict code of self-discipline" that Fox demanded of his brethren and sisters.[26]

Ultimately, the process by which a new religious community was created is significant. To put it another way, the Quakers were not Quakers until they were. All of the Seeking tendencies prior to the Swarthmoor meeting are significant and important to understanding who they were and what they would become. However, it does justice neither to Fell and her efforts nor to all of the people involved in the creation of this new community, to employ Fox's, Braithwaite's, and even Fell's narrative as gospel, when in fact they were attempting to tell the story differently than how it occurred. Therefore, in an effort to properly give credit where it is due, Chapter 2 explores how the letter network ensured that Quakerism succeeded.

The first meeting at Swarthmoor Hall in the summer of 1652 signifies a major change in the development of Quakerism. Unbeknownst to those involved, they established relationships that would allow for future successes that their contemporaries were incapable of achieving. The fanciful goals of radical preachers wandering around the English North and Midlands were not unique to this particular brand of Seekerism; however, Margaret Fell's introduction to Fox, Nayler, and the other itinerants of this movement made them more than they would have been without her. She became something of a steward to this ragtag brood, and in so doing, enabled them to grow into something new.

Growth of the movement: 1653–1655

The traditional narrative provides little insight into Quaker movements for the first half of 1653 until June when Nayler, William Dewsbury, and Richard Farnsworth reported that they were traveling in Yorkshire and having successful meetings there among the Westmoreland Seekers.[27] However, letters from this period give us a glimpse into how the movement spread in these months. Francis Howgill wrote to Fell about his and others' experiences in the Appleby Gaol on January 5.[28] In February, Nayler, who was also jailed in Appleby, wrote to Fox that local anti-Quakers were conspiring against him, but that their accusations were false. Nayler's wife visited and helped denounce the accusations against him, stating that she "hath stoped many movths, and hath conuinced th[e]m of many lies they had rayesed, and was belieued in the covntry."[29] Also in February, Thomas Aldam requested that 200–300 copies of a paper be printed and that he would send payment "by the carrier w[hi]ch bringes the books."[30]

While Braithwaite discusses that Quaker itinerants were apparently also active in Cheshire and around the border of Wales to inquire about Independent minister Morgan Lloyd (who sent members of his congregation into England to learn more about the Quaker message), he does not mention Elizabeth Hooton, Jane Vallance, and Elizabeth Tomlinson's imprisonments in York Castle.[31] The three women sent their love to Fell via Fox on June 11, 1653. It may not be surprising that this commonplace report was omitted; however, Thomas Aldam related that Quakers were being beaten with "clubs and stakes" and one of their supporters was "feld" while riding a horse. Another Quaker defender, Cornet Denham's wife, was threatened by "rude people" who said they would "pull his wife to pieces for harboring Qvakers."[32]

Braithwaite states that Fox sent a group of Westmoreland Seekers to speak on his behalf in Derby. The purpose of this endeavor was to prevent false statements about Fox from circulating among the nascent movement—the accusations of blasphemy had caused some to question his mission, and this proactive effort prevented a potential splinter among his brethren.[33] What this passage fails to mention is Richard Hubberthorne's account of a meeting in Yelland where "weeds was groune over the pvre," and his successful convincements in Westmoreland "w[i]th my 2 systers E and A."[34]

Taken together, the traditional narrative and this letter validate that the Quaker leadership was concerned about the state of the faith in Westmoreland. By just reading Fox's account in Braithwaite, active participants' roles, namely those exhibited by female ministers, were diminished in favor of Fox's orchestration of events. The traditional narrative also ignores the growing influence that Fell had over the mission. Hubberthorne wrote to her that if she felt compelled to write to the community in question, "th[a]t spirit may bee kept downe which judgeth the appearance of the life and motion of god."[35] This suggests that Fell also had the ability to influence the faithful.

Throughout the fall of 1653, there are numerous examples of discrepancies between the traditional and letter narratives. Braithwaite describes Quakers faring well in Cheshire, including Thomas Lawson who found people who were already convinced of the Quaker message—whether that meant they had heard of Quaker ideas or were Seekers who were predisposed to the ideas is unknown. Despite Lawson's successes there, he clashed with locals in Cheshire and was taken to the stocks in October.[36] While jailed in Chester, he converted members of a separatist group that had been meeting in the area. In two letters written by John Lawson (presumed relation to Thomas Lawson but not evident in this correspondence) in November, he states that he was jailed after speaking in Malpasse, Cheshire. During his imprisonment, Lawson was visited by friends like Richard Hubberthorne, Richard Weaver, and the Welsh minister John-ap-John, as well as foes like the "many tempters and provd lvstfull creatures who com to looke at vs and to heare some strange things there are alsoe an other sort of people who are separated from them."[37]

According to Braithwaite, Hubberthorne was in the Northgate prison in Chester in November where he made contacts with Seekers in Mobberly and Morely.[38] By December, Hubberthorne was released, and he subsequently visited Separatist meetings, where he found them divided into two groups, one that met in silence and another that did not.[39] However, on December 4, Hubberthorne wrote to Fell that he was still in the Chester jail. In this letter, he provides some of the best insights into the Quaker experience of being "othered" during their itinerancy. Hubberthorne recounted how he stayed with a man named William Harrison when a Chester lawyer named Richard Golborne inquired if there "was not 2 strangers there the wife answered there was one but the other was gone." Hubberthorne came forward and was subsequently arrested for simply being a foreigner to the city. He stated that he was from Lancashire and was going into Wales, and further he asked why "did not abid in my calling I told him that I was in my calling" and as a result was sent to the city jail.[40]

Meanwhile, perhaps the biggest doctrinal decision made in 1653 was the ordinance that Fox was "to view all books before they are printed, and urges him to send forth his threshing instruments to thresh upon the mountains as the wisdom of God may guide Margaret Fell."[41] There are two astounding claims here: first, that Fox was already censoring Quaker works by the end of 1653 and, second, that Fell was instrumental in the creation of the network. With regards to the first, Braithwaite states that though the decision that Fox should view all books before they were printed had been made, 'other leaders no doubt acted in the same way."[42] Here we have an instance where the narratives are in agreement. Thomas Aldam wrote to Fox in December 1653 that he rejoiced when hearing that Fox would censor all books prior to their being printed. He does not say why he met this announcement with such enthusiasm, but it must have been common knowledge throughout the Quaker community if Aldam heard about this development while in jail in York.

This new censorship policy affected Fell, too. This proclamation was made because Fell, who could not travel herself but had opened her home to Quakers who could, "made it her business to create and maintain close relations of personal friendship between herself and most of the leaders of the new movement."[43] With regards to this development, Braithwaite states: "The extent of her correspondence is amazing, and her careful preservation of the letters received enables us to-day to write much of the early history of the society, as few such books can be written, from the best of all sources, intimate contemporary documents. She took on a leading part in the establishment, development, and administration of the funds collected at Kendal."[44] This is an unusual attribution for Braithwaite, and it begins to hint at her contribution to the movement since the majority of his efforts focus on Fox's sole leadership.

As the movement grew, the role of the traveling minister became increasingly important (with the major exception of Fell who was revered for her management of the movement from home). The itinerant lifestyle affected families in different ways. On February 10, John Audland wrote to Fell of his wife's imprisonment in Banbury. His letter was sent from Bristol, more than 80 miles away. He noted that he had visited her but had to leave to continue his missionary work.[45] In contrast, Anthony Pearson wrote to Edward Burrough on February 21 that he wanted to travel to see Fox but could not because his wife's illness meant that her "condition hitherto hindered" his ability to travel.[46] Despite Pearson's familial obligations, he remained apprised of his brethren's movements in the Quaker network. He had plans to meet friendly justices in Durham who could help him meet up with Fox as he traveled toward Cumberland. Other would-be itinerants did not have the freedom to move about so easily. Pearson noted that others "subkect to parents and masters cannot get so farr as Lancashire and therefore would meet him att the nearest."[47]

Throughout the spring of 1654, numerous Quakers were imprisoned across northern and western England. In March, Thomas Aldam wrote that Thomas Holme was jailed in the Cheshire prison.[48] William Dewsbury wrote to Fell on May 2 to let her know that he was in the York Castle prison with the now imprisoned Thomas Aldam.[49] Roger Hebden wrote to George Fox from the York Castle jail, although he made no mention of Dewsbury or Aldam.[50] Rounding out the month of May, Richard Hubberthorne wrote to Fell twice concerning his imprisonment in Congleton, Cheshire. Both letters were dated May 29. In one, Hubberthorne stated that he was jailed for speaking in the "steeplehouse" but was set free shortly thereafter. In the other, Hubberthorne noted that the letter was written in the jail but spent the majority of the text discussing the need for Fell to send friends into Cheshire. He notes that while some women like Elizabeth Leavens and Elizabeth Fletcher were very serviceable, he felt compelled "to tell thee that Agnes Vairy is not servisable to go forth for lust and filth & darknes rules in her and there is a filthy scandal raysed conseruing her going to Eatrean."[51]

Of these developments, Braithwaite only notes that Dewsbury was jailed for "seducing the people" under suspicion of blasphemy, and that Hubberthorne made vague reference to the need for ministers in Congleton.[52] It is important to note that Braithwaite's omission of the Quaker women's missionary efforts leaves the impression that men's sufferings were considered more significant.

Quakers felt the need to spread their message both near and far by the middle of 1654. An example of important information that Braithwaite omits comes from a July 5, 1654, letter from Edward Burrough to Fox in which he stated that the quality of preaching had been inconsistent throughout the north.[53] This direct plea to Fox shows his significance, yet this potential threat to the stability of the movement is nowhere to be found in Braithwaite's work or Fox's journal. Neither mentions the anxiety that resulted from Isabel Buttery's involvement with the Earl of Pembroke, which Francis Howgill and Anthony Pearson described as "his deceit." Buttery's actions landed her in Bridewell, and they state that everyone (presumably fellow Quakers) suffered for her actions.[54] This description follows Howgill and Pearson's discussion of run-ins with Ranters in London. They further suggested that while some sectarians may have been receptive to the Quaker message, there were many potential difficulties in recruiting them so they were not worth the trouble. They also warned that priests were to be avoided at all costs. Taken together, it seems that they were concerned about corrupting influences penetrating the community.

While Braithwaite notes that on September 7, 1654, Camm and Audland reached Bristol where they met with a community of Seekers, there are no letters to support this. However, Margaret Killam wrote to Fox about meeting with Camm's "maiden" in Cambridge.[55] By this time, James Parnell was imprisoned in Cambridge for the second time; however, he was released almost immediately and was sent out of the city as a vagrant. Somehow the lure of Cambridge could not keep Parnell away because he was back a few months later, had some public arguments with Baptists, and went naked as a sign of his faith.[56] A third brief imprisonment followed, but it could not keep him from his old tricks. Throughout his back-and-forth in the Cambridge jail, various Quakers made a point of mentioning his incarceration.[57]

On September 23, Francis Howgill wrote to Robert Widder that Christopher Atkinson and "2 women" had traveled to France. Later, on October 2, he and Edward Burrough wrote to Fell, but this time only the women's travels were mentioned. It is worth noting here that Atkinson, who was excommunicated from the Quaker community in 1655, was apparently still in everyone's good graces at this point.[58] Burrough and Howgill reported on various itinerants' travels including Hubberthorne and Parnell in Cambridge, Myles Halhead and John Lancaster in the north, John Audland and John Camm in Shrewsbury, Will Dewsbury in Leistershire, and Richard Farnsworth near Leicestershire. They wrote to Fell from London and were able to recount this news despite mentioning that "all letters from

Chester are intercepted."[59] While the incomplete nature of the letters makes it difficult to state with certainty that the traditional narrative is incorrect, Braithwaite places Hubberthorne in Norwich, and Howgill, Burrough, Camm, and Audland in Bristol in early October.[60] It may be that the timing was slightly off because Hubberthorne wrote to Fox that he was jailed in Norwich Castle on November 13. It is also possible that he was jailed earlier in the month but was unable to communicate with Fox until then. By December 21, Christopher Atkinson and John Lancaster joined Hubberthorne in Norwich Castle, and by December 28, George Whitehead was also jailed for disrupting the local church service. Either way, the overreliance on Braithwaite's traditional narrative has allowed for confusion on this point.

Examination of the letters from and concerning the Norwich prisoners also provides insights into another interesting development. On January 11 and 17, Hubberthorne, Whitehead, Lancaster, and Atkinson all wrote to Fell. The majority of these missives concerns what they describe as the unjust cause of their imprisonment, namely Hubberthorne's refusal to take off his hat in front of the magistrate: "show me any written law in England that doth command any to put of any part of his garment either hat or coat or shous before the court."[61] The episode was reiterated in the subsequent letter and was followed by a prescript penned by Whitehead. Beneath both passages, Whitehead, Lancaster, and Atkinson's names are written, but Atkinson's was crossed out. Given his subsequent expulsion from the Quaker community, it seems that Fell or someone else who had access to this letter sought to expunge his name and thereby remove his authorship from the missive. This was a retroactive move since Atkinson was still in favor in the early part of 1655, as demonstrated by another letter written by Hubberthorne to Fox on January 17 that states that Atkinson was unfairly charged.[62]

News of other developments circulated in the beginning of 1655. Friends made progress establishing and expanding meetings in London. George Fox and Dorothy Waugh traveled from Swarthmoor to visit prisoners in Norwich, which resulted in Waugh's imprisonment after speaking in the market. Fell was apprised of this development when Hubberthorne wrote that Fox would be returning "thereawayes" in February.[63] Alexander Parker and Will Caton also wrote to Fell on February 1 about meetings in Drayton, where Fox was "hailed like a king."[64] Other itinerants were preaching throughout the southwest, including Barbara Pattison who was "moued to goe to the steeplehouse," and was likely imprisoned, although the author of the letter, Arthur Cotton, was not sure what had come of her.[65]

Also in February 1655, George Taylor reported to Fell a curious bit of news. First he stated that he had heard that Agnes Ayray and John Spooner had gotten married, but had not received permission from Fox, nor had they had a Quaker ceremony. This tells us that by this point in the mid-1650s, a new system of rituals was being established to replace traditional English customs. It also points to Fox's increasing influence over Quakers' actions. It was noted earlier that censorship of publications was established very early on. This additional example of authoritative behavior denotes the further development of Quaker orthodox behavior centered on Fox's approval. In another peculiar passage in this letter, Taylor states that the wife of printer Giles Calvert had cast some aspersions on Anthony Pearson. Taylor does not say what he was accused of, only stating that "as wee heare hee may it is like goe and cleare them."[66]

As the movement grew, the expansion and problems that itinerant Quakers faced became more pronounced. Braithwaite notes that the wildly successful Bull and Mouth meeting in Aldersgate London had been established, although it is not mentioned in the letters of this period. Burrough and Howgill preached there often, and their presence is noted in March of that year. Some heated exchanges occurred between leading Quakers, such as Fox, and other sectarians who crashed these meetings, like Ranters, Baptists, and Muggletonians.[67] Other ministers were busy throughout England. Howgill wrote from London that Fox was with him, preaching near Whitehall. Hubberthorne and Richard Clayton remained in jail, as did Myles Halhead and Thomas Salthouse in Exeter. Howgill further reported that John Stubbs and Will Caton made their way to Dover to seek passage to Holland, "Two Johns"—John Wilkinson and John Story—were in Kent, and various Quakers were imprisoned in Northampton. While Howgill planned to meet Edward Burrough in the Isle of Ely later in the week, Fox was "hardly free" to go, implying that his obligations in London were too great at that time.[68]

By the middle of March, Nayler and Fox were back in London with Edward Burrough, Francis Howgill, and Will Caton, whose trip abroad must have been delayed. This report came from Hubberthorne and Atkinson who remained jailed in Norwich, although the mood toward Atkinson had somewhat cooled at this point. He responded to a letter that he received from Fell in which she reprimanded him for some undisclosed infraction. Atkinson further stated that he would "lay down in shame" because of her displeasure, but he maintained his innocence of all accusations.[69] By July of 1655, he was no longer considered one of the faithful.

Very important to this development is the fact that when leading male itinerants were managing affairs in the south they still sought advice and direction from Fell in the north. London became the new Quaker headquarters as the base for itinerants in the south. In the first half of 1655, the "Mission of the 70," just like the Apostles, was established with Quakers traveling in pairs around England and beyond. Some pairings were already established, and new ones were created for the expansive mission. Anthony Pearson noted this organizational method on July 18, 1654, when he reported to Fox that ministers traveled in pairs "so they are two & two."[70] Burrough and Howgill were in London; Camm and Audland at Bristol; and John Story and John Wilkinson in Wiltshire. New folks coming from the north included John Stubbs and Will Caton in Dover; Richard Clayton and Thomas Bond in Norwich and Suffolk; Myles Halhead and Thomas Salthouse in Plymouth; John Slee and Thomas Lawson in Sussex; Thomas Robertson and Ambrose Rigge in Surrey and Kent; and Thomas Lancaster and Thomas Stubbs in Bedfordshire.[71] This new level of organization showed the success and growth of the movement. Before 1655, the base of operations was in the remote northwest at Swarthmoor Hall, but by this time a new step was introduced. Itinerants traveling in the south would request help, if needed, from Howgill and Burrough based in London, who in turn wrote to Fell. Like other matriarchs of her day, Fell fashioned a place for herself in the community within which she was unable to travel herself. In *The Patriarch's Wife,* Margaret Ezell states that exchange of correspondence could offer "women who were isolated by either geography or temperament to participate actively in the intellectual controversies of their day and sometimes provide the testing ground for material that was eventually to be published."[72] This was certainly the case with Fell, who circulated information concerning the travel plans of various people to help manage the movement of ideas.

In June 1655, Will Caton wrote from Holland and told of his and John Stubbs's difficulty throughout their trip, which included being put in stocks and whipped in Maidstone.[73] Others faced difficulties, but in the form of encounters with "rude multitudes" who challenged the Quaker faith. John Camm wrote to Fell on June 4 that there was a "rebellious spirit" in Kendal.[74] On June 9, John Killam reported that James Nayler and Richard Farnsworth had multiple run-ins with Manifesterians in York, which resulted in Nayler's imprisonment there.[75] Then on June 18, Alexander Parker informed Fell that both he and Fox had public arguments with Baptists and Independents in Kent.[76]

In July, the basis of Christopher Atkinson's scandal was finally revealed. At the beginning of the month, Nayler wrote to Fell that Atkinson brought disgrace on the community—"It is sadly fallen vp vs here away but the lord will remoue it from the inocent"—but that he would leave it to Burrough and Howgill to explain more thoroughly.[77] The news actually came from Richard Clayton and Richard Hubberthorne on July 12, who stated that Atkinson was a traitor to the faith for indiscretions committed in the Norwich jail. There were numerous witnesses to this undisclosed act, including John Stubbs, Will Caton, and Thomas Simmonds. Those three along with Hubberthorne, Clayton, and George Whitehead subsequently shunned Atkinson.[78] The rumor mill continued when George Taylor wrote to Fell on July 14 that he had received a letter via post that revealed that Atkinson fornicated with a woman in the jail.[79] Atkinson's disgrace must have been so pronounced because he was part of the inner circle before his fall. After July 1655, there is no more mention of him in the letter record except a brief note of the apostate Atkinson on December 10. Hubberthorne wrote to Fox and Nayler that Atkinson appeared in a meeting in Norwich with "the women w[hi]ch was defiled with him and with his spirit and when frends was parted I called them into a chamber and they were brought to owne there condemnation to the filthiness w[hi]ch was amongst them."[80]

The rest of 1655 continued much in the same manner as the beginning of the year. Braithwaite foreshadows the calamitous events of the following year when he states that Nayler was developing a cult-like following of his own, which included Rebecca Travers, who had heard him argue with Baptists at the Glasshouse in Broad Street.[81] However, there is no hint of discord between Nayler and others at this time. Rather, the letters suggest that they were still reeling from the Atkinson scandal and the disappointment of losing one of their most vocal advocates. Furthermore, although some meetings had been established in the Americas by the end of the year, the extant letters do not reflect Mary Fisher or Ann Austin's efforts. Braithwaite suggests that women were the force behind the expansion of itinerancy to distant lands: "As had been the case in the South of England, it was begun by women."[82] This nod to the traditional assertion that female preachers were valued as highly as their male counterparts is not substantiated by the letter record. If we use the letters as our guides, male preachers were beginning to far outweigh the number of women in leadership roles starting in 1654. Margaret Fell, the sole remaining leading female figure by the mid-point in the Interregnum, reinforced rather than challenged seventeenth-century notions of the woman's domestic influence.

Crisis in the Quaker movement: 1656

On January 5, Edward Burrough wrote to Fell about the horrors of spreading the word in Ireland. He claimed that no one lived there except for bands of murderers and thieves. He and Howgill faced great opposition in the form of Baptist missionaries, and Burrough was tried as a Jesuit vagabond. To add insult to injury, the postal service was terribly inconsistent so he felt isolated without a connection to the Quaker network. He claimed that books were greatly needed in the country and asked that Fell send them as soon as possible.[83] George Taylor subsequently substantiated Burrough's feelings of isolation when he wrote to Fell to tell her that the courier who was supposed to take money and supplies from Bristol to Ireland could not be found.[84] But in better news, Anthony Pearson sent £12 from Cumberland to subsidize missionary efforts. When Taylor told him that the Kendal Fund would not be able to pay him back right away, Pearson "saide it mattered not for that but however when thou sends foorth anie notice for a collection lett the note goe first for Bishoppwicke & Yorkshire and for those counties let it come first to our hands because wee know best who to give it first too and who to spare."[85] Additional funds were subsequently received from Yorkshire and Lancashire.

On January 21, Thomas Holme wrote to Fell that he received her letter and was saddened to learn that Fox was angry with him for disobeying some sort of order. The letter does not provide insights into the specifics, but Holme stated that John Abraham would write to her and confirm that he was distraught over displeasing Fox and apparently Fell, as well. Since neither the traditional nor the letter narratives clarify this situation, it is fair to assume that the discord was due to Holme's marriage to Elizabeth Leavens in late 1654. According to Geoffrey Nuttall, she was "of a peculiarly emotional temperament, given to visions and auditions," and their marriage may have been frowned upon by the Quaker leadership.[86] It is curious that Braithwaite does not mention this act of submission as it stands to strengthen Fox's position of authority.

The Quaker movement expanded substantially in 1656. In January, Mary Fisher wrote to Fox from Barbados in a very brief letter stating, "If any friends are free to come over to Barbados, they would be serviceable."[87] News of Edward Burrough's and Francis Howgill's efforts in Ireland continued to circulate. Walter Clement wrote to Fell on January 27 that he learned of six Quakers imprisoned in Dublin.[88] In February, Howgill wrote that he had departed from Burrough, who was in Waterford, while Howgill traveled to Cork. They continued to find the greatest obstacle in Baptist missionaries.[89] Richard Waller wrote to Fell on March 30 that some of the previously imprisoned Quakers in Ireland were on a mission to the Isle of Mann and Wales. Through travels abroad, Quakers learned that they faced similar problems once outside of England. On May 6, William Dewsbury wrote that Samuel Fisher and John Stubbs traveled to synagogues in Amsterdam and Rotterdam looking for someone to translate their works into Hebrew. Along the way, they encountered people who were resistant to their message just like they did in England.[90]

Dedication to missionary efforts was exemplified when personal tragedy struck, yet Quakers continued their work. One such example came on March 7 when Burrough and Howgill wrote to Fox about their travels and noted in a postscript that they had just learned that Howgill's wife had died. It is hard to imagine that he wrote this passage himself because the letter states that the loss was "a little hindrance to him, at presnt, as to settle his children, & the like, but truly he is wholly given up to doe our fathers will."[91] Regardless of the author of this letter, the meaning was clear: the Quaker mission trumped any sense of familial obligations.

One of the more tragic moments in early Quaker history came with the death of James Parnell in the Colchester prison. Braithwaite dates the event to May 5 or 6, but an ambiguously dated letter from sometime in April may move the event a bit earlier. John Audland noted in the midst of a more general newsletter to Fell that Parnell had died. He said this without much sentiment or flourish.[92] This is reiterated on April 26 when George Taylor wrote to Fell that "James Parnell died in Colchester prison about 20 days ago and they seized 94 of his books."[93] However, the fact that multiple missives were sent to Fell concerning Parnell's death suggests that it was quite significant to members of the community at the time, in contrast to the aforementioned death of Howgill's wife.

Meanwhile, what Braithwaite describes as a growing "jealousy of itinerating ministers" had started to develop by April, meaning that those who traveled for the cause were held in greater esteem than others. He cites a letter from Howgill, Audland, and Burrough to Friends in which Howgill and Burrough, just back from Ireland, and Audland, recently returned from Bristol, all met on the 16th at widow Cock's at Birkhagg outside of Kendal. Robert Collinson, of the first members of the Kendal meeting

> denied all that had been said [by Howgill, Audland, and Burrough] as only a form of words without life and power, and bade them to stay at home and be silent and not go idling up and down, and he further charged them with breaking or putting a stop to the power which had been among Kendal Friends before they came. Some seemed to approve his words, and the three Publishers of Truth "seeing the simplicity in many betrayed by the deceit," denied what he had said and afterwards issued a testimony against him as a Friend without the wedding garment, in which they exhorted all the Children of Light to deny fellowship with him until he came to repentance. They also urged all to be aware of being betrayed by the like transformed appearance which was not the power of God.[94]

This coincides with a growing dissent within the movement. In addition to the "jealousy" described above, Humphrey Norton wrote to Fox that he had been to Swarthmoor and was unhappy with what he saw there during their meetings.[95] Clearly nothing came of this, as Fell continued to be a leading figure in the north, but it demonstrates that while some were above reproach, others were not. In juxtaposition to the potential condemnation of Fell's leadership, Thomas Willan wrote to her on April 26 about the need for censorship in general and consulting her opinion on the matter.[96]

Around this time, Thomas Holme wrote to Fell concerning a clash they had about his pregnant wife, Elizabeth Leavens. Previously, Fell had admonished them for causing an undue burden on other Quakers for her to travel while pregnant.[97] This highlights a contradiction to what many have seen as equality of the sexes in the Quaker movement—Fell, a mother herself, argued that the religious community should not be subjected to new mothers, but apparently fathers of small children were not problematic for her. It is also interesting to note that Willan reported to Fell that when Fox saw the young couple in 1655, he said that their mission was going well, thereby not identifying a problem with pregnant itinerants.[98]

Also, taking a retrospective view, one can see the seeds of trouble surrounding Nayler in London several months prior to the incident in Bristol. One of Nayler's supporters, a woman only identified as "Mildred," started causing problems at the Bull and Mouth meeting in London as early as March 20, 1656. Around this time, Nayler had developed something of a cult following in the city that apparently resulted in some of the jealousy that Braithwaite mentions. Richard Hubberthorne expressed some concerns about Nayler's state of mind and behavior and noted in a letter to Fox from March 20 that he showed Fox's last letter to Nayler in the hopes that it would set him straight, noting that he "is coming around."[99] Earlier in 1655, Burrough wrote to Fell that "J. N. is come back into the City and ovr bvrthen and charge is A little abated hee being come."[100] In June, Nayler wrote to Fell that while Fox pled for him to join him in Yorkshire, he would not leave London "for I am not free of the place."[101] Whatever kept him in London, concern grew throughout the summer months, as evidenced by Farnsworth's reiteration that something was wrong with Nayler.[102]

Quaker preaching continued throughout the country, evidenced by letters written from Kendal regarding the disbursement of funds, as well as ministering and preaching in Essex and Sussex.[103] However, Bristol and the surrounding area rapidly became a new hub of activity in the second half of the Interregnum. On April 14, James Myers reported on prolific activity in the southwest. Many Quakers were in jail as a result of speaking in a church. Meetings flourished as far as Lands End, and clashes with other radical sectarians like Baptists occurred as well.[104] On May 9, John Audland started a series of reports when he wrote to Fell that the "two johns in wiltshire" and other leading itinerants like Holme, Burrough, Ann Audland, and Fox were traveling back and forth between Bristol and London.[105] A few days later on May 12, Audland wrote that books sent to Friends in Ireland were lost at sea and that Leonard Fell and Myles Batemen were released from jail in Exeter, although Bateman was too ill to travel at that time.[106] A day later, Audland stated that Howgill and Burrough were back in London after some time in Bristol. Nayler was jailed with 22 others in Exeter, including Priscilla Cotton and Mary and Dorcas Erbury.[107] On May 28, Salthouse and Halhead were released from prison.[108]

By the summer of 1656, Quakers were as far flung as they had ever been. Howgill and Thomas Robertson were in Scotland.[109] Mary Fisher and Ann Austin were in Boston, though they were expelled shortly thereafter along with the eight other Friends who came later.[110] Braithwaite states that William Ames spent 10 weeks in Holland, where he was accused of being a Jesuit.[111] Although this detail is not included in the letter record, John Stubbs wrote to Fell on May 31 that Ames was likely to return from Holland soon and that his brethren hoped that he had escaped danger. Stubbs wrote from Newcastle, where he was unable to find passage to Holland because Spanish pirates seized merchant ships and, as a result, ship owners were scared take to the seas.[112]

This letter also contains a strange reference to Stubbs's tendency toward disobedience and previous reprimands that he had received for his behavior. He stated that he was warned the last time he visited Swarthmoor Hall. Stubbs also expressed concern about what Fox was saying about him, so he requested that Fell let him know if she heard anything regarding Stubbs and his status in the community.[113] On its own, this letter may seem as if Stubbs was paranoid or overly concerned about Fell's and Fox's opinion of him. However, if put into the context of rising jealousies and what we know was on the horizon with Nayler, it seems that ministers would be interested in how they were portrayed by one another in letters that circulated throughout the network.

It was also in June that Fox suggested that Nayler go to Yorkshire, but as stated above, Nayler believed that he was needed in London.[114] This is curious because Braithwaite states that Nayler went to Yorkshire and also visited Quakers in Lincoln. Braithwaite goes on to claim that during Nayler's absence, evidence against him started to mount. The letters do not mention concerns regarding Nayler's behavior until August. According to the traditional narrative, Howgill and Burrough reproached Martha Simmonds and some other women in London.[115] Braithwaite states that when Nayler returned and Simmonds asked him for "justice," he initially refused, and she apparently said, "how are the mighty fallen." This somehow resulted in a depression and period of vulnerability for Nayler, at which time he stayed at Thomas Simmonds's house for a period of three days.[116] There is no mention of this episode in the extant letters. However, they do state that throughout June and July news continued to circulate regarding various Friends' travels, including successes convincing people and also confrontations with the law.[117] In one letter dated July 31, Leonard Fell included Nayler's travels out of London along with several others itinerants' movements.[118]

The first letter that addressed Nayler's shift in behavior came on August 5 when Richard Farnsworth told Fell that their friend was acting oddly.[119] On the 11th, Henry Fell wrote from Bristol that Nayler was in the Exeter Gaol for refusal to don his hat. He did not go into great detail because he assumed that she had heard from Burrough and Howgill concerning Nayler.[120] They actually composed their letter to her on August 13, and they stated that Nayler had left London in mid-July and that they had met up with him at a later point in Bristol. They claimed that he was "under bad influence" there and that Nayler rejected those who came to see him, including his old friends John Audland, Burrough, and Howgill.[121] On August 23, Thomas Rawlinson wrote from Exeter that he was jailed for traveling without a pass and was now near Nayler, who was behaving like a mystic, but Rawlinson did not sound critical of him; however, he noted that others, such as some female prisoners including Mary Howgill, Jane Bland, and James Harrison's wife, had "high flown spirits."[122] In contrast, John Braithwaite wrote to Fell the same day that he knew that she was aware of Nayler's behavior and of the trouble it caused for Quakers, although he did not say anything specific here. He asked that Fell pray for Nayler, indicating that he hoped things would turn around.[123]

In late July 1656, Nayler went to Bristol with two men and two "Shunammite women" who began "to compromise him" by bowing and singing before him.[124] Some in Bristol saw Martha Simmonds, one of the London women who was accused of bewitching Nayler, as a bad influence so they separated her from Nayler. Howgill and Audland were there and reported on these events.[125] Some "sober Friends," John Bolton and Nicholas Ganniclife, accompanied Nayler to visit Fox in the Launceston jail.[126] Fox had already been informed of Nayler's behavior and was reportedly anxious to see him. This moment in the story provides yet another example of inconsistency in Braithwaite's reporting and the letters—he states that Nayler and company were arrested on the road by Devonshire justices for traveling without a pass, and that this was when he was jailed in Exeter. However, as has been noted above, this event was supposed to have occurred months earlier. On August 23, Thomas Rawlinson, either in jail at Exeter or visiting Nayler, wrote to Fell and discouraged her from believing everything she had heard about Nayler.[127] While the letters do not describe a meeting between Burrough, Howgill, and Martha Simmonds, a letter from Richard Hubberthorne to Margaret Fell on August 26 indicates as much. He stated that as soon as he arrived in London, he followed Howgill's lead and went to Simmonds to learn more about Nayler's state of mind. In an improbable encounter, Hubberthorne claimed that Simmonds admitted to putting Nayler under her influence and also implicated Hannah Stringer, as well.[128]

Meanwhile, Fox was jailed in Launceston. From there he wrote to Nayler stating that he disapproved of many of the things he had heard his friend had said and done. Fox instructed Nayler to discard his "bad company," which included Martha Simmonds, Hannah Stringer, and her husband as they "are liars and slanderers."[129] Interestingly, some Quakers continued to speak well of Nayler, including John Stubbs who stated that he was in jail with Nayler in Bristol where they were kept in close quarters with "pirates." He stated: "JN is dear to everyone."[130] Others who were close to Nayler at this time did not mention rising tensions; for instance, Alexander Parker stated that Nayler was with him in Tregangeeves and that Fox had recently been there as well.[131] Stubbs and Parker were not ignorant of the situation, but their failure to mention it to Fell somewhat complicates the idea that the entire community (excepting Nayler's sycophants) was bothered by his actions.

Yet others insisted that Nayler was completely wrong and that he was even receptive to accepting his responsibility for causing the rift between himself and Fox. Hubberthorne wrote on September 16 that he met with Nayler near Exeter and that he was "pretty low and tender." Hubberthorne believed that Nayler was about to open up about how he had been manipulated by the cohort in London, but then the head temptress, Simmonds, called Nayler away and he was "much suiecte to her" once again. Hubberthorne was of the opinion that removing Nayler from Simmonds and the others would restore Nayler's love to his faithful brethren.[132]

On October 4, Walter Clement wrote to Fell that Fox had asked one of the key links in the Quaker network, "W Somers," to let Fox see any letters that may go to the west country, particularly those to Nayler. Clement felt compelled to let Fell know that even her letters to Nayler would first be read by Fox. Clement went on to add that he did not intend to say much about the Nayler situation because John Audland would fill her in when he next saw her. All that he did say was that Nayler was not doing well and he attributed that to Martha Simmonds's constant presence with him. He also noted that Fox had recently met with Nayler.[133] Shortly after their meeting, Fox wrote to Nayler from Reading stating that he acted as if Martha Simmonds was his mother and that she told Fox to bow down before her son. Fox warned Nayler that she was preventing his true friends from being near him, and that Hannah Stringer was a blight on the community too. Three days later, on October 15, 1656, there was a letter from Fell to Nayler admonishing him. She was most likely echoing Fox's sentiments from his angry letter of the previous month.[134] Braithwaite says the letter was probably returned to the sender because Nayler was released from jail shortly after.[135] The reason may have been because, as stated earlier, Fox required that all mail sent to the west go through him first. On October 17, 1656, the eve of Nayler's release, Hannah Stringer wrote to him calling him "the only begotten Son of God."[136] Her husband also signed the letter and included a postscript stating, "thy name shall be no more James Nayler, but Jesus."[137] This letter was found on Nayler when he was arrested; he said that he had kept it because it scared him but did not want anyone to see it.

Richard Roper insinuated in an October 20 letter to Fell that the situation was much worse than others had suggested. He stated that the conflict was not between Fox and Nayler, but rather it started when two camps emerged in London: one saying "I am of James" and the other saying "I am of Francis and Edward."[138] There is no evidence elsewhere of such a division, but all three men were active in London so it is plausible that they all, not just Nayler, may have developed cult-like followings in the capital. Furthermore, Roper's reference suggests that there may have been general tensions within the movement by 1656 and that the episode in Bristol was merely a boiling point rather than an isolated event.

The best description of what came next was written by George Bishope to Fell on October 27. Bishope was in Bristol at the time and provided as reliable of an insider's account as possible. Bishop stated that Nayler's followers

> made drunk w[i]th the indignation that the Lord they brought in J.N. in horseback, whoe rod with his hands before him, our reigne of his bridle Mart: Symds: led & han: string: the other, and some wanton his sides, and Hannah's husband want bare before him, and Dorcas Erbury with a man of the Isle of Eyrod after, & thus they led him, and thus hee rod through the towne, the women singing as they went holy, holy, holy: Hosanah, and soe pass to the White Hart a bad inn wher they lay when they brought him first to Bristoll on the fifth month; multitudes following them (for the whole towne was moued) through

the streets thither, and into their chamber, though it had rayned very hard, before when the woman put of some of their upper garments to drie them at the fire. This mayst soon brought the magistrates together, wher such for them all, & J.N. pockets they search't and found about him _ letters of those women to him, wherein they call him Jesus (and they _ name was noe longer James) the only begotten son of God, the king, of Israelle, the Prince of Peace with such like, by which the mistery of Iniquite ...

The next day J.N. was sent for before the magistrates _ the priests being present, and G.F. letter was read to him sentence by sentence, and asked hee was whither hee would owne it, some of which hee did, and Martha Symonds _ is called your mother, soe _ his mother, but as to their other questions, they obtained nothing of it from him for hee was subtile, few in words, and low of when examination _ of the papers I have endeauord to get copies that soe might _ the certainty which I can procure its like I hay send copies ...

This day, M. was examined alone, and I heare how shee rambled in to declaring how shee spake first to J.N. compase't him, how hee was at Bristoll before with such like, w[hi]ch cleared the innocent the more whoe before this day saw, & _ against this spirit, & G.F. letter was read to her; shee was very confident and boasted with her remark should come, 2 trusted farmer the priest exceedingly but of chuse things I can little enlarge friends staying _ this is wort, and I am not soe certayne of particulars.[139]

News of the Nayler situation traveled far, eventually reaching Will Caton in Holland. Presumably he knew that Fell had greater access to English developments than he did, but he wrote to her in November stating that Nayler was jailed at that time.[140] George Taylor wrote to Fell from London to let her know that Parliament's diurnal stated that Nayler and those with him in Bristol (including Hannah Stringer, Martha Simmonds, and Dorcas Erbury) had been taken to Westminster.[141] Likewise, on November 9, Thomas Salthouse wrote to Fox from Plymouth that a report had been issued by Parliament concerning Nayler's trial.[142]

It is interesting to note that Nayler's sins were not received in the same manner as Christopher Atkinson's. While Fox, Fell, and others admonished Nayler's behavior, they did not appear to want to ostracize him from the community. Anthony Pearson was privy to the trial and stated that Nayler answered all of the accusations "with soe much wisdom, meekness, and clearness to the understanding of all indeferent persons that the whole assemblie except some violent men, of the committee were strangely astonished and satisfied with his answers, hee was accused for being called Christ the Son of God."[143] On November 25, Hubberthorne wrote to Fell that Nayler and the women were jailed in London, although he did not state it with the vitriol that his earlier letters contained.[144]

Braithwaite states that after Nayler was taken into custody, even some of his followers started to question their involvement. On November 1, Thomas Simmonds, despite his prior religious fervor, wrote to his wife that they had been wrong in their conduct. Simmonds particularly blamed his wife because, while he was not at the Bristol entrance, he feared that his wife was leading the activities, stating: "If there was such a glory among you, why were you not silent, and haue let the people cry Hosanna, etc. Your work is soon come to an end: part of the army that fell at Bvrford was your figure."[145] Word of Nayler's "fall" continued to spread. Audland and Halhead started having trouble with meetings in Wales following the episode because they were "overrun with ministers and magistrates."[146] On November 25, Hubberthorne was disapproving of Nayler, but was still "tender toward him" because he had continuously denied that he was Christ.[147] This may have been the major sticking point for Quakers—if Nayler had called himself Christ, his actions would have been unforgivable, but the consensus was that he did not blaspheme in this way. Since Nayler's offense was acceptance of his sycophants' flattery, most in the movement were able to forgive once he recognized his errors. Apparently likening oneself to Christ was behavior reserved exclusively for Fox.

While this episode dominated much of the correspondence of the latter half of 1656 (at least that which was preserved), Quakers continued with their other business, traveling and ministering around the country and throughout Europe and the Atlantic World. Will Caton traveled extensively throughout Scotland in the summer. He claimed that this apparently displeased Fox who had directed him to go to Kent and then Holland. Fox's plans were apparently well known because Henry Fell wrote to Margaret on August 11 that Caton had followed Fox's directive, despite the fact that he stated that he had not.[148] Fox was also angry that Mary Howgill went to Kent in Caton's stead without Fox's approval.[149] Walter Clement reported to Fell that two unnamed Quaker women were imprisoned in Chester—one for marriage (the meaning of this is unclear) and the other for disrupting a priest. He also traveled throughout the southwest and then headed to Swarthmoor with his family. A ship left from Bristol going to Barbados that included Quakers and supplies for those already there.[150] By November, Henry Fell stated that he, Peter Head, John Rous, and Mary Fisher were all there, where they had unpleasant interactions with a Ranter named Joseph Salman.[151] Lancelot Wardell traveled in Durham with Anthony Pearson and others.[152] While traveling to Cornwall, Alexander Parker heard that two women were imprisoned in Plymouth and the jailer would not allow them to see their husbands.[153] In August, John Audland had meetings around Bristol.[154] Also in August, "TC & John Martendall" were jailed in Exeter for refusal to swear oaths.[155] John Stubbs described travails in Holland stating "integrity did not vphold me I should sometimes faint vnder the travels and many tryalls." Yet, he said he considered going on a grand tour to Ireland, Scotland, Flanders, Germany, and Denmark.[156] Apparently,

Caton eventually followed Fox's earlier directive and went to Holland in November.[157] John Slee held several meetings in Skipton.[158] Thomas Salthouse was in Cornwall and next headed to Somersetshire.[159] Richard Hickcocke met up with four Friends in Cheshire who were banished from the Isle of Mann.[160] Arthur Cotton asked Fox to take care of a friend and fellow Quaker who was traveling to London from Cornwall to answer a writ for refusal to pay tithes.[161] In November, Hubberthorne traveled to Essex, Suffolk, and Norfolk.[162] George Taylor was in Carlisle when George Wilson, a former soldier, joined him in his travels and then met up with William Dewsbury. They had books that they were ready to publish, but they were waiting on Fox's permission to move forward with them.[163]

In such a tumultuous period it is difficult to summarize the significance of 1656 to the development of Quakerism. The Nayler Affair exposed the Quakers' vulnerability on a national scale and prompted a retreat of sorts away from wild displays of faith. Fearful of unwanted attention, Quakers became increasingly self-regulating, and nearly everyone fell in line with the idea that Fox was the sole leader of the community.

From sectarian movement to established religion: 1657–1660

While the events in Bristol (and their corollaries in London) challenged the Quakers' efforts, evangelical efforts continued much as they had before. On January 3, 1657, John Stubbs wrote to Fell from Dublin stating that he had not heard from her or his wife in a long time but did not expect to because "any vncertanie abode and for my trauel in the ovtward hath been mvch in this nacon of Ireland."[164] Will Caton wrote from London on January 19 that he had traveled extensively throughout the south of England, including Sussex "where there was seuerall Seekers (soe called) and the most part of two meetings were conuinced."[165] Other Quakers were traveling throughout London and Kent where "strong reports" concerning Nayler were causing difficulties for itinerants at this time.[166] The Bull and Mouth pub became a central meeting place for Quakers, and Caton noted to Fell that he saw Burrough and Howgill there. Thomas Salthouse also wrote that "the seed is great" in northern England, reminding Fell, and other potential readers the letter, of the origins of their movement.[167]

However, the effects of Nayler's behavior continued to be felt. George Taylor wrote to Fell on February 1 that he had read Parliament's diurnal that detailed Nayler's punishment after leaving Bristol. On Saturday, January 17, "Mr. Roach" made Nayler ride into Lawford Gate backwards on a horse. Throughout the course of the ride, Nayler was whipped and then clothed so he could be judged. Robert Rich, "late merchant of London," rode by him bareheaded and singing. Then on January 23, Nayler was taken back from Bristol to London where he was put in Bridewell Prison, which is where he remained for the rest of his sentence.[168] In February, Hubberthorne reported to Fell that Martha Simmonds, John Stringer, and several women went to a meeting in London and continued to cause some distress.[169] Likewise, Edward Burrough wrote on February 12 that some friends "are burdened by some woman's ministry in Bedfordshire." The location suggests that this woman was a separate problem from Simmonds and her group, although Burrough stated that the unnamed woman visited Nayler and his wife in Bridewell.[170]

On February 19, Henry Fell wrote from Barbados that he had been brought before the justices on Christmas Day to give sureties or "I should goe to prison I told them I had not behaued myself isll and therefore I should not give him security."[171] He did not clarify if he spent any time in prison. He did indicate that in February he planned to go to New England via a ship arriving from "Ould England," which had carried Thomas Burden and Mary Dyer who was joining her husband in Rhode Island. Henry Fell later wrote on May 24 that he and John Rous were in Barbados; however, Ann Burden and Mary Dyer were in prison in New England.[172]

In March, others had thoughts of going abroad too. Fox "appointed" Will Caton to go to the west. After that, Caton intended to go to Surrey and then Holland. In contrast to their previous exchange, Caton stated that he would go to Holland without Fox's approval if he did not see him soon.[173] In the same message, written from London, Caton stated that meetings there were sometimes disrupted by "those that adheres after J:N: they are grown very impudent many of them."[174] At the end of the month, John Hall wrote that he had a meeting with Baptists in Inverness, indicating that cooperation may be possible.[175] This contrasted with John Stubbs's experience in London where he and Fox clashed with Baptists.[176] Richard Roper wrote to Fell from Waterford that several Baptists had interrupted Quaker meetings, noting one disturbance in particular that occurred at a Friend's house who had previously been a part of the sect.[177]

The Kendal Fund continued to disburse money throughout the spring of 1657. On May 9, George Taylor wrote to Fell that some traveling through the north were unhappy about the disbursements that they received (or failed to receive).[178] They sent Fell a copy of the receipt for the amount of money that was given to a group of itinerants.[179] Their notices to her not only stated when funds were disbursed but also when donations were made, such as when Taylor notified Fell that the 40 shillings that she sent for Richard Roper and Robert Salthouse had been received and were on their way to their intended recipients.[180]

By mid-1657, sentiments toward James Nayler shifted from anger and frustration to gratitude that his frame of mind seemed to have changed. George Taylor had heard from John Audland that he had visited Nayler in jail and that he was doing rather well. They were able to discuss a variety of matters, indicating to Audland that Nayler was returning to his correct mindset.[181] John Braithwaite wrote that "some hurt" from Martha Simmonds's company could be felt as far away as the greater Bristol area; however, he stated that the Lord "gave us dominion over them."[182] In addition, Richard Waller and Richard Roper stated that meetings in Ireland had received letters from Nayler's followers who tried to persuade the community of their position. He was pleased to note, though, that Elizabeth Morgan intercepted the letters and stopped the spread of their ideas before the newly converted in Ireland heard from them.[183]

In November of 1657, Henry Fell wrote from London about his trip to Barbados. On the return trip to England, his ship was taken by Spanish pirates and then sent to Rochelle, France. From there he somehow found passage to Norfolk and then London.[184] After retelling his woes, he relayed that Hubberthorne, Burrough, and Fell's son George were in London. Martha Simmonds was at the Bull and Mouth meeting and several Quakers returned from Paris.[185] Elizabeth Coward and Elizabeth Hooton had gotten aboard a ship to some undisclosed location.

Problems with "that imprudent lasse" continued in 1658. Hubberthorne wrote to Fox that Simmonds "th[a]t said shee was above the apostles and shee makes it her common practice to goe vpon the first dayse to the bull and mouth and to Woster house but heare is many great peaceable meetings in the citie."[186] He warned Fox that no one would be in London for a while because Howgill intended to go to Essex, Suffolk, and Norfolk, although Hubberthorne did not say why he would not be available. By mid-March, Hubberthorne was back in London (from wherever he had gone) and stated that he had many meetings in London. All had gone well except those at the Bull and Mouth, Woster House, and sometimes the Strand where two new nuisances, "Mildred and Judy," frequented.[187] It seems that the old burden of Martha Simmonds and the other Nayler followers had dissipated and been replaced by newly bothersome women that Hubberthorne, in particular, seemed to have problems with.

Even as the Interregnum drew to a close, Quakers continued to report on conflicts with other sectarians. Richard Hickcocke wrote to Fell from Chester about meetings amongst Ranters and Familists, although it is difficult to believe that the second group actually still existed in 1658. He stated that Burrough argued with them, and, according to Hickcocke, of course overcame them.[188] Likewise, Alexander Parker encountered many Baptists and Brownists in Scotland in January.[189] Richard Clayton spoke with some Baptists in Dublin on his way to Waterford.[190]

1659 continued the course of what the Quakers had been building throughout the rest of the Interregnum. Friends traveled throughout England, including Fox, Burrough, and Caton who came and went through London. However, travels continued to extend to new territories such as Rome, where John Perrot and John Lose went—Lose died in jail there, although Perrot noted that he did not die at the hands of the Inquisition.[191] In February, Alexander Parker went back to Lands End. Thomas Salthouse was in Cornwall.[192] And although Henry Fell said that he would go back to England if God wanted it, he had traveled throughout the Caribbean, establishing meetings in Surinam where he found Indians who were "worse than the English," which was a true condemnation.[193]

Fox's authority was firmly established at this point as reflected by Elizabeth Adams's letter where she said that she feared he was ashamed of her "if I have mis behaued my selfe in any thing as to intarrning the truth if thou haue a word from the lord."[194] This point is one of the most important aspects of both the traditional narrative and what we learn from reading the letters: that Fox became the leader despite multiple schisms and difficulties. However, he did not attain this position alone. Fell and those who remained faithful to Fox throughout the Interregnum protected both their leader and the narrative that kept him in power. The traditional narrative omits some of the early conflicts and shapes the way modern readers assess the 1656 Nayler episode in Bristol. However, the letters cannot tell a coherent narrative on their own, so a reassessment of the early Quaker story in light of additional resources that have often been overlooked can provide a much more complicated but comprehensive narrative. This allows us to better assess the early years of this religious community and in so doing, acknowledge the essential role that Fell played in shaping the early Quaker faith.

Notes

1. Joseph Besse's work is discussed at length in Chapter 6.
2. Sydney V. James, *Review of The Beginnings of Quakerism by William C. Braithwaite*, revised and annotated by Henry J. Cadbury (New York: Cambridge University Press, 1955) in *The William and Mary Quarterly* 19 no. 2 (April 1962): 302. This is a review of the 1955 reissue of the original 1912 publication.
3. Ibid., 303.
4. Elsa F. Glines (ed.), *Undaunted Zeal: The Letters of Margaret Fell* (Richmond, IN: Friends United Press, 2003).
5. Jane Couchman and Ann Crabb, *Women's Letters Across Europe, 1400–1700: Form and Persuasion* (London: Ashgate, 2005), 4.
6. Overall, this study does not rely heavily on published sources with the major exception of Joseph Besse's eighteenth-century work, *A Collection of the Sufferings of the People Call'd Quakers*, which is the subject of Chapter 6.
7. Braithwaite, *The Beginnings of Quakerism*, 45.
8. For a full discussion of the centrality of the inner light to Quaker theology see Hilary Hinds's impressive work *George Fox and Early Quaker Culture* (Manchester: Manchester University Press, 2011).
9. In 1653, Margaret Fell referred to the Quakers as "Children of Light": MSS vol. 378/131. Margaret Fell to Unknown: Location unknown?, 1653.
10. Braithwaite, *The Beginnings of Quakerism*, 46.
11. George Fox, *The Journal of George Fox*, ed. John L. Nickalls (Cambridge: Cambridge University Press, 1952), 10, and Braithwaite, *The Beginnings of Quakerism*, 55.
12. Fox, *The Journal of George Fox*, 81.
13. Braithwaite, *The Beginnings of Quakerism*, 57. However, Braithwaite states that the term was used as early as 1647 to refer to "a sect of women (they are at

Southwark) come from beyond sea, called Quakers, and these swell, shiver and shake, and when they come to themselves,—for in all this fit Mahomet's Holy Ghost hath been conversing with them—they being to preach what hath been delivered to them by the Spirit." Braithwaite cites Clarendon MSS No. 2624.
14. Ibid.
15. Michael Watts, *The Dissenters* (Oxford: Clarendon Press, 1978), 300.
16. Sally Bruyneel "Margaret Fell: Historical Context and the Shape of Quaker Thought," *Quaker Religious Thought* 95, no. 4 (2000): 29.
17. Braithwaite, *The Beginnings of Quakerism*, 100.
18. Ibid., 103.
19. MSS vols. 323–24/16. Thomas Aldam and Elizabeth Hooton to George Fox: York Castle, July 1652.
20. MSS vol. 352/373. Thomas Aldam to George Fox and Others: York, July 1652.
21. Ibid.
22. MSS vol. 354/65. James Nayler to George Fox: Appleby, November 1652.
23. MSS vol. 354/45. Richard Farnsworth to Margaret Fell and Others: Balby, December 2, 1652.
24. MSS vol. 354/40. Thomas Aldam to Friends: York, November 1652.
25. MSS vol. 354/36. Thomas Aldam to George Fox: York, 1652.
26. Watts, *The Dissenters*, 193.
27. Braithwaite, *The Beginnings of Quakerism*, 113.
28. MSS vols. 323–24/74. Francis Howgill to Margaret Fell: Appleby, January 5, 1653.
29. MSS vol. 354/66. James Nayler to George Fox: Appleby, February 1653.
30. MSS vols. 323–24/15. Thomas Aldam to Captain Amor Stoddard: York Castle, February 19, 1653.
31. Braithwaite, *The Beginnings of Quakerism*, 122.
32. MSS vols. 323–24/17. Thomas Aldam to Captain Amor Stoddard: York Castle, June 21, 1653.
33. Braithwaite, *The Beginnings of Quakerism*, 127.
34. MSS vol. 352/341. Richard Hubberthorne to Margaret Fell: Lancaster, September 13, 1653.
35. Ibid.
36. MSS vol 355/66, John Lawson to Margaret Fell: Chester, November 1653; and MSS vol. 355/69, John Lawson to Fell and Others: Chester, November 1653.
37. Ibid.
38. Braithwaite, *The Beginnings of Quakerism*, 125.
39. Ibid.
40. MSS vol. 352/339. Richard Hubberthorne to Margaret Fell: Chester, December 4, 1653.
41. Braithwaite, *The Beginnings of Quakerism*, 134–35.
42. Braithwaite, *The Beginnings of Quakerism*, 304.
43. Ibid.
44. Ibid., 134–35.
45. MSS vol. S81/141. John Audland to Margaret Fell: Bristol, February 10, 1654.
46. MSS vol. 354/35. Anthony Pearson to Edward Burrough: Location unknown, February 21, 1654.
47. Ibid.
48. MSS vol. 354/42. Thomas Aldam to Margaret Fell: York, March 1654.

36 The making of Quakerism

49. MSS vol. 355/131. William Dewsbury to Margaret Fell: York, May 2, 1654.
50. MSS vols. 323–24/22. Roger Hebden to George Fox: York Castle, April 27, 1654.
51. MSS vol. 355/1. Richard Hubberthorne to George Fox: Frandley, Great Budworth, May 29, 1654.
52. Ibid.
53. MSS vols. 323–24/161. Edward Burrough to George Fox: Chester, July 5, 1654.
54. Ibid. Ariel Hessayon describes their relationship as being literary and financial: "In July 1654 the Quaker Isabel Buttery was apparently given £20 by Pembroke, using some of it to finance the printing of books which she distributed in London on a Sunday." Ariel Hessayon, *"Gold Tried in the Fire": The Prophet Theaurau John Tany and the English Revolution* (Aldershot, England: Ashgate, 2007), 321.
55. MSS vol. 351/2. Margaret Killam to George Fox: Cambridge, September 1654.
56. Braithwaite, *The Beginnings of Quakerism*, 188–193.
57. MSS vol. 351/89. Francis Howgill to Robert Widder: London, September 23, 1654; MSS vol. 355/5. Richard Hubberthorne to Edward Burrough: Location unknown, September 27, 1654; MSS vol. S81/109. Richard Hubberthorne and James Parnell to Margaret Fell: Oakington, Cambridgeshire, September 28, 1654; MSS vol. S81/68. Edward Burrough and Francis Howgill to Margaret Fell: London, October 2, 1654.
58. Fuller discussion of Christopher Atkinson's fall from grace and subsequent shunning in the Quaker community is discussed later in this chapter as knowledge of it unfolded in the letter narrative.
59. MSS vol. S81/68. Edward Burrough and Francis Howgill to Margaret Fell: London, October 2, 1654.
60. Braithwaite, *The Beginnings of Quakerism*, 186.
61. MSS vol. 352/354. Richard Hubberthorne and Christopher Atkinson to Margaret Fell: Norwich, January 11, 1655.
62. MSS vol. 355/2. Richard Hubberthorne to George Fox: Norwich, January 17, 1655.
63. MSS vol. 352/346. Richard Hubberthorne to Margaret Fell: Norwich, February 1, 1655.
64. MSS vol. 356/234. Alexander Parker and William Caton to Margaret Fell: Higham-on-the-Hill, February 1, 1655.
65. MSS vol. 354/94. Arthur Cotton to George Fox and Others: Plymouth, February 20, 1655.
66. MSS vol. 352/214. George Taylor to Margaret Fell: Location unknown, February 26, 1655.
67. Braithwaite, *The Beginnings of Quakerism*, 182–85.
68. MSS vol. S81/72. Francis Howgill to Margaret Fell: London, March 1655.
69. MSS vol. 352/347. Richard Hubberthorne and Christopher Atkinson to Margaret Fell: Norwich, March 15, 1655.
70. MSS vol. 354/34. Anthony Pearson to George Fox: London, July 18, 1654.
71. Braithwaite, *The Beginnings of Quakerism*, 185.
72. Margaret Ezell, *The Patriarch's Wife: Literary Evidence and the History of the Family* (Chapel Hill and London: The University of North Carolina Press, 1987), 76.

73. MSS vol. S81/9. William Caton to Margaret Fell: Location unknown, June 1655.
74. MSS vol. 355/119. John Camm to Margaret Fell: Camsgill, Preston Patrick, June 4, 1655.
75. MSS vol. 355/88. John Killam to Margaret Fell: York, June 9, 1655.
76. MSS vol. S81/94. Alexander Parker to Margaret Fell: Hawkhurst, Kent, June 18, 1655.
77. MSS vol. 354/81. James Nayler to Margaret Fell: London, July 1655.
78. MSS vol. 351/30. Richard Clayton and Richard Hubberthorne to Margaret Fell: Wramplingham, July 12, 1655.
79. MSS vol. 352/239. George Taylor to Margaret Fell: Location unknown, July 14, 1655.
80. MSS vol. 355/7. Richard Hubberthorne to George Fox and James Nayler: Norwich, December 10, 1655.
81. Braithwaite, *The Beginnings of Quakerism*, 201.
82. Ibid., 402.
83. MSS vol. 354/16. Edward Burrough to Margaret Fell: Waterford, Ireland, January 5, 1656.
84. MSS vol. 352/265. George Taylor to Margaret Fell: Kendal, January 19, 1656.
85. Ibid.
86. "Dictionary of Quaker Biography" in Friends House, London, note by Geoffrey Nuttall, 63.
87. MSS vol. 356/193. Mary Fisher to George Fox: Barbados, January 30, 1656.
88. MSS vol. 351/178. Walter Clement to Margaret Fell: Olveston, January 27, 1656.
89. MSS vols. 323–24/61. Francis Howgill to George Fox and James Nayler: Cork, Ireland, February 18, 1656.
90. MSS vol. S81/164. William Dewsbury to Margaret Fell: Essex, May 6, 1656.
91. MSS vols. 323–24/176. Edward Burrough and Francis Howgill to George Fox: Lancaster, March 7, 1656.
92. MSS vol. S81/136. John Audland to Margaret Fell: Bristol, April 1656.
93. MSS vol. 352/272. George Taylor to Margaret Fell: Location unknown, April 26, 1656.
94. Braithwaite, *The Beginnings of Quakerism*, 345.
95. Ibid.
96. MSS vol. 352/272. Thomas Willan and George Taylor to Margaret Fell: Kendal, April 26, 1656.
97. MSS vol. 354/150. John Audland to Margaret Fell: Bristol, May 9, 1656. See Chapter 3 for additional discussion of Fell's attitude toward female preachers.
98. MSS vol. 352/274. Thomas Willan to Margaret Fell: Kendal, May 31, 1656.
99. MSS vol. 355/12. Richard Hubberthorne to George Fox: London, March 20, 1656.
100. MSS vol. S81/73. Edward Burrough to Margaret Fell: London, 1655.
101. MSS vol. 354/82. James Nayler to Margaret Fell: London, June 1, 1656.
102. MSS vol. 354/56. Richard Farnsworth to Margaret Fell: Kendalshire, August 5, 1656.
103. MSS vol. 352/272. George Taylor to Margaret Fell: Location unknown, April 26, 1656; MSS vol. 354/32. Thomas Taylor to James Nayler: Market Harborough, April 28, 1656; MSS vol. 352/394. Katherine Evans to Margaret

Fell: English Batch, April 22, 1656; MSS vol. 352/274. Thomas Willan to Margaret Fell: Kendal, May 3, 1656; MSS vol. S81/164. William Dewsbury to Margaret Fell: Essex, May 6, 1656.
104. MSS vol. 352/360. James Myers to Friends: Launceston, April 14, 1656.
105. MSS vol. 354/150. John Audland to Margaret Fell: Bristol, May 9, 1656.
106. MSS vols. 323–324/110. John Audland to Edward Burrough: Bristol, May 12, 1656.
107. MSS vol. 351/12. John Audland to Margaret Fell: Bristol, May 13, 1656.
108. MSS vol. S81/49. Myles Halhead and Thomas Salthouse to Margaret Fell: Exeter, May 28, 1656.
109. Braithwaite, *The Beginnings of Quakerism*, 238.
110. Ibid., 402–405.
111. Ibid., 407.
112. MSS vol. 355/25. John Stubbs to Margaret Fell: Newcastle-upon-Tyne, May 31, 1656.
113. Ibid.
114. MSS vol. 354/82. James Nayler to Margaret Fell: London, June 1, 1656.
115. Braithwaite, *The Beginnings of Quakerism*, 244.
116. Ibid.
117. MSS vol. S81/149. John Audland to Margaret Fell: Bristol, June 20, 1656; MSS vol. 351/179. Walter Clement to Margaret Fell: Olveston, July 15, 1656; MSS vol. 352/277. Lancelot Wardell to Margaret Fell: Sunderland, July 18, 1656; MSS vol. 351/165. Alexander Parker to Margaret Fell: Plymouth, July 22, 1656; MSS vol. 352/313. William Caton to Margaret Fell: Launceston, July 23, 1656; MSS vol. 351/120. Leonard Fell to Margaret Fell: Beckerings Park, Ridgmont, July 31, 1656.
118. MSS vol. 351/120. Leonard Fell to Margaret Fell: Beckerings Park, Ridgmont, July 31, 1656.
119. MSS vol. 354/56. Richard Farnsworth to Margaret Fell: Kendalshire, August 5, 1656.
120. MSS vol. 351/81. Henry Fell to Margaret Fell: Bristol, August 11, 1656.
121. MSS vol. S81/61. Francis Howgill and Edward Burrough to Margaret Fell: London, August 13, 1656.
122. MSS vol. 354/12. Thomas Rawlinson to Margaret Fell: Exeter, August 23, 1656.
123. MSS vol. 354/86. John Braithwaite to Margaret Fell: Salisbury, August 23, 1656.
124. 2 Kings 4:27 and 4:37. See also Braithwaite, *The Beginnings of Quakerism*, 245.
125. MSS vol. S81/149. John Audland to Margaret Fell: Bristol, June 20, 1656.
126. Braithwaite, *The Beginnings of Quakerism*, 247.
127. MSS vol. 354/12. Thomas Rawlinson to Margaret Fell: Exeter, August 23, 1656.
128. MSS vol. S81/116. Richard Hubberthorne to Margaret Fell: London, August 26, 1656.
129. MSS vol. 354/195. George Fox to James Nayler: Location unknown, September 1656.
130. MSS vol. 355/27. John Stubbs to Margaret Fell: Bristol, September 2, 1656.

131. MSS vol. 351/167. Alexander Parker to Margaret Fell: Tregangeeves, St. Austell, September 13, 1656.
132. MSS vol. 354/153. Richard Hubberthorne to Margaret Fell: Location unknown, September 16, 1656.
133. MSS vol. 351/181. Walter Clement to Margaret Fell: Olveston, October 4, 1656.
134. Braithwaite, *The Beginnings of Quakerism*, 249.
135. Ibid.
136. Ibid., 248.
137. Ibid.
138. MSS vol. 354/131. Richard Roper to Margaret Fell: Woburn, October 20, 1656. The "Francis and Edward" implied here are Howgill and Burrough.
139. MSS vol. 351/188. George Bishope to Margaret Fell: Bristol, October 27, 1656.
140. MSS vol. S81/3. William Caton to Margaret Fell: Location unknown, November 1656.
141. MSS vol. 351/94. George Taylor to Margaret Fell: Location unknown, November 1656.
142. MSS vol. 354/157. Thomas Salthouse to George Fox: Plymouth, November 9, 1656.
143. MSS vol. 354/78. Anthony Pearson to George Fox: Westminster, November 18, 1656.
144. MSS vol. S81/117. Richard Hubberthorne to Margaret Fell: London, November 25, 1656.
145. Braithwaite, *The Beginnings of Quakerism*, 256.
146. Ibid.
147. MSS vol. S81/117. Richard Hubberthorn to Margaret Fell: London, November 25, 1656.
148. MSS vol. 351/81. Henry Fell to Margaret Fell: Bristol, August 11, 1656.
149. MSS vol. 352/313. William Caton to Margaret Fell: Launceston, July 23, 1656.
150. MSS vol. 351/179. Walter Clement to Margaret Fell: Olveston, July 15, 1656.
151. MSS vol. 351/66. Henry Fell to Margaret Fell: Barbados, November 3, 1656.
152. MSS vol. 352/277. Lancelot Wardell to Margaret Fell: Sunderland, July 18, 1656.
153. MSS vol. 351/165. Alexander Parker to Margaret Fell: Plymouth, July 22, 1656.
154. MSS vol. 351/81. Henry Fell to Margaret Fell: Bristol, August 11, 1656.
155. MSS vol. 352/361. James Myers to Margaret Fell: Launceston, August 14, 1656.
156. MSS vol. 355/27. John Stubbs to Margaret Fell: Bristol, September 2, 1656.
157. MSS vol. S81/3. William Caton to Margaret Fell: Location unknown, November 1656.
158. MSS vol. 355/110. John Slee to Margaret Fell: Scalehouse, Skipton, November 8, 1656.
159. MSS vol. 354/157. Thomas Salthouse to George Fox: Plymouth, November 9, 1656.
160. MSS vol. 351/141. Richard Hickcocke to Margaret Fell: Middlewich, November 12, 1656.

40 *The making of Quakerism*

161. MSS vol. 355/163. Arthur Cotton to George Fox: Plymouth, November 18, 1656.
162. MSS vol. S81/117. Richard Hubberthorne to Margaret Fell: London, November 25, 1656.
163. MSS vol. 352/293. George Taylor to Margaret Fell: Kendal, December 6, 1656.
164. MSS vol. 355/24. John Stubbs to Margaret Fell: Dublin, Ireland, January 3, 1657.
165. MSS vol. 352/314. Will Caton to Margaret Fell: London, January 19, 1657.
166. MSS vol. 352/314. William Caton to Margaret Fell: London, January 19, 1657.
167. MSS vol. 354/185. Thomas Salthouse to Margaret Fell: Plymouth, January 30, 1657.
168. MSS vol. 352/300. George Taylor to Margaret Fell: Kendal, February 1, 1657.
169. MSS vol. S81/118. Richard Hubberthorne to Margaret Fell: London, February 10, 1657.
170. MSS vols. 323–24/ 36. Edward Burrough to George Fox: London, February 12, 1657.
171. MSS vol. 351/68. Henry Fell to Margaret Fell: Barbados, February 19, 1657.
172. MSS vol. 351/79. Henry Fell to Margaret Fell: Barbados, May 24, 1657.
173. MSS vol. 352/316. William Caton to Margaret Fell: London, March 17, 1657.
174. Ibid.
175. MSS vol. 355/65. John Hall to Margaret Fell: Scotland, March 31, 1657.
176. MSS vol. 354/160. John Stubbs to Margaret Fell: Location unknown, April 1657.
177. MSS vol. 355/23. Richard Roper to Margaret Fell: Waterford, Ireland, July 24, 1657.
178. Further discussion of the Kendal Fund may be found in Chapter 2.
179. MSS vol. 352/297. George Taylor to Margaret Fell: Kendal, May 9, 1657.
180. MSS vol. 352/298. George Taylor to Margaret Fell: Location unknown, May 22, 1657.
181. MSS vol. 352/299. George Taylor to Margaret Fell: Kendal, July 18, 1657.
182. MSS vol. 354/129. John Braithwaite to Margaret Fell: Christian Malford, August 3, 1657.
183. MSS vols. 323–24/24. Richard Roper and Richard Waller to Margaret Fell: Waterford City Jail, September 4, 1657.
184. MSS vol. 351/71. Henry Fell to Margaret Fell: London, November 3, 1657.
185. MSS vol. S81/123. Richard Hubberthorne to Margaret Fell: London, November 1657.
186. MSS vol. 355/15. Richard Hubberthorne to George Fox: London, February 16, 1658.
187. MSS vol. 355/13. Richard Hubberthorne to George Fox: London, March 16, 1658. Prior to the Nayler Affair a woman named Mildred was reported as causing some trouble in London. While it seems likely that this is the same woman, there is no way to confirm or deny that.
188. MSS vol. 351/148. Richard Hickcocke to Margaret Fell: Chester, April 6, 1658.
189. MSS vol. 354/140. Alexander Parker to George Fox: Leith, January 13, 1658.

190. MSS vol. 351/28. Richard Clayton to Margaret Fell: Dublin, Ireland, June 10, 1658.
191. MSS vol. 355/269. William Caton to Richard Weaver: London, January 3, 1659.
192. MSS vol. 354/142. Alexander Parker to George Fox: Plymouth, February 21, 1659.
193. MSS vol. S81/82. Henry Fell to Margaret Fell: Barbados, May 8, 1659.
194. MSS vol. 354/118. Elizabeth Adams to George Fox: Whitfield, Kent, May 6, 1659.

2 The Quaker letter network

Prior to the establishment of the Quaker church, the people who became leading members of the emergent faith sought spiritual fulfillment in a variety of forms. The plurality of sectarian communities that permeated the Interregnum is well-covered territory; however, the would-be Quakers shared a seeking tendency that underlined their membership in various sectarian groups.[1] These communities were often quite small—possibly a single congregation or a segment of one. Furthermore, participants moved easily between groups, which meant that future Quakers brought elements of these various sects into the formation of the Quaker faith. Or put another way, the journey to Quakerism involved different paths and therefore included a myriad of theologies and practices that influenced how the faith was shaped. Not all who flirted with Quakerism fully committed—some joined briefly and then moved on to other sects or congregations. It was a fluid environment during the Interregnum that briefly allowed people to try out all sorts of godly religious experiences. Yet, while not always described as Seekers, nearly all eventual Quakers were seeking similar religious fulfillment, even leaders like George Fox. I argue this not simply to identify the religious proclivities of various future Quakers, but to demonstrate the significance that settling on Quakerism had on these early members.

The beginning of this chapter explores the Seeker roots of Quakerism. The second half examines the communication network that Fell established, which tied distant Quakers together by informing one another of the activities of the movement throughout England and abroad on the continent and in the American colonies. Without this system in place, the Quakers may have fallen by the wayside like some of their contemporary sectarians. Fell received letters from itinerant ministers who reported on their activities. Occasionally letters included directives about who should receive copied letters, but generally Fell determined which ones warranted copying and should be sent on to others. This responsibility was not given to her. Rather, she assumed it of her own volition, making her much more than the secretary described by Braithwaite, or even the proto-feminist described more recently by her enthusiasts.

Seeker and sectarian heritage

It is important to note that "Quaker" did not mean any one specific thing in the earliest phase of the movement—or arguably even throughout the

Interregnum. Because people came to the movement from different faith backgrounds, they brought different traditions, approaches to scripture, attitudes toward sacraments and ritual, and perspectives on the roles that women and men of lower social standing should play in the emergent faith. Part of the intention of this book is to show how Fell and Fox created a coherent religious movement out of seemingly disparate backgrounds. But, in the early years, there was no single way to be a Quaker. For most, a brief stint as a Seeker was part of their journey to Quakerism.

Seeker is a term that applies to religious nonconformists of the mid-seventeenth century who sought spiritual fulfillment outside of existing structured religion.[2] The Interregnum was primed for such non-specific religious aspirations; with no official state church or censorship, many people found themselves in "a seeking state," where people "rejected all forms of organized worship," but were unsure of where to go.[3] While some godly folk moved between sects, others did not formally separate from their parish churches yet sought out more satisfactory answers than most parishes provided.[4] However, like early Quakers, at no point did all self-proclaimed Seekers share an identical set of beliefs.

Seekerism was more of a state of mind or attitude than a belief system.[5] Some were content with the absence of a formal church institution while others were "waiters" who sought to find a community that fit their notion of the truth.[6] All varieties shared some qualities, including a mystical view of the world, belief in "inward religion" as opposed to outward displays of faith, and disdain for educated and paid ministers, as well as disdain for church structures or "steeplehouses" and sacraments.[7] Furthermore, while many rejected strict Puritanism, they spoke of the "eternal seed" and belief in apostolic purity, or what T. L. Underwood describes as the primitivism that would define early Quakerism.[8]

This vagueness does not allow for an exact genealogy of Seekerism, but Michael Watts argues that it may be traced as early as 1590 to Henry Barrow who "felt it necessary to counter the opinion that 'all extraordinary offices [in the church] have ceased, and so must all the building of Christ's church and the work of the ministry cease, until some second John the Baptist, or new apostles, be sent us down from heaven.'"[9] Watts identifies a Seeker lineage with brothers Walter, Thomas, and Bartholomew Legate who were all vocal proponents of "renegade Baptist" Edmund Jessop's ideas in the early seventeenth century. Furthermore, Watts looks to mid-seventeenth-century sectarians William Erbery and Thomas Edwards for contemporary characterizations of Seekerism. Erbery found that "the essence of the Seeker position was a belief that the powers and authority granted to the apostles in the New Testament had been so corrupted and destroyed by Church of Rome that no true church could be constituted until God had raised up a new race of apostles."[10] Unlike contemporary millenarians who sought a "glory without," Erbery and his ilk waited for "glory to be revealed in us."[11] In a less approving manner, Thomas Edwards wrote in 1646 in *Gangraena*: "The sect of Seekers grows very much, and all sorts of sectaries turn Seekers;

many leave the congregations of Independents [and] Anabaptists, and fall to be Seekers, and not only people, but ministers also."[12]

At times, Seeker communities would merge or tap into the same populations. Sectarian membership between Quakers and Baptists was fluid, as it was with Seekers and other smaller groups of the period.[13] Subsequent Quakers adopted many Seeker ideas, such as distrust in formal structures of churches and the belief in a seed or inner light. Furthermore, most of the concentrations of Seeker communities correlated with future Quaker centers—the Midlands, Yorkshire Dales, Bristol, London, and Lancashire. David Como states these were the areas where antinomianism took root in the seventeenth century.[14] This also corresponds to Margaret Spufford's findings of "descent of dissent" in parts of northern and central England. Quakers incorporated the ideas of many earlier groups, repackaging antinomian and even Lollard ideas in new ways that allowed them to join forces with other extant communities and recruit new members by echoing dissenting ideas of previous generations.[15] As a result, Quakers became an answer to the spiritual dilemma posed by the Seekers.[16]

Some Seekers may have been aware of one another, but none sustained continual communication like the Quakers would. This is in part because Seekers often thrived due to the charisma of an individual in a particular parish, rather than being part of a larger movement. Not all sought to create a universal mission, and they did not all operate on the same trajectory. At different times throughout the Interregnum, Quaker itinerants came upon Seeker communities that were convinced of the Quaker message. As Quakerism changed over the years, they became more amenable to the communities they encountered so that what was appealing to some Seekers (certainly not all) at one moment may not be appealing to another group at another point in time. The "Seeker network" that Michael Watts describes also hints of future Quaker behaviors.[17] However, Seekers, by nature, were less apt to preserve a memory of who they were at any given moment because they hoped to be something else in the near future. Therefore, in the years before 1652, we have to rely even more than at other points on retrospective analysis—in particular Fox's journal and eighteenth-century histories that largely depend on his memoir.

As discussed in the previous chapter, the problem that Braithwaite and others have with identifying the original moment that the movement began is that Fox's recollections are inconsistent and heavily biased. He paints a rosy picture of his own role and is dismissive of anything that may contradict his centrality to the early movement. This indicates a more general problem with telling the story of Quaker origins. From a very early point, Quakers were conscious of the creation of a narrative; therefore they were mindful of their legacy as they recorded events, even in letters to one another. Carla Gardina Pestana argues that Quakers, like their Puritan counterparts in New England, "selectively recounted their pasts to convey symbolically significant images."[18] This is further enhanced by the subsequent "endorsement" or censorship employed by Fox, Fell, and others as early as the 1650s.

Elsa Glines states that "someone decided which of [Fell's] letters to retain," although she does not state with certainty who that may have been: "It may have been Margaret herself, or George Fox, or other persons." The endorsement issue is described as someone identifying or verifying the authenticity of the letter "often on the verso of the letter, the writer, the recipient, and the date."[19]

While the endorsement process is not described in the letters themselves, some of the letter writers provided glimpses into this process, including comments regarding the oversight of the letter network indicating that both Fell and Fox were perceived as regulators of information to be circulated and published to the wider world. James Daybell has shown that "examination of networks of correspondents helps to map the ambit of women's social worlds."[20] This is illustrated by a letter written on July 7, 1653, in which James Nayler sought out Fox's advice and permission to forward news to others in the movement.[21] Later in December of 1653, Thomas Aldam declared his support of Fox's oversight when he was pleased to learn that Fox had implemented a policy of pre-approving all Quaker publications.[22] When George Taylor wrote to Fell on December 6, 1656, he stated that they had books ready to print but said that Fox needed to provide permission for them to go to the press.[23] Fox was not the only one who approved what should be circulated in the movement. In October of 1655, George Taylor sent a bundle of letters to Fell in order for her to be able to determine which ones should be circulated and preserved.[24] The process of endorsing letters separated the emergent Quakers from their Seeker ancestors because it identified both a sectarian hierarchy and systematic beliefs that were not distinguishable in Seekerism.

The question remains: What did Fox and Fell hope to persuade others to believe and what was the conversion process to accepting his truth? Many scholars have discussed the tenets of the Quaker faith and have acknowledged its similarities to other earlier Christian reform movements. Watts notes that while Seeker communities provided the fertile ground for the expansion of Quakerism in the north—coming from Independent, Anabaptist, and various other sectarian congregations—in southern England, the Baptists were the most amenable to Quaker ideas.[25] The subsequent letter record also suggests this was the case, given the sharp increase in the number of encounters with Baptists described by Quaker itinerants in the post-1652 letters after the movement had spread south. This is likely due to the apparent desire that existed at this time for a new age of Apostolic Christianity, as William Erbery described, a desire for a new John the Baptist to show the way to the "glory revealed in us," which sounds a lot like the Quaker inner light. Prior to the 1650s, others had espoused similar ideas. Perhaps it was the Baptist literalism "which was the chief cause of Baptist losses to the Quakers."[26]

This heritage aligned Quakers with sixteenth-century Protestants who also traced their lineage to the Lollards. However, a more direct connection is apparent between groups like the Family of Love and the Quakers. In addition to similarities in the mystical quality of their theologies, their focus on the "inner self," and the nomenclature used by the groups (Friends and Family of Love), the Familists also foreshadowed Quaker practices in ways such as meeting in houses or anywhere they could outside of churches and disdain for the high-church practices of their contemporaries. Christopher Marsh describes the Quakers as one of the inheritors of Familist theology. He notes that a self-proclaimed member of the Family of Love remarked in the 1680s that they were "a sort of refined Quakers," or rather that they "recognized a certain affinity, but saw themselves as the purer and more sophisticated exponents of illuminist theology."[27] In 1675, Quakers Henry More and Lady Conway of Ragley debated and corresponded over the influence Familism had on the early Quaker church. Henry More wrote: "The carriage of James Naylour, who was then at least equall with Fox, is to me a demonstration of how much at least many of [the early Quakers] were tinctured with Familisme ... that they are hardly come from all points of Familisme, is plaine."[28] Geoffrey Nuttall concludes from this seventeenth-century insight that "the soul of infant Quakerism struggled between two theological camps: Apostolic Christianity and Familism."[29] One of the Familists' main distinctions from the Quakers was their secrecy, which stood in stark contrast to the flagrant behavior that Quakers used to draw attention to themselves. Despite this difference, Marsh attributes the disappearance of the Family of Love as a distinct religious sect to their being all but subsumed into seventeenth-century groups like the Quakers and Baptists.[30] In 1656, Will Caton referred to the Quakers as a "Family of Love"; however, it could have just been used without intentional connotation to the previously named religious sect.[31]

Like the subsequent early Quakers, the sixteenth-century Family of Love emphasized the "true light" that could be found in "godded men."[32] Familist Henry Nicholas stated: "The true Light therefore consists not in knowing this or that, but in receiving and partaking of the true being of the eternal life, by the renewing of the mind and spirit and by an incorporation of the inward man into this true Life and Light so that the person henceforth lives and walks in the Light in all love."[33] This quotation can be found nearly verbatim in any number of Interregnum Quaker letters. Furthermore, similarities can be found in both Anabaptist and Baptist communities concerning oaths, egalitarian attitudes toward preaching, some interpretations of Scripture, and infant baptism. However, the Quakers and Baptists would obviously divide on this last point, as the various manifestations of Quakerism would reject all forms of baptism in water, whether for infants or adults. The lack of ecclesiastical oversight espoused by Independents drew some of their members into Quakerism early on, as they too seemed much more individualized than Presbyterians or other sects with a governing system. To the Quakers' chagrin, they also proved to be easily conflated with Ranters due to their laxity of social norms, although Quakers maintained stricter rules of behavior than Ranters, even if their members were accused of belonging to the other community.[34] Braithwaite states:

> The Ranter position afforded no test by which the individual could distinguish between the voice of the Spirit and the voice of his own will. The Quakers, on the other hand, were "Children of Light," and insisted that there could be no guidance of the Spirit apart from a walking in the light. Accordingly their message became an antidote to Ranterism, and reclaimed many of the Ranters themselves to a truer type of spiritual religion.[35]

Furthermore, Watts states, "It was [Fox's strict code of conduct] which enabled him to weld his disparate band of disillusioned Baptists, former Seekers, and near Ranters into one of the most remarkable missionary movements in English history."[36] It is important to note that Quakers were quite reluctant to acknowledge any similarity to older or contemporary groups as is best seen in Fox's affirmation that he did not inherit these ideas from anywhere.[37]

Defying Fox's assertion, Henry More states in *Enthusiasmus Triumphatus*: "Ranters and Quakers took their original from Behemenism and Familism."[38] Braithwaite acknowledges that while there are no direct connections between Familism and Quakerism, Fox would have been unlikely to acknowledge that fact in his journal, where most foundational information of the sect comes from. This points us to the larger issue of reliability of Quaker sources for these early years: while they are all we have to go on, they must be doubted because many of these early "histories" like the journal were written retrospectively. Letters, which were written at the time events occurred may be more reliable, but even these contain dubious claims because they included an agenda to preserve their image in a particular way.

If the majority of Quaker theology was not original in the 1640s, how did people join efforts with Fox? Quakers discussed the process of convincement in vague terms; however, it essentially constitutes their meaning of conversion in a less formal manner, or the individual's "convincement of truth," which was less of a rational decision, and more spiritual or even mystical in nature. This problem of nomenclature has been defined within the Society of Friends in the following manner:

> Conviction, convincement and conversion are words that have some resemblance to each other in appearance, and a close relation to each other in meaning. Keen and searching conviction sometimes follows speedily after the commission of sin, but if this conviction be not accepted and cherished it may become dissipated, and the good fruit that shou'd follow may be lost; yet if it be accepted and prayerfully cherished, with a corresponding abhorrence of all sin, these emotions will help the sinner on a hair's breadth nearer to convincement of the

> duty, first, to "cease to do evil," then, "learn to do well;" and if this convincement be abode under, in the fear of the Lord, "with prayer and supplication," and "with groaning that cannot be uttered," a slight of the land of conversion may be occasionally granted, cheering the weary soldier in the warfare in which he is engaged, with the hope that if he be "not weary in well-doing," he will "in due season reap if he faith not."[39]

This description of acceptance of the Quaker faith is far from daunting, but Fox described it differently regarding his own "openings," or religious experiences:

> These openings soon took him beyond the current outward religion of his day. Profession was not enough: the true believer was one who was born of God, and had passed from death to life. Learning was not enough—though commonly supposed to be—for, as he was walking in a field one Saturday 'the Lord opened unto me that being bred at Oxford or Cambridge was not enough to fit and qualify men to be ministers of Christ, and I stranged at it, because it was the common belief of people.'[40]

In summary, opening oneself to the truth of Christ's message made one capable to be convinced by others who had already been opened. This is why Seekers were so susceptible to the Quaker message—they were open and waiting for a new inward religion.

Acceptance of this truth could be approached in a variety of ways. This is because the theology is quite simple, and in many ways it is the logical conclusion of Protestantism—there is a covenant between the faithful and God that one achieves by recognition of Jesus as one's savior, without intercession on the part of a priest or spiritual advisor.[41] If salvation is ultimately an individual's responsibility, then awareness of the light within becomes, for those with Quaker-like sensibilities, all that is necessary to be part of the community of the faithful. In an environment that allowed for the proliferation of godly ideas without censorship by a national church, many people were able to develop their own theologies by reading works and hearing preachers who would have been censored prior to the Civil Wars and Interregnum. Therefore, it is not surprising that many Seekers came to the Quaker truth via their own paths and not through the influence of a single prophet.

How the network worked

Once in the Quaker fold, believers quickly adapted to the development of a system that protected and promoted their new religious community—a network of letters that united the faithful despite being physically scattered.

Unfortunately we cannot know exactly how Margaret Fell decided which letters to copy. Elsa Glines states that there were many copies of most letters, and at times the originals were sent to the recipient and the copy was retained at Swarthmoor.[42] Further, Glines states:

> When two copies exist, my assumption has been that the manuscript at the Friends House Library contains the earlier version and thus is closer to Margaret Fell's own words. This may not always be the case. It seems likely that sometimes the copy is a draft, and a later version was the one that was actually sent. In a number of instances, there are several copies of a given letter that seem to be contemporary, and it is remarkable how similar they are. Most scribes were evidently careful when they made their copies.[43]

The extant letters reflect different ways of being a Quaker. One could be at the center, making decisions and running the show, but there were also members of the flock who were less involved and therefore less revered. Quaker letters also illustrate how imprisoned individuals rose in influence within the young group and how news of sufferings traveled throughout the national (and international) network of first-generation Quakers. Early Friends debated important issues concerning their sect and the environment in which they lived. Through their writing, Quakers in distant parts of the kingdom were able to participate in discussions centered in the capitol and elsewhere. While many authors demonstrate in these letters that they felt physically separated from fellow Quakers, the sharing of ideas and news from far away enabled them to remain informed and therefore to participate actively in their religious community. Over time the letters became more like newsletters, containing information concerning fellow travelers and highlighting the suffering that they all invariably experienced.

These letters were not suffering accounts that discussed the problems and actions of early Quakers at large; rather, Fell maintained a contemporary record of itinerant ministers commenting on their travels and sufferings and discussing the state of the faith.[44] Those who traveled to spread the word and risked their lives for the faith were also most likely to have altercations with local authorities and to agitate parishioners and townsmen. Thus, the inner circle was comprised of the preachers who were also often the sufferers. In a culture that placed a premium on suffering, these elite Quakers were valued more than those who passively accepted their faith with no risk to themselves or their own well-being. Those who actively suffered either generated the most letters or had the best-preserved letters, which provide essential information about the early years of Quakerism.[45] Generally, these letters demonstrate evidence of particular traits of the early movement such as how inchoate members traveled around the country and interacted with other people; letters also provide insights into key figures of the movement. Collectively, these letters give us more insights into how members of the faith communicated with one another and the choices they made to progress than any other materials from this period.

People wrote to friends and strangers in distant parts of the kingdom, Europe, and throughout the Atlantic World because they heard tales of their heroic duty for the faith or because they were revered leaders of the movement. There are a handful of trans-Atlantic messages among early Quakers. The most prolific writer in the New World was Henry Fell, who often wrote lengthy letters to Margaret Fell mainly concerning his personal suffering.[46] However, he also outlined the mechanics of communication from England to the colonies. Henry Fell described the process of receiving news from England, providing insights into the time it took to send and receive letters across the Atlantic:

> Dear Friend since the wrieting of my Letter (which I haue kept by mee vnsealed the shippe not being fully ready to goe away) I receiued A Letter from thee dated the 10 of the 12 M: by A London shipp: And truly it was exceedingly welcome to me and much Refreshment it was to my life of thy owne hard thy voyce and did Rejoice in it, for it was sweet & pleasant euen as the voyce of my beloued by which my hard was made glad and my joy full filled.[47]

Henry Fell's response to Margaret Fell was dated May 8, 1659, nearly two months later. Given the isolation that he felt, he surely replied in a timely fashion. Problems with trans-Atlantic correspondence were prevalent in the seventeenth century so one may determine that it took several months for letters to reach their trans-Atlantic recipients. This is understandable, given that this letter indicates that Margaret Fell, living in a remote part of Lancashire, sent her letters through an uncertain number of hands before they reached London and then continued on to Barbados. This may be why he gave more specific directions than most others to make sure that safeguards were preserved. He provides the only instance that I have found of a specific directive that limits who may see the letter, although it should be noted that it was not written to Fell, but rather was shared with her by Thomas Rawlinson: "This letter may keepe by thee & lett none see it but whom it concernes."[48] Once again Henry Fell said to Margaret Fell in 1656: "When thou writes let[te]r by way of London or Bristoll lett it be subscribed to Leut. Collnonell Rousson the backside of his house on the Barbadoes and soe it is like I may receiue it."[49]

Quakers often requested that their news be spread to fellow believers, but they rarely indicated how this should be done. A typical directive sent respect to Fell, her family, or those close to her at Swarthmoor Hall. In 1654, Edward Burrough and Francis Howgill asked that Fell "salute us in the eternall bowells of Love to all thy children and seruants & to all our dear Friends, and to all the church of christ with thee."[50] Likewise, in 1655, Ann Audland ended her missive by stating "soe dear sister in the bowells of tender Love to thee & to thy daughter Mar: & to all the rest of thy Famelly, and Friendes thereawayes doe I Remaine."[51] And yet again in 1657, Will Caton said "Remember mee dearly to Friendes according to thy freedome."[52] Far less common were instances of requests for specific people to hear about their whereabouts or information to be sent to them. This is so rare that one may wonder if it was particular to certain individuals, such as when Alexander Parker wrote in 1656, "Deare I desire thee to send the inclosed to Thomas Bond or to my Brother Chrofer,"[53] or again when he gave very specific instructions for corresponding with him: "from Tregangeeves in the parish of Austell in Cornwall: if thou (or any) write to me (w[hi]ch would much reioyce me) direct thy letter to Nicholas Cole, a shopkeeper in Plymouth and it is like it may come by my hands: _ paper subscribed Geo Fox is a copie of Geo: not sent to Generall Disbrowe Send these 2: inclosed as soon as thou canst as they are directed."[54] When authors did mention specific people, it was usually a plea to "be remembered" to those with whom they knew Fell was in communication. In 1654, Richard Hubberthorne asked that Fell "Remember mee to my dear bro: Geo:" and "desire him to write us or send to us as he is moued."[55] In 1659, Henry Fell asked that "My dear love is dearly remembered to dear T. Salthouse and W. Caton."[56] However, far more often, there were also general statements like when Francis Howgill asked in March 1655 to "Salute me to all the Saintes that way, and to all that loue the Lord Jesus."[57]

In addition to demonstrating why this method of communication was important, the letters provide insights into the mechanics of the network as well. As a useful basis of comparison, work on trans-Atlantic networks identifies the difficult circumstances religious dissenters faced when writing to one another.[58] While some letters followed the classical form of salutation, narration, request, and conclusion, not all did.[59] Rather, the standard format of the letter that David Cressy describes in *Coming Over* is essentially the same for Quaker correspondence. It began with a greeting and religious sentiment, which was followed by the purpose of the letter, including any news or comments about the state of the movement. This was often followed by concluding remarks that included greetings and respects to the recipient's family or neighbors.[60] The following is from the Swarthmore Manuscript Collection that typifies the format Cressy describes:

> M. Everlastingly beloued and longed for, Thy letter I haue receiued the last 7[th] day after much expectation, like vnto the husbandman that waiteth for the former and the latter Raine, I did admire the house of thy silence, but I find (as before I iudged) that thou art clear and th[a]t I am not in any measure blotted out of thy Remembrance, but that thou art as ready to nourish the tender plant after it be remoued out of the Norsery, as well as in it therefore refraine not they selfe, from imparting some spirituall gift vnto mee, neither let the bowels of thy Compassion be Refrained for is not thy strength my strength, thy life,

my life, hast not thou eased when I was burdened & heavy Laden, fed mee when I was hungry, Cloathed mee when I was naked, and strengthened me when I was weake & feeble, And euen vntill this very day I know thou art sensible of my suffering & of my weightes & burdens, which I partake of with the rest of the bretheren, which hath come more vpon us then ordinary, but by the same word which changed us, are we vpheld, and by it are brought thorrow our suffering & with it supported & Comforted in the midst of our tribulations & prayers be to the Living God for euermore.

And Conscerning my health, I am pretty well in body only A Cough doth strike fast. I haue bene in Hampshire Surry & Sussex & hath had very good seruice, A dore was opened mee in A Corner of Sussex where there was seuerall Seekers (Soe called) the most part of two meetings were Convinced. I have thoughts of passing into Kent where GF & TR is. Amsterdam is sometimes set before mee for what I know as yet, there may be Another opportunity for mee to passé thither: but I perceiue the Truth hath noe Comelynes in it in there eye, but appears odious vnto them the woman that did interpite for Margret Wood is gone distracted & strong Reports Conserning JN is gone ouerthat soe many stumbleing blockes is laid in the way: Friends hereawayes is pretty well, & shakes of the mire and the dirt, which hath come & bene cast vpon them: I can say very little to thee Conscerning passages, I came but to this City the last day of the last weeke & yesterday being the first day Tho: Goodayre & I was at the Bull & Mouth E.B: & F:H is in Towne, Friendes keeps their meettinges & are Reasonable peaceable.

If thy husband and Geo: be at home remember me to them, if thou be free and to all th[a]t Abide faithfull in the famelly, I desire to hear from thee as often as thou art free, for thereby am I refreshed yea abundantly: Thine Will Caton[61]

The above includes the requisite complimentary language directed to Margaret Fell, followed by a desire to remain strong in the face of suffering. The author, Will Caton, then described the travels and work of itinerant ministers throughout the countryside, detailing suffering and imprisonment in particular. The letter concludes by asking Fell to give Caton's greetings to his loved ones near Swarthmoor Hall.

The main difference between Cressy's missives and those discussed here is the issue of what he calls the "heart of the matter."[62] While the colonists' letters to their English friends and families generally dealt with the practical matters of their lives, most Quakers' correspondence focused on accounts of sufferings. This single dissimilarity demonstrates that both types of letters reflected the customs of the day, but that authors emphasized the most pressing matters for each of their contexts. For colonists separated from loved ones, seeking financial success and reports on their fiscal needs was the main focus; for the Quakers, the experiences that made them feel closer to God were what they reported.

Despite the differences of circumstances between colonists writing to loved ones in England and itinerant ministers reporting on their travels throughout the British Isles, the authors' situations presented them with similar difficulties. Cressy notes that the poor quality of mail delivery made it difficult to share news not only across the Atlantic but within England as well.[63] Writing to Fell at her home in Ulverston required sending correspondence to the remote corner of northeastern England. Letters would be sent to her or other friends visiting the area; in turn, they would be copied and sent on to others throughout the country. One such example comes from Henry Fell writing to Margaret in November 1656: "When thou writes let[te]r by way of London or Bristol lett it be subscribed to Leut. Collnonell Rousson the backside of his house on the Barbadoes and soe it is like I may receiue it."[64]

The northwest of England included people from wide-ranging dissident religious backgrounds. In order to ensure that letters arrived to their intended recipient in a timely fashion, the network had to depend on reliable, likeminded or sympathetic people to cooperate in moving information. In November of 1653, John Lawson wrote to Fell with detailed instructions for future letters to him and others throughout the country. When writing to Lawson, she should send missives to "Edward Moore, shopkeeper in Repam and he will get them to me thou may get a copie of this to frends in Westmerland if thou can send _ bokes printed papers to me in Wales." For letters to John Lawson in Chester, she "may inquire to William Harrison dwelling in _ courte who is louing and owns us and ofrnge much kindness to the prisoners."[65] These types of directions were common. On July 1656 Walter Clement wrote to Fell that he had difficulty getting letters to Friends in London so he left them with "C Gouldsney" and suggests that she take similar precautions.[66] In September of 1656, Alexander Parker stated that letters to London should be sent to Arthur Cotton in Plymouth and they would find their way to Parker.[67] In November of 1656, Henry Fell wrote from Barbados with instructions for trans-Atlantic correspondence. Letters to Fell in Barbados should be sent via either London or Bristol.[68] However, the methods of reaching Henry Fell changed because in 1657 he stated that her letters to Barbados should be addressed to either Thomas Rous at Winward or Peter Evans at Indian Bridge, and they would forward her news to him.[69] In 1657, Thomas Salthouse wrote to Fell from Plymouth stating that her response should be sent via London rather than going directly to the southwest of England.[70] Complicated directions also came from itinerants in Ireland, such as when Richard Roper wrote from Waterford that if she wrote to them, her letters needed to be sent to George Laythom in Dublin "next door to poole gate" and then they would find their way to Roper and his traveling companion, Richard Waller.[71] Thomas Morford in Southampton could be reached via Thomas Golden in Bristol.[72] These sorts of instructions continued throughout the Interregnum.

Fell also maintained letters written to other Friends that came through the Swarthmoor hub. James Daybell notes that this practice was commonplace in the sixteenth century: "certain types of letters were intended to be read by people other than the addressee. Letters were sometimes sent open for other family members to read, seal, and then send on to the addressee."[73] Certainly this was the intention of letters that were sent to Quakers who did not reside at Swarthmoor Hall though letters were addressed to them there. Thomas Aldam's letter to "Friends" in 1652 does not specify an intended recipient; however, at one point he indicates that it may have been for Fox when he said "deare brother thou mayest let frends see this if it bee thy freedome, for these spirits wich lighe cloase by us doe seeke to make demishion."[74] In November 1652, Nayler wrote to Fox from the Appleby prison concerning a warrant for his arrest in Newcastle.[75] Some of the letters to recipients other than Fell also indicated how letters should be sent or where the authors hoped they would eventually end up. When Thomas Ollive wrote to Fox in 1658, he stated that if he had time to reply, "thou may direct it to Will Hoiknell at Church Brampton." In a rare personal note, Ollive stated that it was not safe to write directly to him at his father's house because his parents would keep anything from him that came from a Quaker.[76] Under less dramatic circumstances earlier in 1657, George Whitehead told Fox that any correspondence should be sent to Robert Duncan of Mendlesham in Suffolk.[77]

Reporting on developments not only kept members of the community informed but also allowed for planning of future missionary efforts. In a few instances itinerants wrote to either Fell or Fox suggesting that Friends go to specific communities to proselytize the Quaker message. In August of 1654, William Dewsbury told Fell that John Audland or another Friend going toward London should go as soon as possible, as there were important developments there.[78] In 1656, Mary Fisher wrote to Fox from Barbados with the more grandiose request that Friends should travel to the Caribbean.[79] In the same year, George Taylor forwarded a letter to Fell requesting that ministers go to Scotland, as they were greatly needed there.[80] Finally, in November Arthur Cotton implored Fox to send "wisdome" to Cornwall and Devon in the aftermath of the Nayler Affair, and "there may be some sent w[i]th power and wisdom guide and rather men frends for they doe not care to have any women friends."[81]

Some Quakers of the 1650s traveled to the Caribbean and New England and their missives are quite similar to those written within England.[82] The experience of communicating to unknown persons even within England consisted of transporting letters across large regions, often under duress. For Quakers in England, that duress was often the threat of prison. At times, news could be delayed and letters would not be able to be sent because jailers prohibited correspondence from coming into or going out of the prison.

Swarthmoor Hall, which had historically welcomed traveling ministers, remained a hospitable port for Quakers throughout the Interregnum and beyond. Furthermore, people wrote to Fell because she was well respected due to her socio-economic status as the wife of a gentryman and because her home was the figurative center of the Quaker movement. Furthermore, since she was not an itinerant minister in this period, her stasis provided stability for an ill-defined movement during the Interregnum. In 1656, itinerant minister Alexander Parker stressed Fell's importance to the early movement as an example of strength through suffering: "Deare Sister knowing thy tender care ower the flock of God and joy, to hear of the florishing of Truth that thou dost suffer with them that suffer, and reioice with them th[a]t doe rejoice & in the Lord."[83] Fell was considered a "vessel of honour for his owne names sake,"[84] and "A pillar in the temple of our god,"[85] despite the fact that she did not take up an itinerant ministry or suffer like many of her brethren. Fell's suffering was spiritual in nature, rather than physical, and her devotion to the maintenance of the letter network earned her prestige and reverence.[86]

Fell responded to such praise with news of others' sufferings and exploits of the road, thereby continuing the thread of communication from minister to Fell to minister. During the early years, the Quakers did not have formal meetinghouses, so they met wherever they could—homes, alehouses, and fields. But because the leaders traveled constantly, the only way to produce any sort of consistency of faith or practice was to write to one another about news from abroad. Newsletters became the best way to communicate about changes in theology and ideas about behavior. John Gibson notes that "letters can be classified rather vaguely as 'newsletters': 'news' of all kinds was retailed, inter alia, between friends and family, from servant to master," and that "many letters, of course, performed more than one function."[87] Newsletters were also efficient means of reporting about the ever-expanding lists of Quaker sufferings. In 1655, John Audland reported that many Quakers were in prison and that "verily our Lyberty is pretious, truth reignes and the same spreades: two Johns are in Wiltshire Myles Halhead & Tho: Salthouse is yet in Exetor prison; Tho: Robertson and Amb: Rigg are in prison at Bayzingstook in Hampshire, one Friend hard by (A pritty young man) is Committed to Ilchester prison: Jan Waugh at Banbery other Friends and some at Oxford committed."[88] These reports not only kept far-flung friends aware of the news, but also created a sense of community. While Margaret Fell and others who were unable to travel did not suffer imprisonment or physical torture, they could pray for those who did. Newsletters allowed co-religionists to feel connected to those who were thrown in jail and putting themselves in harm's way by challenging priests and running naked through the streets.[89]

People came to expect that Fell knew of developments in the movement and said as much in their letters to her. On January 22, 1656, Alexander Parker mentioned that Leonard Fell had successful meetings in Manchester, but assumed that she was already aware of them.[90] Likewise, in April of 1656, Katherine Evans stated that she need not mention some developments in the movement because "I believe thou art better informed by thoase that are better able to declare it."[91] Other times Quakers noted the manner in which she would have heard of their news, such as when Richard Hunter wrote to Fell that he assumed that Oliver Atherton had informed her of Hunter's wedding.[92]

The Nayler Affair generated an abundance of letters that mention Fell's likely awareness of a situation circulating throughout the network. On August 11, as the scandal was still enfolding, Henry Fell wrote to Margaret saying that he was sure that Edward Burrough and Francis Howgill had told her about Nayler's behavior and that they were better able to give her specific details, although that letter apparently did not survive.[93] Later in the same month, John Braithwaite stated in a letter to Fell that he knew that she was aware of the Nayler situation and the trouble that it had caused for the Quaker community.[94] All of these examples, including those regarding Nayler's episode in Bristol, indicate that Fell's knowledge of events was both expected and demonstrative of her significance. Throughout the Interregnum, itinerants made sure that Fell was aware of news and assumed that she knew about developments from her remote location in the northwest.[95]

Despite being kept abreast of developments via newsletters, Quakers often requested to hear from specific Friends. As early as 1653, Richard Hubberthorne made such a plea to Fell to write to Quakers in Lancaster "that spirit may bee kept downe which judgeth the appearance of the life and motion of god."[96] On May 1, 1655, Thomas Salthouse and Myles Halhead asked for Fell to write to them as soon as possible.[97] In 1656, Lancelot Wardell complained that he had sent Fell a letter concerning himself and Anthony Pearson but still had not heard back from her. Wardell added that he sent another of Fell's letters on to other Friends but had not heard back from them either.[98] It appears that Wardell felt rather isolated at this point.[99]

While the network reflects the relative reliability of sending and receiving letters in the seventeenth century, there are a few examples of missed communication. In March of 1655, Thomas Taylor wrote to Fox from Leicester stating that he had written to him twice recently but had not heard anything back.[100] Later in September, Edward Burrough wrote from Dublin stating that not only had Quakers in Ireland not heard from Fell, but they had not received any mail from Friends from anywhere in the north or London despite writing repeatedly.[101] Likewise, in January of 1657, John Stubbs complained that he had written to Fell often but had not heard anything from either her or his wife. Stubbs, unlike some others, noted that he was not surprised because "any uncertanie abode and for my trauel in the outward hath been much in this nacon of Ireland."[102]

Quakers often mentioned the utility and necessity of copying letters in their correspondence. Sometimes authors would ask the recipient to make copies to be sent to specific people or to be circulated throughout the community. In 1653 Richard Hubberthorne requested that Margaret Fell send a copy of his letter to other Friends. "lett vs heare from you all Shortly as you are moved: send A copie of these to Yellands: & Kellat."[103] Letters like this mainly concerned the business of the group and relayed information concerning suffering and convincements. Requests for copies were also made by those hoping that their loved ones might know of their well-being, as in the case of Richard Clayton who wrote to Margaret Fell in 1655 stating: "& as for the noote th[a]t thou writs of I know not whether I have receued it or not, for I have but receued 3 from thee sence I came into this contry but as for out ward things there is noe want, soe deare one if thou be free A copye of this then may send to my deare mother and sister at Lancaster."[104] This example demonstrates that the network was a useful tool to convey personal messages or to keep distant relatives in touch with itinerant ministers. As early as July 1652, Thomas Aldam and Elizabeth Hooton wrote to George Fox about prisoners in York. Aldam stated that he did not have any letters "but single coppie of what I have send forth for what hee was would to write or my selfe I keepe copies, I am _ kept to writeinge and my eyes are much, as I have done, a rume is come into."[105] In November of 1653, Nayler asked Fox to copy his letter so that it "may be sent into Furnass," the Cumbrian region where Swarthmoor Hall was located.[106] In the same month, Gervase Benson wrote to Nayler and Fox and included a copy of the message that he sent to Parliament.[107] This demonstrates that copied materials could be used to maintain records with the wider world, as well.[108]

Some of the most fruitful resources available from the Interregnum are the Caton Manuscripts, a collection of copied letters.[109] William Caton served as Fell's secretary at Swarthmoor, and at some point after the 1650s Caton transcribed several letters for posterity. Examples from this collection include many written by Caton himself, as well as numerous other letters that had been maintained at Swarthmoor. Some of these missives also denote the importance of copying and maintaining records. On September 6, 1655, John Camm wrote to Fell from Gloucestershire. There is nothing particularly remarkable about this letter—it follows the form of many newsletters in that it contains information about various prisoners, including Fox and Nayler, amongst others.[110] Another letter in the collection from John Audland to Fell, written October 20, 1655, similarly reports on itinerants' travels and imprisonments.[111] In yet another example, Caton copied and preserved an August 13, 1656, letter from Francis Howgill and Edward Burrough to Fell concerning the Nayler Affair.[112] However, not all denote such a straightforward provenance. A May 6, 1656, letter from William Dewsbury to Fell contains a copy of a copy. Within the body of the letter, Dewsbury states that he received a letter from Friends in Holland, which was addressed to Fell. Here we have a curious insight into the inter-workings of the network: Caton copied a letter written to Fell but received by Dewsbury, which was itself a copy. Clearly the information contained in these letters was significant to Fell, Dewsbury, Caton, and those interested in the preservation of the formative years of the movement.[113]

Copies were circulated so that more people would be able to read them. Margaret Ezell discusses this phenomenon in *The Patriarch's Wife*:

> An interesting feature of this period's correspondence is the quantity that has been preserved, not only in the original letters, but also in letter books and transcribed copies. Such practices argue that correspondence of a certain type was viewed not as a discreet communication between two people only, but a formal composition to be preserved and perused by others as well.[114]

Evidence of copies is threefold. First, there were requests for letters to be sent, such as in 1655, Ann Clayton wrote to Margaret Fell on behalf of her meeting in Lancaster, asking for a copy of news from London: "wee would haue thee to send vs A copie of th[a]t letter w[hi]ch thou receued the last from London as shortly as thou canst conueniently."[115] This missive is a mere four lines long and the request is the only issue discussed here. Presumably Fell or someone else had mentioned receiving news from London in a previous letter, thus prompting the request from the Lancaster Friends. A second type of request for copies can be seen when occasionally duplicating letters is explicitly stated, such as when William Dewsbury wrote to Fell from Northampton in 1655 and told her "I haue sent a paper when thou art free it may be Read amongst frinds."[116] And a third use of copies is less explicitly described but evident in the letter record. Letters to people other than Fell, including Fox, were presumably copies that were kept at Swarthmoor. For example, Richard Hubberthorne wrote to Edward Burrough in 1654 describing various itinerants' whereabouts and the conditions of those imprisoned in Cambridge. Once again we have support for Fell making choices in what to record for the long-term memory of the group.[117]

Fell's agency is apparent in letters where directives were explicitly stated that contradict her actions. In a postscript from an August 1656 letter, Henry Fell wrote to Thomas Rawlinson: "As thou art free Remember my deare love to J:N: J:B: N:G: and the rest of thy fellow prisoners. And when thou sees G:F: remember me. This letter thou may keepe by thee & lett none see it but whom it concernes."[118] Either Rawlinson must have determined that Fell was one of the concerned parties, or someone he considered relevant shared the letter with her. In any case, upon receipt of the letter, a copy was made for her records.

On numerous occasions Quakers enclosed original or copied letters with their missives to be kept at Swarthmoor. These letters could presumably have been copied and circulated further, although this next phase of movement is not always verifiable. Throughout the Interregnum, Quakers gave us examples of enclosed letters, some of which were meant for specific recipients. On July 22, 1656, Alexander Parker enclosed a letter to Fell that was intended for Thomas or Christopher Bond.[119] There is no mention in this missive as to whether Fell or anyone else could see Parker's letter or Fell was merely the go-between in the network. However, on February 16, 1658, Richard Hubberthorne wrote to Fox and enclosed a letter from Humphrey Horton that stated that only Fox should see its contents. At some point, however, Fox or whoever came to possess it gave it to Fell who presumably read it in the process of preserving the letter.[120]

Fell maintained the letters that were enclosed in missives written to other members in the community. On July 14, 1658, Richard Hubberthorne stated to Fox, "I haue sent heare in cloased something of the usadge of friends at Maksfield in Cheshire if thou see it conuenient: they may get it sent to OP."[121] In an unusual case of preserved letters to and from Quakers other than Fell or Fox, Will Caton wrote to Richard Weaver and enclosed a letter that Fox "put into my hands" so he could send it by the post to "JS." However, Caton stated "wee considering how that it might have come to his house in his absence and soe to his wifes hands, therefore have wee thought it best to inclose it to thee."[122] The Interregnum rounded out with two examples of letters to Fox regarding the printing of letters.[123] All of these examples provide further evidence of Fell's efforts to maintain a record of Quaker events in the Interregnum. Furthermore, it shows that others trusted her with their correspondence. They sent not only their own letters to her but also messages sent to others for her to keep for the community's recordkeeping.[124] This points to a more general issue that once letters were put in motion in the network, the author had little expectation of control over where they would end up. James Daybell's work on sixteenth-century women's letters notes the convoluted concept of privacy within letter networks. He describes the various ways that privacy could be maintained: "the manner by which letters were dispatched; instructions outlining by whom letters were to be opened and read; requests for letters to be burned or returned and use of codes and ciphers."[125] For Quakers, generally there was no expectation of privacy unless a specific note regarding who could read the letter was included.

While some letters focused on the transmission of news, others also kept the community apprised of tangible goods that circulated throughout the Quaker network. Usually these notices concerned "papers" or published works like books. The exact difference between published papers and books is not clear, but the topics of papers were wide ranging, like one concerning the donning of hats.[126] Most letters did not discuss the topic of the papers but mentioned that they were being sent or should be circulated throughout the community.[127] In one particularly specific example, Thomas Aldam asked the recipient of his letter to print 200–300 copies and promised to pay for the costs by "the carrier which bringes the books."[128] Letters discussing the publication of books could be just as vague as those regarding papers.[129] However, some references to books provide deeper insights into the network. Richard Farnsworth wrote to Fell in December of 1652 requesting that 300 books be printed with instructions that Friends should read them in "steeplehouse yarthes" and the markets. He further asked her to "send one of the books to Robert Widder, one to Underbarrow, and one to Gray Rigg."[130] In May of 1656 John Audland wrote to Edward Burrough in Ireland to apologize that they did not receive the books that were sent to them. Audland speculated that they were lost at sea.[131] In possibly the most famous letter regarding the publication of books, John Stubbs updated Fell on the translation of one of her books into Hebrew in Amsterdam. It has been speculated that the unnamed Jewish translator was the Dutch philosopher Baruch Spinoza and that his translation of her book was his first publication.[132] And in a final, rare example, an order of pies from London was noted in a letter. In February of 1657, George Taylor reported on her pie order: "The one of the Charr Pies is mad upp & boxed readie for goeing but, this last weeke they haue not nor told not get anie charges soe that we feare the other will hardly be gotten redie this weeke though we have earnestly formaled th[e]m with those that gets and will bring them if possible."[133]

As the letter network grew, Quakers became increasingly aware of itinerant ministers' financial needs. They required funds for food, shelter, and transportation, but also for maintenance in prison and occasionally for bond or assurances for release. To that end, in 1654, Margaret Fell, Thomas Willan, and George Taylor established the Kendal Fund, a charitable organization to aid traveling ministers and prisoners throughout England. The fund was yet another example of how the young sect developed a relationship between those at home and those abroad. It is no wonder that Margaret Fell was key to its creation given that she was the prime example of a non-traveling leader of the faith. Several letters addressed the needs and thanks of recipients of the fund to enable them to continue their mission.[134] Early in the movement, there were letters requesting funds for itinerants such as when Margaret Newby asked for money to be sent to Tewkesbury and to send it to "Samuel Mosses in Tewxtbury 9 miles from Havisham."[135] However, over time more of the letters were reports to Fell on requests and payments made to itinerants and prisoners, such as when George Taylor told Fell that the money she contributed had been sent to Cambridge.[136] Taylor also reported on others' contributions such as when Taylor received money from an unreported donor and it was sent to Lancaster to pay for prisoners' fees.[137]

In general the missives provide very few explicit insights into the organization of this network and thus require one to infer much about how the process worked. The letters that are the most illuminating either mention the ways that information is disseminated (e.g., someone sends word of someone else's activities) or, more commonly, report difficulties in transmitting correspondence because the network was being watched or its missives were being intercepted by authorities. John Audland wrote to Margaret Fell in 1656 that: "G.F. sent word to mee to send to Friendes that they send noe letters to them; [the prisoners of Launceston] For watches being set in the Country they are taken: soe doe thee giue notice to Friendes carefully that awayes."[138] This letter highlights the need for care in disseminating information and also specific directives about with whom the author hoped to share his news. Thus, while Fell had a great deal of liberty in determining when and to whom to copy letters, she was also aided by itinerants in this effort.

There are a few instances that discuss the mechanisms used to send messages other than utilizing Quaker or religiously sympathetic carriers. The post is mentioned frequently in the correspondence of George Taylor and rarely in other missives. Taylor, along with Thomas Willan, wrote frequently to Fell concerning the Kendal Fund, and his interactions with the post give us insights into how the letter network operated. On January 19, 1656, Taylor added to the end of a note that he would send her anything that came for her via post as soon as they received it.[139] On April 20, Taylor informed Fell that he and Willan received a letter for Henry Fell the previous day, but the carrier was out to Bishopwick so they could not forward it yet.[140] A letter dated roughly the same time included more insights. They received a letter from London via the post that states there was much "rage" concerning Edward Burrough's latest publication, which was seized and taken to Whitehall. A Quaker approached Oliver Cromwell to find out what had come of it, but they did not know the answer. They asked Fell to see if she had a copy of the paper at Swarthmoor and if not to let them know and they would send it to her via next week's post.[141] Other excitements came by post, such as George Taylor's report that Nayler was returning to his old self in July of 1657 and that Oliver Cromwell died and that "his sonn Richard chosen Protector in his stead."[142] Less dramatically, Taylor also informed Fell when there was no new news for her.[143]

The fear of the network being watched and letters being intercepted was mentioned repeatedly throughout the Interregnum. In February of 1654, Anthony Pearson told Edward Burrough that letters and papers were intercepted throughout the network.[144] Later in 1654, Burrough and Francis Howgill wrote to Fell from London but wanted her to know that all letters from Chester were being intercepted so not to expect any news from there.[145] On December 11, 1654, George Taylor told Fell that he heard that writing to Leicestershire was too dangerous so no one should write to Friends there.[146] A year later Taylor warned Fell to be careful writing to Dublin as their messages may be intercepted.[147] In a final example, in 1656, John Audland told Fell that Fox stated that no one should write to him in Launceston because the network was being watched.[148]

Quakers may have roused suspicions through the use of initials rather than spelling out someone's whole name. Initials afforded some anonymity in case unwanted eyes saw a letter. In 1656, Thomas Willan wrote to Margaret Fell to follow up on previous correspondence concerning funds for itinerants James Nayler, Edward Burrough, Henry Fell and uproars over Burrough's publications: "we shall send thee the money thou sends for J:N: and E:B: is still in great seruice in the Citie & H:F: in Kent."[149] In this instance, several of the most high-profile members' initials were listed in a letter written at the end of the decade. Margaret Fell, the recipient of this correspondence, was personally familiar with all of these people, thus their identity would have been quite apparent to her. However, initials were also used in place of full names of lesser-known Quakers in letters from their early, formative years. In 1653, prisoners in York signed a letter: "Prisoners of the Lord at Yorke on Owse Bridge A:W: B:P: and A:N:."[150] One may argue that in the early phase of the movement there were so few members that initials could easily identify specific individuals; however, the identity of those people would only have been known to those participating in the movement. It is reasonable to assume that inchoate Quakers in 1653 would not have been widely known as such, and therefore the use of initials in lieu of full names may have provided some anonymity.

As James Daybell states: "delivery is at once impersonal, plural and ad hoc."[151] Quakers also passed news through multiple mail carriers as an early modern safeguard against confiscation. John Gibson states that messengers were "like secretaries, they were extensions (and sometimes traitors) of the will of the letter writer. The ideal messenger was someone close to the writer—a friend or close personal servant whose presence could go some way toward compensating for the writer's absence and who could be trusted."[152] George Taylor wrote to Margaret Fell in 1657 with a rare account of detailed instructions for sending news: "If that Eliz: Stubbe wold haue anie Stuffe she may now send for what shee neede by this Carrier to Tho: Symmonds who is here now, and inteds for Noridge shortly; we had nothing by this poaste, neither anie to thee, here was som for F:H: but we did not open th[e]m because both F:H: & John Audland was at Crostande this last night."[153] This letter's instruction to send money and "papers" suggests that it is more explicit than most missives in the collections. This document originated in Kendal, Lancashire, and was sent a short distance to Margaret Fell at Swarthmoor. However, George Taylor discussed sending materials to people as far away as London and Norfolk, thus demonstrating the geographic distances between members of the faith, as well as indicating that the network included reliable people throughout all of England.[154]

In 1655, Thomas Salthouse and Myles Halhead wrote to Margaret Fell from Exeter. They provide some insights into the process by which some people attained letters and passed them along to others: "If the Judge bee at home Salute us dearly to him wee wrote to him by Tho. Aldam to London for he had sent to enquire of J.T.S. wanted anything for the outward by A man that was to supply mee with anything I needed, soe I wrote to him satisfie him I had noe want for the outward, but to see his love which I received as from the Lord I was Refreshed."[155] In addition to demonstrating the stoic face Quakers put on their suffering, this letter describes the layers of communication required to pass information from one person to another. Salthouse and Halhead wrote to Fell to ask her to send their salutations to her husband (rather than writing directly to him since he was not a convinced Quaker). Furthermore they ask her to pass information along concerning the activities of other itinerants. They tell Margaret Fell that they wrote to another Quaker to have him relay information to her husband, Judge Fell, because the justice had inquired about Salthouse and Halhead's prison conditions via the network, but once again, not to one another directly. This letter demonstrates the web of communication that was required to send news effectively.[156]

Letters of this era also reflect the emergence of key figures who were seen as best exemplifying the life of a suffering Quaker. George Fox and James Nayler, along with Fell, stood out as inspirational leaders of the faith. It is important to note that during the formation and duration of the sect, no one person was isolated as the sole leader of Quakerism. Leadership was a responsibility and honor shared by many individuals, denoted most often by the frequency and severity of their suffering. It was only after all other potential leaders fell away that George Fox assumed the role of "founder of the faith," and even that was largely because of Fell's efforts to promote him.

By the end of the Interregnum, Fox and Fell began the process of selecting which documents should be preserved for posterity, namely the letters that she had chosen and circulated throughout the 1650s. Quaker letters, like those of other literary circles, "were often deliberately written to be passed on."[157] In addition to censoring the manuscript record, this was also accomplished through the Committee on Sufferings, which determined what could be published based on whether or not it reflected Fell and Fox's agenda. Certainly by the time of the Restoration, they knew that part of ensuring their position in the church involved manipulating the historical record. They endorsed letters to indicate that they were authentic, but also kept those that put Fox in a favorable light and tarnished the image or erased the memory of those who opposed his authority. The most obvious examples include Nayler and Simmonds, but presumably others fell victim to the endorsement system.

Once endorsed and preserved, the letters and documents that remained became the basis of subsequent recordkeeping, such as the Great Book of Sufferings and later Joseph Besse's eighteenth-century martyrology, *A Collection of Sufferings of the People Call'd Quakers*.[158] Fell biographer Bonnelyn Young Kunze and Fox biographer H. Larry Ingle both acknowledge that Fell and Fox worked to construct a memory of the early years of the movement that highlighted his role as "founder of Quakerism."[159] Both Kunze and Ingle claim that this was a forward-thinking action—Fell and Fox wanted to control the future of the religious community by ensuring they, or at least Fox, had firm authority over the group's development. In order to be able to control the record in the future, thus recreating the memory of the past, Fell and Fox had to control the letter record, which was the basis of subsequent histories; however, neither Kunze nor Ingle see that while this may have been done in Fox's interest, it was largely done by Fell. As architect of the letter network, or less prestigiously as Braithwaite's recording secretary, Fell possessed a great deal of power when she maintained the letters.[160] Fox demonstrated the inconsistency of his memory of the Interregnum in his journal that was written in the 1680s and as Carla Pestana states: "George Fox's journal selectively edited to create an impression of continuity on principles."[161] For example, despite the "Two Johns," John Story and John Wilkinson, being revered members of the Valiant Sixty, whose efforts were recounted numerous times in the letter network, Fox changed his tune about them when discussing their involvement in the first years of Quakerism. In his journal, Fox recounts his first meeting with Story: "It came into my mind that the lad might think I had not unity with the creation, for I saw he had a flashy, empty notion of religion; so I took his pipe and put it into my mouth and gave it to him again to stop him lest his rude tongue should say I had not unity with the creation."[162] And then in 1670, two years before his schism with Story, Fox recalled that "Ann Curtis told me that John Story stayed there a great while, and had many meetings in prison; and I told her that was nothing to me."[163] Fox's dismissive attitude toward Story was clearly clouded by their subsequent rift. The letter record supports this idea. Despite being mentioned in others' reports, there were no letters to or from Story or Wilkinson available for this study.

Thus, the arc of this early period of Quakerism was confined to the decade of the Interregnum. In the following century, a narrative emerged that highlighted the valiant suffering and superiority of Fox and his cohort. While Nayler and other Quaker dissenters were discussed, they were remembered largely for their failings and how their behavior tried the church's ability to survive the difficult early years. Eighteenth-century works, like Joseph Besse's *Collection*, echo Fox's memories of the 1650s. Besse uses many letters from the Interregnum Quakers for his book, and it should be noted that the majority of Besse's sources come largely from the manuscript collections housed at Swarthmoor Hall.[164] The absence of an abundance of other letters that may tell a different story about the struggles for domination of the movement reiterates the point made here: that the winning faction, driven by Fell's efforts, maintained its records in order to tell a retrospective narrative of the group originating with them.

Notes

1. A small sample of works on seventeenth-century sectarianism includes, but is not limited to: Christopher Hill, *The World Turned Upside Down*; Christopher Marsh *The Family of Love in English Society, 1550–1630* (Cambridge: Cambridge University Press, 1994); Michael Watts, *The Dissenters*; Margaret Spufford *The World of Rural Dissenters: 1520–1725* (Cambridge: Cambridge University Press, 1995); Richard Greaves and Robert Zaller, *Biographical Dictionary of British Radicalism in the Seventeenth Century* (Brighton: Harvester Press, 1983); David Como, *Blown by the Spirit: Puritanism and the Emergence of an Antinomian Underground in Pre-Civil-War England* (Stanford, CA: Stanford University Press, 2004); Christopher Durston and Judith Maltby, *Religion in Revolutionary England* (Manchester: Manchester University Press, 2006).

The Quaker letter network   65

2. Rufus Jones, *Mysticism and Democracy in the English Commonwealth* (New York: Octagon Books, 1965), 59.
3. Jacqueline Eales, "'So many sects and schisms': religious diversity in revolutionary Kent, 1640–1660," in *Religion in Revolutionary England*, ed. Christopher Durston and Judith Maltby, (Manchester, England: Manchester University Press, 2007).
4. Ibid., 228.
5. Rufus Jones, *Mysticism and Democracy in the English Commonwealth*, 76.
6. Rufus Jones, *Studies in Mystical Religion* (New York: Macmillan and Co., 1909), 80.
7. Rufus Jones, *Mysticism and Democracy in the English Commonwealth*, 79.
8. T.L. Underwood, *Primitivism, Radicalism, and the Lamb's War: The Baptist-Quaker Conflict in Seventeenth-Century England* (Oxford and New York: Oxford University Press, 1997).
9. Henry Barrow, "Writings of Henry Barrow," in *Elizabethan Non-Conformist Texts*, Vol. III, ed. Leland H. Carlson (London: Routledge, 2003). Also in Watts, *The Dissenters*, 185.
10. Watts, *The Dissenters*, 185.
11. William Erbery, *Apocrypha* (London, 1652).
12. Thomas Edwards, *Gangraena* (London, 1646).
13. Adrian Davies, *The Quakers in English Society, 1655–1725* (Oxford: Clarendon Press, 2000), 136.
14. Como, *Blown By the Spirit*, 266.
15. Spufford, *The World of Rural Dissenters*.
16. Rufus Jones, *Studies in Mystical Religion*, 78.
17. Watts does not describe a coherent network of communication. Rather, by describing the fluidity of sectarian interaction in this period, he suggests that there was an informal system of transferring information from one Seeker congregation to another.
18. Carla Gardina Pestana, "The Quaker Executions as Myth and History," *The Journal of American History* 80, no. 2 (September 1993): 443–44.
19. Glines (ed), *Undaunted Zeal*, xx.
20. James Daybell, "Letters," in *The Cambridge Companion to Early Modern Women's Writing*, ed. Laura Lunger Knoppers (Cambridge: Cambridge University Press, 2009), 183.
21. MSS vol. 354/64. James Nayler to George Fox: Location unknown, July 7, 1653.
22. MSS vol. 354/39. Thomas Aldam to George Fox: York, December 1653.
23. MSS vol. 352/293. George Taylor to Margaret Fell: Kendal, December 6, 1656.
24. MSS vol. 352/252. George Taylor to Margaret Fell: Baddesley, October 1, 1655.
25. Watts, *The Dissenters*, 204.
26. Watts, *The Dissenters*, 205. This will be explored further in Chapter 4 when discussing Baptist and Quaker approaches to reading Biblical Scripture.
27. Marsh, *The Family of Love in English Society, 1550–1630*, 260.
28. "Conway Letters" in Geoffrey Nutall, "*James Nayler: A Fresh Approach*," *Journal of the Friends' Historical Society*, Supplement to Issue 26 (London: Friends Historical Society, 1954), 2.
29. Nuttall, *The Beginnings of Nonconformity* (London: J. Clarke, 1964), 2.
30. Marsh, *The Family of Love in English Society*, 248.

31. MSS vol. 352/313. William Caton to Margaret Fell: Launceston, July 23, 1656.
32. Henry Nicholas in Braithwaite, *The Beginnings of Quakerism*, 23.
33. Ibid.
34. D.G. Greene, "Muggletonians and Quakers: A Study in the Interaction of Seventeenth-Century Dissent," *Albion: A Quarterly Journal Concerned with British Studies* 15, no. 2 (Summer 1983).
35. Braithwaite, *The Beginnings of Quakerism*, 22.
36. Watts, *The Dissenters*, 193.
37. Fox, *The Journal of George Fox*, ed. John L. Nickalls, 84.
38. Henry More, *Enthusiasmus Triumphatus* (1656), in Braithwaite, *The Beginnings of Quakerism*, 40.
39. Enoch Lewis and Samuel Rhoads, *Friends' Review: A Religion, Literary and Miscellaneous Journal*, Vol. 20, (Charleston, SC: Reprinted by Nabu Press, 2011).
40. Braithwaite, *The Beginnings of Quakerism*, 33.
41. Henry J. Cadbury, "A Quaker Approach to the Bible," (1953), Guilford College, http://universalistfriends.org/printable/cadbury_printable.html.
42. Glines, *Undaunted Zeal*, xx.
43. Glines, *Undaunted Zeal*, xxi.
44. James Daybell's work on women's letters and privacy shows that the preservation of letters was a common practice: "Several women carefully retained letters that had been sent to them." "'I wold wyshe my doings myght be … secret': Privacy and the Social Practices of Reading Women's Letters in Sixteenth-Century England," in *Women's Letters Across Europe, 1400–1700*, eds. Jane Couchman and Ann Crabb (Aldershot and Burlington, VT: Ashgate, 2005), 152.
45. Suffering is discussed in detail in Chapter 5.
46. MSS vol. 355/260. Henry Fell to William Caton: Location unknown, May 11, 1656; MSS vol. 355/265. Henry Fell to William Caton: Location unknown, May 27, 1656. MSS vol. 351/81. Henry Fell to Margaret Fell: Bristol, August 11, 1656; MSS vol. 351/42. Henry Fell to Thomas Rawlinson: Bristol, August 19, 1656; MSS vol. 351/66. Henry Fell to Margaret Fell: Barbados, November 3, 1656; MSS vol. 351/67. Henry Fell to Margaret Fell: Barbados, December 19, 1656; MSS vol. 351/69. Henry Fell to Margaret Fell: Barbados, April 14, 1657; MSS vol. 351/79. Henry Fell to Margaret Fell: Barbados, May 24, 1657; MSS vol. 351/70. Henry Fell to Margaret Fell: Barbados, September 17, 1657; MSS vol. 351/71. Henry Fell to Margaret Fell: London, November 3, 1657; MSS vol. 351/72. Henry Fell to Margaret Fell: Barbados, October 7, 1658; MSS vol. S81/81. Henry Fell to Margaret Fell: Location unknown, December 1658; MSS vol. S81/82. Henry Fell to Margaret Fell: Barbados, May 8, 1659; MSS vol. 351/74. Henry Fell to Margaret Fell: Thetford, July 14, 1660; MSS vol. 351/77. Henry Fell to Bridget Fell: London, August 11, 1660; MSS vol. 351/68. Henry Fell to Margaret Fell: Barbados, February 19, 1657; MSS vol. S81/86. Henry Fell to Margaret Fell: London, February 7, 1660.
47. MSS vol. S81/82. Henry Fell to Margaret Fell: Barbados, May 8, 1659.
48. MSS vol. 351/42. Henry Fell to Thomas Rawlinson: Bristol, August 19, 1656.
49. MSS vol 351/66. Henry Fell to Margaret Fell: Barbados, November 3, 1656.
50. MSS vol. S81/68. Edward Burrough and Francis Howgill to Margaret Fell: London, October 2, 1654.

51. MSS vol. S81/142. Ann Audland to Margaret Fell: Banbury, November 23, 1655.
52. MSS vol. S81/172. William Caton to Margaret Fell: Leyden Holland, March 15, 1658.
53. MSS vol. 351/165. Alexander Parker to Margaret Fell: Plymouth, July 22, 1656.
54. MSS vol. 351/166. Alexander Parker to Margaret Fell: Tregangeeves, August 19, 1656.
55. MSS vol. S81/126. Richard Hubberthorne to Margaret Fell: Congleton, June 13, 1654.
56. MSS vol. S81/86. Henry Fell to Margaret Fell: London, February 7, 1660.
57. MSS vol. S81/72. Francis Howgill to Margaret Fell: London, March, 1655. There are numerous other examples of authors asking to be "remembered" to another Friend, including the following: MSS vol. 355/33. Gervase Benson to George Fox: Sedbergh, December 23, 1653; MSS vol. 352/359. Margaret Newby to Margaret Fell: Tewkesbury, November 25, 1655; MSS vol. 323–24/110. John Audland to Edward Burrough: Bristol, May 12, 1656; MSS vol. 354/12. Thomas Rawlinson to Margaret Fell: Exeter, August 23, 1656; MSS vol. 323–24/24. Richard Roper and Richard Waller to Margaret Fell: Waterford City Jail, September 4, 1657; MSS vol. 351/70. Henry Fell to Margaret Fell: Barbados, September 17, 1657; MSS vol. S81/86. Henry Fell to Margaret Fell: London, February 7, 1660.
58. David Cressy, *Coming Over: Migration and Communication between England and New England in the Seventeenth Century* (Cambridge: Cambridge University Press, 1987), 222.
59. John Gibson, "Letters," in *A Companion to English Renaissance Literature and Culture*, ed. Michael Hattaway (London: Blackwell, 2002), 615.
60. Ibid.
61. MSS vol. 352/314. William Caton to Margaret Fell: London, January 19, 1656.
62. Cressy, *Coming Over*, 222.
63. Ibid., 233.
64. MSS vol. 351/66. Henry Fell to Margaret Fell: Barbados, November 3, 1656.
65. MSS vol. 355/66. John Lawson to Margaret Fell: Chester, November 1653.
66. MSS vol. 351/179. Walter Clement to Margaret Fell: Olveston, July 15, 1656.
67. MSS vol. 351/167. Alexander Parker to Margaret Fell: Tregangeeves, St. Austell, September 13, 1656.
68. MSS vol. 351/66. Henry Fell to Margaret Fell: Barbados, November 3, 1656.
69. MSS vol. 351/68. Henry Fell to Margaret Fell: Barbados, February 19, 1657.
70. MSS vol. 354/185. Thomas Salthouse to Margaret Fell: Plymouth, January 30, 1657.
71. MSS vol. 355/23. Richard Roper to Margaret Fell: Waterford, Ireland, July 24, 1657.
72. MSS vol. 355/79. Thomas Morford to Margaret Fell: Southampton, August 7, 1657.
73. Daybell, "Letters," 155, and "'I wold wyshe my doings myght be ... secret': Privacy and the Social Practices of Reading Women's Letters in Sixteenth-Century England," 151.
74. MSS vol. 354/40. Thomas Aldam to Friends: York, 1652.
75. MSS vol. 354/65. James Nayler to George Fox: Appleby, November 1652.

76. MSS vol. 355/166. Thomas Ollive and George Fox: Brampton, November 9, 1658.
77. MSS vol. 355/91. George Whitehead to George Fox: Great Yarmouth, February 26, 1657.
78. MSS vol. 355/133. William Dewsbury to Margaret Fell: Location unknown, August 1654.
79. MSS vol. 355/193. Mary Fisher to George Fox: Barbados, January 30, 1656.
80. MSS vol. 352/234. George Taylor to Margaret Fell: Kendal, March 17, 1656.
81. MSS vol. 355/163. Arthur Cotton to George Fox: Plymouth, November 18, 1656.
82. The only exception to this is that letters from the New World often included a lengthy description of their surroundings and the customs of Native Americans. This, however, did not detract from the overall purpose of the letters to communicate news along with reports of persecution at the hands of "heathens," whether they were indigenous peoples or autocratic ministers.
83. MSS vol. 351/166. Alexander Parker to Margaret Fell: Tregangeeves, St. Austell, August 19, 1656.
84. MSS vol. S81/47. Myles Halhead to Margaret Fell: No Date or Location Given.
85. MSS vol. S81/9. William Caton to Margaret Fell: Location unknown, June 1655.
86. Chapter 5 discusses the role of suffering in the Quaker movement in detail.
87. Gibson, "Letters," 616.
88. MSS vol. S81/147. John Audland to Margaret Fell: Location unknown, July 1655.
89. There are far too many examples of newsletters to detail them all here. However, for those interested in a sampling, the following provide a good starting point for inquiry: MSS vol. 352/210. George Taylor to Margaret Fell: Location unknown, December 11, 1654; MSS vol. 354/17. Edward Burrough to Margaret Fell: Dublin, Ireland, September 1655; MSS vols. 323–24/176. Edward Burrough and Francis Howgill to George Fox: Lancaster, March 7, 1656; MSS vol. 352/360. James Myers to Friends: Launceston, April 14, 1656; MSS vol. 351/164. Alexander Parker to Margaret Fell: Near Stockport, April 20, 1656; MSS vol. 351/12. John Audland to Margaret Fell: Bristol, May 13, 1656; MSS vol. 351/166. Alexander Parker to Margaret Fell: Tregangeeves, St. Austel, August 19, 1656; MSS vol. 352/315. William Caton to Margaret Fell: Steyning, February 13, 1657; MSS vol. 354/146. Alexander Parker to George Fox: Nantwich, June 27, 1660; MSS vol. 351/12. John Audland to Margaret Fell: Bristol, May 13, 1656; MSS vols. 323–24/110. John Audland to Edward Burrough: Bristol, May 12, 1656; MSS vol. 351/164. Alexander Parker to Margaret Fell: Near Stockport, April 20, 1656; MSS vol. 355/238. Thomas Loe to George Fox: North of Ireland, August 17, 1660; MSS vol. 355/200. Thomas Robertson to George Fox: Horsham, May 9, 1656; MSS vol. 352/361. James Myers to Margaret Fell: Launceston, August 14, 1656; MSS vol. S81/08. Richard Hubberthorne to Margaret Fell: Cambridge, August 25, 1654; MSS vol. 352/354, MSS vol. 352/346. Richard Hubberthorne to Margaret Fell: Norwich, February 1, 1655; MSS vol. 355/217. Lady Margaret Hamilton to George Fox: Ayr, June 20, 1659; MSS vol. S81/72. Francis Howgill to Margaret Fell: London, March 1655; MSS vol. 352/347. Richard Hubberthorne and Christopher Atkinson to Margaret Fell: Norwich, March 15,

1655; MSS vol. 354/48, Richard Farnsworth to Margaret Fell: Baddesley, May 16, 1655; MSS vol. 354/118. Elizabeth Adams to George Fox: Whitfield, Kent, May 26, 1659; MSS vol. 355/88. John Killam to Margaret Fell: York, June 9, 1655; MSS vols. 323–324/58. John Audland to Francis Howgill and Edward Burrough: Bristol, July 7, 1655; MSS vol. S81/97. Alexander Parker to Margaret Fell: London, September 3, 1655; MSS vol. 352/350. Richard Hubberthorne to Margaret Fell: Norwich, December 14, 1655; MSS vol. 352/200. Thomas Holme to Margaret Fell: Frandley, January 21, 1656; MSS vol. 352/201. Thomas Holme to Margaret Fell: Newport, Monmouthshire, March 3, 1656; MSS vol. 351/187. Walter Clement to Margaret Fell: Olveston, October 20, 1659; MSS vol. S81/133. John Audland to Margaret Fell: Bristol, January 26, 1656; MSS vol. S81/82. Henry Fell to Margaret Fell: Barbados, May 8, 1659.
90. MSS vol. 351/161a. Alexander Parker to Margaret Fell: Frandley, January 22, 1656.
91. MSS vol. 352/394. Katherine Evans to Margaret Fell: English Batch, April 22, 1656.
92. MSS vol. 352/358. Richard Hunter to Margaret Fell: Bickerstaffe, November 21, 1656.
93. MSS vol. 351/81. Henry Fell to Margaret Fell: Bristol, August 11, 1656.
94. MSS vol. 354/86. John Braithwaite to Margaret Fell: Salisbury, August 23, 1656.
95. Additional examples of letters that state Fell must be aware of news include: MSS vol. 352/317, MSS vol. 355/218, and MSS vol. 354/130.
96. MSS vol. 352/341. Richard Hubberthorne to Margaret Fell: Lancaster, September 13, 1653.
97. MSS vol. 354/155. Thomas Salthouse and Myles Halhead to Margaret Fell: Wiltshire, May 1, 1655.
98. MSS vol. 352/277. Lancelot Wardell to Margaret Fell: Sunderland, July 18, 1656.
99. Additional examples of Quakers requesting to hear from Fell and others include: MSS vol. 355/27. John Stubbs to Margaret Fell: Bristol, September 2, 1656; MSS vol. 352/315. William Caton to Margaret Fell: Steyning, February 13, 1657; MSS vol. 355/134. William Dewsbury to Margaret Fell: Evesham, March 1660; MSS vol. 355/45. Robert Widder to George Fox: Location unknown, March 1655; and MSS vol. 355/260. Henry Fell to William Caton: Location unknown, May 11, 1656.
100. MSS vol. 354/30. Thomas Taylor to George Fox: Litchfield, March 16, 1655.
101. MSS vol. 354/17. Edward Burrough to Margaret Fell: Dublin, Ireland, September 1655.
102. MSS vol. 355/24. Other examples of failure to successfully communicate with other Friends include MSS vol. 352/265 and MSS vol. S81/81.
103. MSS vol. 352/339. Richard Hubberthorne to Margaret Fell: Chester, December 4, 1653. The name at the end of this quotation may be some sort of code as it does not appear elsewhere in the letter record.
104. MSS vol. 351/30. Richard Clayton (and Richard Hubberthorne, but not this portion) to Margaret Fell: Wramplingham, July 12, 1655.
105. MSS vols. 323–24/16. Thomas Aldam and Elizabeth Hooton to George Fox: York Castle, July 1652.

106. MSS vol. 354/69. James Nayler to George Fox: Location unknown, November 1652.
107. MSS vol. 355/32. Gervase Benson to George Fox and James Nayler: London, November 29, 1653.
108. Numerous examples of letters that discuss the copying of letters also include: MSS vol. 352/263. George Taylor to Margaret Fell: Location unknown, December 20, 1655; MSS vol. 354/187. William Caton to Margaret Fell: Edinburgh, May 27, 1656; MSS vol. 354/193. George Fox to James Nayler: Reading, October 12, 1656; MSS vol. 352/316. William Caton to Margaret Fell: London, March 17, 1657; MSS vol. 354/160. John Stubbs to Margaret Fell: Location unknown, April 1657. MSS vol. 352/297. George Taylor to Margaret Fell: Kendal, May 9, 1657; MSS vol. 355/145. Ann Dewsbury to Margaret Fell: Wakefield, November 3, 1657; MSS vol. 354/96. John Harwood to Luke Howard: Paris, June 28, 1658; MSS vol. 352/303. George Taylor to Margaret Fell: Kendal, September 7, 1658; MSS vol. 351/170. Alexander Parker to Margaret Fell: Nantwich, August 22, 1660; and MSS vol. 352/318. William Caton to Thomas Willan: Near Warrington, February 8, 1660.
109. The Caton collection exemplified by the "letter-books" described in Gibson, "Letters," in *A Companion to English Renaissance Literature and Culture*.
110. MSS vol. S81/154. John Camm to Margaret Fell: Gloucestershire, September 6, 1655.
111. MSS vol. S81/131. John Audland to Margaret Fell: Bristol, October 20, 1655.
112. MSS vol. S81/61. Francis Howgill and Edward Burrough to Margaret Fell: London, August 13, 1656.
113. MSS vol. S81/164. William Dewsbury to Margaret Fell: Essex, May 6, 1656.
114. Ezell, *The Patriarch's Wife*, 73.
115. MSS vol. 352/398. Ann Clayton to Margaret Fell: Lancaster, 1655.
116. MSS vol. 355/139. William Dewsbury to Margaret Fell: Northampton, September 3, 1655.
117. MSS vol. 355/5. Richard Hubberthorne to Edward Burrough: Location unknown, September 27, 1654.
118. MSS vol. 351/42. Henry Fell to Thomas Rawlinson: Bristol, August 19, 1656.
119. MSS vol. 351/165. Alexander Parker to Margaret Fell: Plymouth, July 22, 1656.
120. MSS vol. 355/15. Richard Hubberthorne to George Fox: London, February 16, 1658.
121. MSS vol. 355/16. Richard Hubberthorne to George Fox: Congleton, July 14, 1658.
122. MSS vol. 355/269. William Caton to Richard Weaver: London, January 3, 1659.
123. MSS vol. 352/349. Richard Hubberthorne to Margaret Fell: London, November 29, 1659; MSS vol. 355/271. William Caton to George Fox: London, August 13, 1660.
124. Fell received numerous other examples of enclosed letters being mentioned in other correspondence. Additional examples include: MSS vol. 351/188. George Bishope to Margaret Fell: Bristol, October 27, 1656; MSS vol. 352/321. Walter Clement to Margaret Fell: Olveston, June 10, 1660; MSS vol. 351/74. Henry Fell to Margaret Fell: Thetford, July 14, 1660; MSS vol. 352/298. George Taylor to Margaret Fell: Location unknown, May 22, 1657.

125. Daybell, "I wold wyshe my doings myght be ... secret," 151.
126. MSS vol. 354/94. Arthur Cotton to George Fox and Others: Plymouth, February 20, 1655.
127. MSS vol. 352/297. George Taylor to Margaret Fell: Kendal, May 9, 1657; MSS vol. 351/79. Henry Fell to Margaret Fell: Barbados, May 24, 1657.
128. MSS vols. 323-24/15. Thomas Aldam to Captain Amor Stoddard: York Castle, February 19, 1653.
129. MSS vol. 354/96. John Harwood to Luke Howard: Paris, June 28, 1658; MSS vol. 352/271. George Taylor to Margaret Fell: Location unknown, April 20, 1656; MSS vol. 354/44. Thomas Aldam to George Fox: York, July 1654; MSS vol. 354/16. Edward Burrough to Margaret Fell: Waterford, January 5, 1656; MSS vol. 355/5. Richard Hubberthorne to Edward Burrough: Location unknown, September 27, 1654.
130. MSS vol. 354/45. Richard Farnsworth to Margaret Fell and Others: Balby, December 2, 1652.
131. MSS vols. 323-24/110. John Audland to Edward Burrough: Bristol, May 12, 1656.
132. MSS vol. 354/152. John Stubbs to Margaret Fell: London, August 10, 1657.
133. MSS vol. 352/300. George Taylor to Margaret Fell: Kendal, February 1, 1657.
134. MSS vol. 352/310. Anne Clayton to Margaret Fell: Lancaster, October 1655.
135. MSS vol. 352/359. Margaret Newby to Margaret Fell: Tewkesbury, November 25, 1655.
136. MSS vol. 352/260b. Other examples include: MSS vol. 352/259, MSS vol. 352/263, MSS vol. 352/265, MSS vol. 352/234, and MSS vol. 352/274.
137. MSS vol. 352/270. George Taylor to Margaret Fell: Kendal, April 12, 1656.
138. MSS vol. S81/149. John Audland to Margaret Fell: Bristol, June 20, 1656.
139. MSS vol. 352/265. George Taylor to Margaret Fell: Kendal, January 19, 1656.
140. MSS vol. 352/271. George Taylor to Margaret Fell: Location unknown, April 20, 1656.
141. MSS vol. 352/272. George Taylor to Margaret Fell: Location unknown, April 26, 1656.
142. MSS vol. 352/299. George Taylor to Margaret Fell: Kendal, July 18, 1657; MSS vol. 352/303. George Taylor to Margaret Fell: Kendal, September 7, 1658.
143. MSS vol. 352/294. George Taylor to Margaret Fell: Location unknown, November 1656; MSS vol. 352/297. George Taylor to Margaret Fell: Kendal, May 9, 1657. There are only three other letters that reference the post in this selection: MSS vol. 351/145. Robert Benbricke to Margaret Fell: London, June 21, 1659; MSS vol. 351/81. Henry Fell to Margaret Fell: Bristol, August 11, 1656; MSS vol. S81/74. Francis Howgill and Anthony Pearson to Margaret Fell: London, July 10, 1654.
144. MSS vol. 354/35. Anthony Pearson to Edward Burrough: Location unknown, February 21, 1654.
145. MSS vol. S81/68. Edward Burrough and Francis Howgill to Margaret Fell: London, October 2, 1654.
146. MSS vol. 352/210. George Taylor to Margaret Fell: Location unknown, December 11, 1654.
147. MSS vol. 352/263. George Taylor to Margaret Fell: Location unknown, December 20, 1655.
148. MSS vol. S81/149. John Audland to Margaret Fell: Bristol, June 20, 1656.

149. MSS vol. 352/274. Thomas Willan to Margaret Fell: Kendal, May 3, 1656.
150. MS Box P2/15/1. Agnes Wilkinson to Unknown: York Castle, 1653.
151. James Daybell, *The Material Letter in Early Modern England: Manuscript Letters and the Culture and Practices of Letter Writing, 1512–1635* (Basingstook, Hampshire: Palgrave Macmillan, 2012), 8.
152. Gibson, "Letters," 617.
153. MSS vol. 352/297. George Taylor to Margaret Fell: Kendal, May 9, 1657. The Thomas Simmonds mentioned in this letter may not be the same as the one involved in the Bristol Affair and was married to Martha Simmonds. That connection is unclear.
154. Another example of a letter making multiple stops is MSS vol. 355/261. Will Caton and Richard Hubberthorne to Thomas Willan: London, May 1660.
155. MSS vol. S81/44. Thomas Salthouse and Myles Halhead to Margaret Fell: Exeter, February 9, 1655.
156. Additional examples of dissemination of letters include MSS vol. 355/33. Gervase Benson to George Fox: Sedbergh, December 23, 1653; MSS vol. 355/66. John Lawson to Margaret Fell and Others: Chester, November 1653; and MSS vol. 355/91. George Whitehead to George Fox: Great Yarmouth, February 26, 1657.
157. Gibson, "Letters," 617.
158. Joseph Besse, *A Collection of Sufferings of the People Call'd Quakers for the testimony of a good conscience, from the time of their being first distinguished by that name in the year 1650 to the time of the act commonly called the Act of Toleration granted to Protestant dissenters in the first year of the reign of King William the Third and Queen Mary in the year 1689* (London: Luke Hind, 1753).
159. Bonnelyn Young Kunze, *Margaret Fell and the Rise of Quakerism* (Basingstoke: Macmillan, 1993) and H. Larry Ingle, *First among Friends: George Fox and the Creation of Quakerism* (Oxford: Oxford University Press, 1994).
160. Pestana states that "the restoration of the monarchy indicated to most radicals that the last days were not, in fact, at hand; this realization alone seriously undermined the apocalyptic hopes and related prophetic activity of most early Quakers. At the same time, the danger of persecution encouraged Quaker leaders (principally George Fox and Margaret Fell) to systematize the sect's beliefs and practices and to publicize a newly articulated commitment to the principle of pacifism." "The Quaker Executions as Myth and History," 450.
161. Pestana, "The Quaker Executions as Myth and History," 451 note 17.
162. Fox, *The Journal of George Fox*, ed. John L. Nickalls, 110.
163. Ibid., 567.
164. Besse is discussed at length in Chapter 6.

3 Margaret Fell reexamined

Amongst the many biographies of nascent Quakers on the shelves of the Quaker Center Bookshop in London, there is a standout work: *In Search of Margaret Fell*. This is not a historical account of Fell, rather it is a "reimagination" of her life, focusing on both her spiritual journey and love affair with George Fox. This work is hard to fit into a genre, as "story, rather than history," author Judith Hayden sought to "find out not who she was, but who she might have been" by combining Fell's story with her own personal journey.[1] In so doing, Hayden found many similarities between her own life and that of the "Mother of Quakerism." There are two main motifs in Hayden's work. First, that Fell, an emotionally neglected, seventeenth-century housewife, found both love and spiritual fulfillment in her relationship with George Fox and second, that Fell's efforts in the religious community emboldened her to assume a feminist attitude about early modern women that was far beyond her time. The result is that Hayden combines the two main threads of Fell historiography: "nursing mother" of Quakerism and proto-feminist preacher.

These two threads summarize the problem of Fell historiography. In the past, Fell has been limited to the role of maternal figure or proto-feminist, neither of which is a satisfactory description because it is insufficient to describe Fell as entirely traditional or progressive. Many Quaker itinerants of the 1650s described Fell as a maternal figure, and she often encouraged this notion, as well; however, her efforts were not simply to nurture the men of the movement. Furthermore, while Fell organized and managed a letter network, created a charity for itinerant ministers, and developed the Women's Monthly Meeting, she was reluctant toward female preaching. During the Restoration, Fell preached and advocated that women should be allowed to be ministers as well, but her later efforts must not be used to assess her Interregnum character. Her personal circumstances changed tremendously from the early years of the movement when she remained at home and chastised those who fell out of line with the approved message, and later when, as a widow, she was free to experience the ministerial lifestyle. Scholars have appropriated moments in Fell's life to simplify and celebrate the figure they seek to describe. By questioning not only the ways she has been discussed, but also the methods used to understand her, we can begin to complicate this important member of the early Quaker faith and ultimately find a more accurate representation of her role in her religious community.

Mother of Quakerism

Scholars often tend to focus on Fell's responsibilities that support her moniker of "mother of Quakerism." This title dates from as early as the 1650s, when itinerants wrote to her as a "nursing mother." The concept of Fell as mother of the movement was employed by numerous Quakers writing throughout the Interregnum. In 1653, John Lawson began his missive referring to Fell as his sister and migrated to maternal language: "Deare sister in the eternall union of my fathers loue whose loue and care comes out to all the saints to supply there nesseseties and another comforting the children of god by the breaste of devin consolation."[2] By the next year, the term "nursing mother" gained traction. Thomas Salthouse stated: "thou who art an nurseing mother, to all the babes which are tender & younge, the liuing in mee breathes forth."[3] In 1655, many letters began with the concept. Ann Cleaton addressed her letter to: "Dear nvrsing mother my dear loue salutes thee."[4] John Audland, likewise, evoked Fell's maternal attributes when he wrote: "my life, loue hart and soul breathes after thee, who art a tender mother to mee, and to all who loue the Lord."[5] Thomas Salthouse and Myles Halhead expanded the moniker to cover not just Quakers, but all of the Judeo-Christian tradition: "Dear sister and beloued of the Lord whom hee hath set as a nursing mother in Israel to watch over and feed the flock."[6] Perhaps a more natural example came from someone who grew up in her household. Will Caton took a more personal tone when he wrote: "My D: M A nursing mother indeed; I above all may call thee, and that which thou hast nourished and soe often sustained."[7] In 1657, Richard Waller wrote from Ireland that Fell was a "Deare and tender nurseinge Mother often thou aret on my rememberance of loue unto thee in writinge I cannot expres who at first did bee git mee by the immortall word of life."[8] In 1658, Robert and Thomas Salthouse both utilized this idea: "How I loue thee and thy offspring the lamb of thy fould and children of thy table who are nursed at thy side and brought up at thy feet,"[9] and "Dearely beluved of my sole and honoured in the lord as a nursing mother unto mee as also unto many of my deare brethren and sisters begtn by the lord."[10] Rounding out the Interregnum, Walter Clement provided one of the most explicit examples of Fell as mother to all Quakers: "Deare Margarett Whoe hast beene as a other to me in the daies of my infancy how should or can I forget thee in my yeares, can the captaine forget him whoe hath directed & an instrument wrought his deliverance, without in him and in gratitude, or can the childe forget the nurse at whose breasts he hath been suckled."[11]

This term was adopted by scholars, including John L. Nickalls, editor of Fox's journal, who describes her as "Margaret Fell (1614–1702), wife of Judge Thomas Fell. Her home now became the cradle of the new movement and she its nursing mother."[12] It is impossible to miss the motherly overtones here; even beyond his use of the term "nursing mother," he refers to her home as a cradle, suggesting that the young faith was nourished by her care. This idea was reiterated in the postscript to Fox's journal by Henry J. Cadbury who simply describes her as "the mother of Quakerism."[13] Braithwaite propelled the use of the term in his characterization of her as a nurturing, supportive figure, calling Fell a "nursing mother who served the First Publishers of Truth," though he did not credit her as a publisher of truth in her own right.[14] *Mother of Quakerism* by Isabel Ross further solidified this idea of Fell as Fox's helper by focusing on her devotion to Fox and efforts to encourage the development of the faith by hosting itinerants and providing for their needs while they were on the road and imprisoned.[15] Ross stresses the things that Fell, as a gentry woman and mistress of a manor, did that made her typical of her age. According to this depiction, Fell did not challenge any social mores by leading a public life; rather she enabled the men of the movement, particularly Fox, to further their work.

Proponents of the traditional narrative, such as Braithwaite and Ross, interpreted the Kendal Fund as indicative of her nurturing role. They contended that her responsibilities as mistress of Swarthmoor Hall prepared her in managing money and being responsible for a large number of people. However, others, like Bonnelyn Young Kunze and R. Tudor Jones see this as a way in which Fell broke with traditional female roles by creating a national charity that supported male itinerants through their travels and imprisonment.[16] While not denying that her past gave her the skills required to manage such a fund, Kunze says that Fell was in some ways more of a "mother superior" than nurturing mother and that she bullied those who disagreed with her concerning the Kendal Fund, Fox's preeminence, or even regarding business and personal conflicts.[17] In one instance, a group of Fell's Ulverston neighbors, including Isabel Gardner, Peter Moser, and Thomas Wilson, accused her of "departing from the living God." Fell wrote to Isabel and Peter calling them Judas and stating: "I alsoe will laugh at yo[u]r destruction and will mocke when yo[u]r feare cometh & when yo[u]r desolation & calamity cometh, and anguish & distresse cometh vpon you as a whirlwind, in the day of yo[u]r callamitie, then shall yee remember me."[18] As seen here, Fell's "sometimes abrasive nature" shaped some contemporary perceptions of her.[19] Thus, despite the overwhelmingly positive responses to Fell's nurturing nature, not everyone appreciated her maternal role in the community.

There were other approaches to Fell's mothering role. Phyllis Mack and Su Fang Ng both focus on the "elders" or mothers and fathers of the faith.[20] Mack and Ng say this is because the first generation, like early Christians during the Apostolic period, functioned like parents of the movement. Therefore, while Fell remained a maternal figure, she was not alone because there were female preachers in the first generation. More importantly, parental figures included men, as well, which diminishes the significance others have placed exclusively on Fell. Mack does not clarify who was included as an "elder," so it is possible that she means the first generation generally (known as the Valiant Sixty), or that her intention is more specifically the mother and father figures, Fell and Fox.

Playing with the idea of "Mother of Quakerism," Margaret Hope Bacon identifies Fell as a matron of another nature in *Mothers of Feminism: The Story of Quaker Women in America*.[21] Building on traditional assessments of Fell's position in the early Quaker faith, Bacon argues that Fell was the first of a long line of Quaker women who sought to create gender equality, beginning first with their religious community. For Bacon, Fell is significant because she anticipated the goals of subsequent generations of feminists and established a precedent for Quaker women. Thus, Fell's attitude was more important than any one specific, tangible achievement during her tenure as "Mother of Quakerism."

One of those tangibles that acknowledge Fell's innovation is the Kendal Fund. As the letter network grew, Quakers became increasingly aware of itinerant ministers' financial needs. They required funds for food, shelter, and transportation, but also for maintenance in prison and occasionally for bond or assurances. To that end, in 1654, Margaret Fell, Thomas Willan, and George Taylor established the charitable organization to aid traveling ministers and prisoners throughout England. The fund was yet another example of how the young sect developed a relationship between those at home and those abroad. It is no wonder that Margaret Fell was essential to its creation, given that she was the prime example of a non-traveling leader of the faith.

Thus Margaret Fell not only embodied the matron of the early Quaker movement, but she also encouraged others to think of her as a nurturing figure. However, just as scholars cannot agree on what this meant for her or the Quakers, we should not limit our understanding of Fell's role to simply that of a nurturing mother. While men also nurtured itinerants through the Kendal Fund and by offering legal support and hospitality where they could, none are described with traditionally feminine language that reduces them to "helpers" of the movement. The next section of this chapter considers an extreme alternative to viewing Fell's contribution to early Quakerism.

The feminist Fell

An alternative approach to the "nursing mother" is to see Margaret Fell as a forward-thinking example of female empowerment. Scholars who emphasize her innovation rather than her nurturing role tend to focus on four aspects of her contributions to Quakerism: the structure of Quaker meetings, female preaching, female writings, and most recently, Fell's theology. Arguments range from the statement that Fell had the forethought to find a meaningful place for women in the movement's structure to the notion that she was an advocate for a public role and ministry for women from the onset of the faith to the idea that Fell's theology, even more than many of her male contemporaries', was foundational to the creation of a Quaker belief system. These claims are not unrelated: The meeting allowed women to speak to one another, possibly enabling them to spread the faith to a wider audience and therefore disseminate a pro-woman theology. It is a nice idea. However, it does not really reflect Fell's goals to celebrate and protect George Fox and his position in the religious community. When female preachers failed to follow Fox's directives in the early years of the Interregnum, Fell was quick to reprimand them, supporting Fox's ambitions instead. My intention is not to argue that her role was insignificant in any of these areas; rather by shifting attention away from previous conversations of this early Quaker figure, I hope to integrate Fell into the larger discussion of what happened in the first phase of this religious movement. As a result, I hope to take Fell out of the narrow, limited way that she has been discussed thus far.

By 1671, with the creation of the Women's Monthly Meeting at Swarthmoor Hall, women's roles became more clearly defined. Prior to this period, men and women met together in monthly administrative meetings where the business of the church was discussed. However, Fell and Fox believed that there was a necessity for a meeting that specifically addressed the needs of women and allowed them to discuss philanthropic issues in the northwest. Braithwaite quotes extensively from Fox's journal on this matter. He begins by recounting Fox's miraculous curing of a woman's sick child and then goes on to describe Fox's subsequent conversation with this woman and others:

> So I spoke to her, to bid about sixty women to meet me about the first hour in the afternoon at the sign of the Helmet at a Friend's house And they did so accordingly, such as were sensible women of the Lord's truth and fearing God. And what the Lord had opened unto me I declared unto them, concerning their having a meeting once a week, every second-day that they might see and inquire into the necessity of all Friends who was sick and weak and who was in wants, or widows and fatherless, in the city and suburbs. And so they blessed the Lord for the wisdom of God that had settled such a meeting in His power amongst them.[22]

According to Fox's description of the origin of the Women's Meeting, its purpose was for them to attend to the needs of the "sick and weak and who was in wants, or widows and fatherless."[23] Su Fang Ng claims that this meeting was a positive, "empowering" change for women by allocating specific responsibilities and leadership opportunities for female Quakers.[24] It seems, however, that the creation of the meeting gave women a purpose that fell in line with traditional Christian assumptions about women's roles in the church: as caretakers. There is no mention of leadership, itinerancy, preaching, or other progressive opportunities. In reality, few women outside of the Fell family enjoyed such roles.

But not everyone agreed with the idea of a Women's Monthly Meeting—neither Fell's contemporaries nor subsequent scholars. "The Two Johns," John Wilkinson and John Story, were vocally opposed to the creation of the meeting.[25] Fox and Fell were the main advocates of the meeting, and given Fox's virtual supremacy over the faith by that time, few raised objections to the creation of a separate meeting for women.[26] However, Wilkinson and Story believed that a women's meeting would relegate women to the outside of the center of the faith and result in diminished role for them in the church. Henry Cadbury credits Fox with the establishment of the Women's Meeting and states that it was met with "general approval, but two Westmoreland men, John Story and John Wilkinson, 'publishers of Truth' in an earlier day, strongly objected to this innovation and found supporters in their own country and later elsewhere, especially in Wiltshire and Bristol." He goes on to say that as the schism grew, the Two Johns proceeded to make personal attacks on Fox's character "and perhaps even more on Margaret [Fell] Fox."[27] Braithwaite suggests that Story and Wilkinson not only opposed the idea of a women's meeting, they balked that they had to defer to Fell in the situation because Fox was traveling in the Americas and unable to arbitrate.[28] In their own words, Story and Wilkinson outlined their complaints about the new governance of the Quaker church: Story claimed that the argument that the women's meeting would deal with concerns of the poor did not apply to most communities, excluding London and Bristol. Instead he called a separate meeting for general worship "monstorous and ridiculous."[29] Here Story criticized Fell when he stated that when she prayed, she groaned and sang and that others could not concentrate because "of the noise of deceit" coming from her.[30] They also seem to have resented Fell's singular prominence in the burgeoning faith because of her closeness to Fox and the resulting limitation of opportunities for other women. In this instance, like with the Nayler Affair, challenges to Fell and Fox's control resulted in the opponents being ostracized from the community. This schism, if it can even be considered that given the small support on the opposing side, further solidified Fox's authority and Fell's position as his second in command.

Fell's role expanded as most Quaker women had fewer opportunities in the religious community after the Restoration.[31] This may be because during the Interregnum there were few institutionalized rules for either men or women; however, with the creation of the Women's Monthly Meeting, their function in the community became more clearly defined. Once kept busy tending to the needs of the sick, poor, and downtrodden, women did not have time to assume the more controversial roles of jailbird preachers. Most Quaker women began to appear more like their Protestant contemporaries in terms of their religiosity. In contrast, once again, Fell's role remained prominent—during the Interregnum she was the backbone of the letter network; in the Restoration, she promoted preaching and was the central figure and advocate of the meeting.

A recent area of Fell historiography deals with her contribution to the development of a Quaker theology. This is the latest area of Fell-revisionism to be found in the works of Sally Bruyneel. These works tend to focus on Fell's doctrinal contributions to the Quaker faith as described in her published works. Bruyneel's *Margaret Fell and the End of Time* focuses on Fell's theology, in particular her eschatology. This work contains some extreme claims—such as that Fell had articulated a pacifist position as early as 1653—but by and large this work contributes a much-needed study of Fell's positions on theological matters, particularly that she was a doctrinal driving force in the movement.[32] Another interesting claim made is that Fell's social status allowed the religious community to flourish and made her a more viable source of authority. Bruyneel states:

> It is helpful to remember that this affluent and personally dynamic, upper-class woman was the one whom George Fox first encountered. This will be born out in the new argument that Margaret Fell's intervention and protection, along with that of her husband and children, is primarily responsible for Fox's survival when so many of his counterparts met early deaths.[33]

Despite some over-generalizations, and while there is no doubt that Fell's station in life and access to powerful men provided opportunities for her faith group, Bruyneel's argument somewhat undercuts Fell's contribution. Bruyneel suggests that her wealth and status made her ideas acceptable; however, I argue that her skills, as well as who she was in the world, helped make Quakerism what it became—or rather helped make Fox who he became. Bruyneel rightly points out that Fell's "firebrand ways" lost her favor among the upper crust of English society, and Fell's devotion to the Quakers "cost her the love and loyalty of her only son."[34]

Fell's attitude toward women's roles in the Quaker movement seems to have been motivated by her personal experiences in it. When she was at home, women should stay at home. When she traveled and suffered imprisonment, then it became acceptable for women to preach. Finally, when she created a separate meeting for women, it was expected that women be relegated to their own realm. This narrative demonstrates that she was always off the feminine norm, allowing her to stand out as different from other women in the movement. In the beginning, Fell was less a representative of what women in the movement should or could be and more of the exception to the rule. Or rather, over time she made the rules for other women to follow. She began advocating for female preachers once the time of prominent women in the ministry had passed.[35]

The Quakers, while not unique, were quite unusual in their allowance of female preachers. This issue has arguably generated the most discussion of Fell's proto-feminist tendencies. Elizabeth Hooton, one of the earliest members of the movement, preached as a Quaker as early as 1652 and as a Baptist and Seeker prior to meeting Fox. Hooton's experience as a preacher may have given her credibility. That she was likely Fox's first convert sanctioned her role as an early itinerant.[36] This also made her an acceptable juxtaposition to Fell's stationary role as architect of the movement. Other women took up itinerant ministries in the early years of the movement; however, it was Fell who became synonymous with the ideal Quaker woman, not by preaching or abandoning traditional early modern female roles, but by maintaining a center for the religious community. In fact, despite assertions based on her later work "Women's Speaking Justified," at times Fell reprimanded female preachers during the Interregnum either for failing to fulfill their traditional female duties or for challenging Fox's authority. In 1655, writing to the Friends in Grayrigg, she admonished women in the community that she felt had strayed from the guidance of the Valiant Sixty. She singled out two women, "Widdow Gardner and her sister," telling them to:

> Keep in the pure fear of the Lord and dwell low in the power, and keepe Downe all that would be exalted above the pure in the low and in the humble waite and in the pure obedience to your measures of the Lord God be faithfull, and there you will read the love of God, and be low and subject and willing to cast your [c]rowns at the feet of Jesus soe the lord God Allmighty of life and power preserue you faithfull and obeydient, and look not out at others words, but in the pure power of the lord god Dwell.[37]

This last phrase "look not out at others words" tells us much of the reprimand that she gave her fellow females. Through their travels (like itinerant men), they would have come into contact with other prophets' ideas that Fox and Fell would have wanted them to avoid. Yet despite the fact that male preachers faced the same challenges, only these female itinerants apparently warranted the warning. Fell let them know that their responsibility was to the faith prescribed by Fox and that their place was to remain "faithfull and obeydient" at all times.[38] This sentiment reflects what Catie Gill identifies as a general anxiety about women's position in the Quaker movement.[39] Women could preach, but in the mid-1650s, Fell expected them to remain faithful to Fox's leadership. Male preachers were expected to stay in line, too, but female preachers appeared more vulnerable to corruption, so they received instructions that men could apparently intuitively understand.

The most famous example of Fell's criticism of female preachers stemmed from the Nayler Affair.[40] As described in Chapter 1, rumors circulated throughout the Quaker community in the months leading up to Nayler's infamous entry into Bristol. It has been a common trope, dating to the earliest assessments of the event, that Nayler was bewitched or somehow led astray by beguiling women, such as Martha Simmonds, Dorcas Erbury, and Hannah Stringer.[41] It is possible that Fell and others were reluctant to place the blame on Nayler because he was their beloved friend who had been with

Margaret Fell reexamined 81

the religious movement since the beginning, and they hated the idea of his doing anything to threaten their success, much less the movement's existence. However, it contradicts much of the celebratory rhetoric of the early Quakers to see that they actually reprimanded those who fell outside the parameters of what an ideal woman should be, even if their definition was much broader than most of their contemporaries. Ultimately, how the Nayler Affair affected Quakers is more important than the event itself. It gave Fell and Fox the opportunity to close ranks and begin building a platform for his singular control of the movement. While painful at the time, the Nayler Affair was arguably the best thing that could have happened for the pair.

The party line that rogue female preachers led the formerly faithful Nayler astray became a cautionary tale. Richard Hubberthorne writing to Fell said Martha Simmonds was an arrogant and corrupting presence who sought to sway the influential Nayler by encouraging him to challenge Fox's authority and set out on his own. He said that "she being the party which was as the cause ... sought to have the dominion." Hubberthorne goes on to describe Nayler's corruption:

> [Simmonds] & the other woman Hanah Stringer she alsoe went to James, and said that he had iudged the Innocent, and not iudged righteously, and something to that effect did she & Martha speake to him, which word he receiued to bee the word of the Lord, And comeing vnder the power of their wordes, Judgem[en]t came vpon him, and much trembleing night and day, while he was in London, for some nightes lyeing vpon A table, And then they reigned and deceipt got vp especially in Martha to glory, and boast ouer all, And now an exceeding filthy spirit is gott vp in her, more filthy then any th[a]t yet departed out of the Truth, And with it Laboures to breake and destroy the meettinges if it were possible, when I spoke to her and told her how the deceipt entered she could not bear it nor stand And I see it was the will of the Lord that I should come hither soe soon.[42]

Hubberthorne followed up this notice with another on September 16, 1656, which stated that he had visited Nayler, who was "opening up" his pleas to return to a right way of thinking and behaving when Simmonds arrived and ushered him away. Hubberthorne described Nayler as "much suiecte to her."[43] Fox echoed these sentiments in his letter to Nayler later that month. Fox stated that Nayler was keeping company with a bad crowd, particularly calling out Simmonds and Hannah Stringer as "lyars and slanderers," although not mentioning Stringer's husband who was also in their cohort.[44]

These reports were followed on October 4, 1656, the eve of the shameful event when Walter Clement wrote to Fell concerning Simmonds's constant presence around Nayler, stating that their friend suffered from her influence. Clement was hopeful that Nayler could be released from his trance, stating that he had not had Fox's positive influence since Simmonds came back to see him.⁴⁵ On October 12, Clement's hopes that Nayler would turn around were dashed when Fox wrote to Nayler angrily expressing concern. He stated that Nayler treated Simmonds like his mother, clearly misplacing his affections. Fox cited Simmonds's refusal to allow Howgill to see Nayler, while commenting that Hannah Stringer was a terrible influence, too. Here the maternal issue is brought up; although there is no direct comparison to Fell, it is hard for the modern reader of this letter not to see that a comparison could easily be made. Fell, as a nurturing influence contrasts sharply with Simmonds as a temptress who led Nayler astray.⁴⁶

Concern about the impact that Simmonds and the other women had on the community as a whole continued long after Nayler's imprisonment and separation from their corrupting influence. In August of 1657, John Braithwaite reported that Simmonds caused trouble for Quakers from London to Wiltshire. He said that their efforts were "some hurt" because of Simmonds and company, but that the Lord "gaue us dominion over them."⁴⁷ Later in November, Richard Hubberthorne felt compelled to mention Simmonds's presence at a Quaker meeting, even though he did not go on to describe any of her terrible deeds.⁴⁸ Regardless of whether or not Simmonds actually attributed to Nayler's downfall and the resulting fracture in the movement, she remained threatening enough to warrant reports on her whereabouts well after the episode was over.

Eventually, these fears motivated Fox and Fell's efforts to close ranks within the movement. Margaret Fell's opinions on the episode are also known from the letter record. She wrote to Nayler in jail, stating that "it hath greeved my Spiritt" to hear that he denied Fox even though "Thou hath confessed him to be thy Father." She went on to ask, "How will thou answer this to him who hath giuen him a name Better then euery name to w[hi]ch euery knee must bow."⁴⁹ Here Fell had clearly made her allegiance known and chastised Nayler for refusing to do the same.

Fell's attitude toward Simmonds could be perceived as an isolated event given the severity of the Nayler Affair; however, her earlier criticism of the Friends of Grayrigg suggests that she did not have a magnanimous attitude toward early Quaker women who chose a different path than she did. Following this epistle, Fell worked hard to promote Fox to the position of undisputed leader of the Quaker faith. Her correspondence with other itinerants echoed the sentiment here. From 1656 on, there is little information available about Nayler, while Fox's star continued to rise. As administrator of the letter network, Fell was in the unique position to influence the movement's official rhetoric through this most important of Quaker media. She was able to transform the way the movement thought about their leadership—the early years of several key leaders were replaced by Fox as a single "founder of Quakerism." Therefore, it was Fell's work that made the creation of a Quaker orthodoxy possible. Fox—a single leader without a real threat to his authority—was able to put forth an authoritative message, largely due to Fell's efforts.

This episode has generated much debate among scholars. Traditional narratives, like those of Braithwaite and Ross, claim that Martha Simmonds controlled Nayler through her sexually bewitching ways.[50] Nayler had been one of the most respected members of the early group and therefore must have become victim to ill-intentioned feminine wiles to fall so far from grace. According to Ross, Simmonds was a "hysterical woman" who led Nayler astray.[51] The traditional take on this episode juxtaposes Simmonds as the antithesis to Fell—a fallen, brazen woman versus the Quaker feminine ideal. In one timely, contrasting example, Fell was called "Virgine daughter of Sion who hath layd downe thy crowne at the fette of the lambe and hath followed him through tribulation."[52] Furthermore, all records of a possible alternative view of Simmonds were eliminated by the Fox camp at Fell's hands through her access to and control of the historical record. Therefore, it is no wonder that this has been the prevalent view of Nayler and Simmonds throughout much of Quaker history.

However, this is not the only view. Patricia Crawford and Christine Trevett argue that the Braithwaite-Ross narrative not only unfairly maligns Simmonds, but also misplaces the significance of the conflict.[53] Crawford and Trevett argue that the heart of the issue was between Nayler and fellow itinerants over the leadership of the London meetings. Nayler found himself at odds with Fox's supporters in London and as a result became surrounded by more subversive people in the movement. Arguing that devious women manipulated Nayler really misses the point of the episode in Bristol and reduces influential women, who disagreed with the Fox-Fell camp, to negative female stereotypes.[54] It also takes Fell out of the story. She played a part in shaping the way the other women of the movement are remembered.

Attitudes toward female preaching and the Quakers in general changed during the Restoration. With a new regime on the throne, Quakers experienced a new relationship with the state. During the 1660s, Charles II instituted a clampdown on radical sects, in part seeking to punish those who rebelled against his father in the Civil War. The national temperament also cooled toward groups like the Quakers because they had grown tired of their antics during the Interregnum. Fell's personal situation changed too when her husband, Thomas, died in 1659, apparently freeing Fell of her domestic responsibilities because she began to pursue a more public life. In 1660 she traveled to London to petition the king for George Fox's release from prison. She also went back to London in 1662 to ask for lenience when Quakers experienced intensified persecution due to the Fifth Monarchist Uprising and passage of the Quaker Act.[55]

James Daybell describes the "act of writing a letter" to be a "way of going public, especially when a wider audience was anticipated."[56] In that sense, Margaret Fell was a public figure throughout the Interregnum. She assumed a more public life in 1660 that included continuing management of the letter network as well as preaching, although Fell was never much of an itinerant. However, she fully joined the ranks of Quaker "elders" when she was first imprisoned in 1664. While never a preacher on the level of Fox, Nayler, or even Elizabeth Hooton, Fell's public life during the Restoration differed tremendously from her period of relative isolation at Swarthmoor Hall. As a public figure, she met with monarchs, instigated judges (no longer under the protection of her justice husband), and perhaps finally came to appreciate the difficulties of the itinerant life firsthand.[57] But even this was unusual as the average itinerant's experience was much more mundane.

One may expect a favorable use of feminine language in Fell's letters, but she was quite complicated in this regard. Most of the language that Fell evoked concerning women was negative, partially because so much biblical language about women is negative. Writing to Justice John Sawrey in 1653, Fell evoked Luke 15:8–9: "Either what woman hauing ten pieces of silver, if she lose one piece, doeth not light a candle, & sweepe the house, and seeke diligently till she finde it: And when she hath found it, she calleth her friends, and neighbours, saying, Reioyce with me: for I haue found the piece which I had lost." In turn, Fell stated: "but thou art the woman that goes abbroade and dost not abide in thy owne house, and if thou could wittnesse the parable, the woman that sought for the groate, and when the Candle was lighted and the house swept shee found it in her owne house and shee rejoiced with her Neighbors, but thou art ignorant of the parables."[58] It is important to note here that while the passage utilizes the idea of a woman, Fell did not use it in this instance to chastise a rogue itinerant. Rather, it was used to criticize a male preacher for a variety of offenses.

Fell's public persona was further enhanced when she published her most famous pamphlet, "Women's Speaking Justified," which is often referenced as evidence of her proto-feminism. Published in 1666, this work challenges the traditional Pauline subjugation of women and prohibition on female preaching. Jeanne Shami and others have pointed out that Fell disregarded Paul's directive for women to remain quiet in church by focusing on the roles that Old Testament women like Esther and Judith played as "holy prophetic women." Further, Shami notes that Paul's prohibition was not a general condemnation, but rather it was directed at "a church in confusion," specifically in Corinth.[59] In this tract, Fell goes beyond the excessively quoted 1 Corinthians 14:34, which states that women should remain silent in church. She responds with 2 Corinthians 12:9 by emphasizing Paul's point that those who are perceived as weak will "confound the things which are mighty" and those who "are despised, hath God chosen, to bring to nought things that are."[60] Hilary Hinds cites further biblical evidence in support of female preaching from Acts 21:8: "And on my servants and on my handmaidens I will pour out in those days of my Spirit; and they shall prophesy."[61]

What may surprise some is Fell's use of 1 Corinthians 14:34: "Let your Women keepe silence in the Churches: for it is not permitted vnto them to speake: but [they ought] to be subiect, as also the Lawe sayeth."[62] When writing to a Quaker detractor, she said:

> If thou will but seriously Consider thou wilt see thy blindness, & Ignorance of God, & of his truth: for verily the living God thou art Ignorant of: and yet thou takes the Apostles words, and saith, that he forbids a

woman to speake in the Church, but thou knows not the life & Substance which was in him: for he knew the woman Clothed with the sonne & the woman that sits upon the many waters, which thou dost not, nor cannot put a difference betwixt the pretious & the vile.[63]

This example indicates that Fell's attitude regarding female preaching changed considerably before she wrote "Women's Speaking Justified" in 1666. Fell experienced an epiphany after she undertook a ministering effort of her own. Therefore, her sentiments in the Restoration text that she is so famous for should be considered as a reflection of her evolving theology and not as emblematic of an unwavering position on female preaching.

Elizabeth Clarke states that Fell's work "discredits all external authority and allows only the power of the Spirit and the verbal authority of the Bible, which may be conferred on women as well as men."[64] Some scholars use this tract to argue that she was a progressive, feminist figure throughout her career in the Quaker movement. For instance, Kunze argues that Fell was "a new paradigm of radical Protestant womanhood."[65] Kunze points to the pamphlet as evidence that Fell was the new ideal as female minister, rather than the more mystical prophetess figures of the medieval and early modern periods. But it seems that Fell's very limited experience as a minister was not her most defining characteristic. As the most esteemed female member of the faith, she was certainly celebrated for all of her activities that served Quakerism, but the fact that she is remembered as a minister is almost an ironic twist given her earlier stance on preaching women.

Margaret Olofson Thickstun makes an even stronger case for Fell's position as a minister, stating that she "interprets Scripture as an empowering feminist force." Thickstun's reading of Fell's pamphlet suggests that "feminist biblical criticism as we know it began two centuries earlier in the work of a woman who understood, as we do today, the subversive power of the remembered past."[66] This does not really represent Fell's character or position on preaching in general, which was ambiguous at best in the years before she preached herself. She may have developed a more progressive position over time, but her views were certainly less feminist in the Interregnum and arguably less progressive and more self-serving in the Restoration.

Ultimately, it is problematic when scholars argue that Fell's most defining characteristic was her feminist tendency as indicated by the publication of this tract. Rather than demonstrating Fell's feminism (not to mention the problematic nature of calling a mid-seventeenth-century woman a feminist to begin with), it shows her self-interest. Fell became an advocate of female preaching once she was a minister. This does not diminish the significance of the pamphlet; however, it does require further consideration of the context in which the work was written. Certainly she may have changed her mind— the experience of preaching may have changed her perspective; however, it does not necessarily make her a symbol of progressive womanhood, as defined by twentieth- and twenty-first-century scholars.

The letter network and myth making

In his seminal work, *The Beginnings of Quakerism,* William Braithwaite dubs Fell a "recording secretary," adding to her collection of mediocre titles. Braithwaite acknowledges the importance of Swarthmoor Hall as a location to send letters to and from.[67] However, Fell's function in this process was far more central than Braithwaite recognizes because her role was much more than a secretary. People wrote to Fell because she was well respected and her home was the figurative center of Quakerism. Furthermore, as she was not an itinerant minister in this period, her stasis provided stability for an ill-defined, Interregnum movement.

Taking Braithwaite's lead, scholars have largely ignored the significance of Fell's creation and administration of the network. Some, like Phyllis Mack, have called Fell a "great organizer of early Quakerism" along with Fox. Mack further states that the early Quakers had "an informal but effective international postal system, and it was organized and directed by a woman, Margaret Fell, who used her home at Swarthmoor as a clearinghouse for letters and who was the chief correspondent of almost every leading male and female Quakers."[68] This is a parenthetical reference in Mack's work, denoting the aside intention of this statement—the Quaker letter organization, and Fell's role in starting and maintaining it, is not her primary concern. When other scholars discuss Fell's organization, they generally adopt Braithwaite's assessment and leave it at that.[69] However, the present work is the first to reassess Fell's role as the chief selector of which letters to maintain, copy, and circulate amongst the Quaker community. Thus, even those historians who elevate Fell's role beyond "recording secretary" still seem to miss what may have been her most profound contribution to the religious movement.

By the end of the Interregnum, Fell and Fox began the process of choosing which documents should be preserved for posterity, namely the letters that she had selected and circulated throughout the 1650s. In addition to protecting Fox's prominence in the movement, Fell kept hundreds of letters that dealt with a wide array of topics, as discussed in Chapter 2, including the role of women in the Quaker community. While we cannot attribute the ideas of others to Fell, we can learn about general attitudes toward women publicly demonstrating their faith. And Fell's preservation of these letters suggests that they held some value, if not to her personally, then to the memory of the early years of the faith.

Condemnation of women for various offenses was far from rare. Braithwaite states, "Local Friends were sometimes burdened, especially by one or two unsuitable women ministers," some of whom, in the words of Edward Burrough, were better suited as "servants" than ministers.[70] On July 10, 1654, Francis Howgill and Anthony Pearson described Isabel Buttery's wanton ways and susceptibility under the influence of the Earl of Pembroke. In the only instance found in this study, a Quaker's imprisonment is described with disdain for the shame it could bring on the community, rather than the typical hagiographic tone of pride in suffering for the faith.[71] In 1656,

Thomas Rawlinson reported that another group of women had caused trouble in prison, as well. Mary Howgill, Jane Bland, and James Harrison's wife had "high flown spirits" that were disruptive and upsetting the Quakers around them.[72]

The most surprising condemnation concerned Mary Howgill, possibly the sister of "first publisher of truth" Francis Howgill and who one may have assumed would have been immune to such criticism given her connection to a member of the inner circle.[73] Mary's behavior was discussed in numerous letters from the middle of the Interregnum. In February of 1655, George Taylor told Fell that Howgill had gone into Kent and her behavior had upset Fox in one way or another.[74] On March 20, Richard Hubberthorne reported that she had been in Essex, Suffolk, and Norfolk "where she hath done hurt for she ministereth confusion among friends soe that some now will not appoint a meeting for her."[75] Braithwaite states that Howgill suffered from a fever, which explained her odd behavior, but there is no hint of concern for her in the letters. Rather, she was derided for bringing unwanted attention to the movement.

Another woman who was at times praised for her devotion but later condemned for her behavior was Agnes Wilkinson. Thomas Aldam wrote to Fell on October 30, 1654, to let her know that he had sent Wilkinson to see her at Swarthmoor and that she was accompanied by an unnamed female Friend. Aldam states that she "acted contrary to the light in filthynes and is cast out with the light with them who was partakers with her."[76] While he did not describe her actions in this letter, he mentioned that another letter was enclosed and sealed (so Wilkinson could not open it). He reiterated that Wilkinson had been made to "owne her condemnation diuers times" but had never redeemed herself. The situation had gotten so bad that he had tried to send her to Wilkinson's mother, but she would not have her. Therefore, he depended on Fell, as a shining example of femininity, to set her straight. Agnes Vairy was also described as filthy when Hubberthorne stated in May of 1654 that "it lay upon mee to tell thee that Anges Vairy is not serviceable to go forth for lust and filth and darknes rvles in her and there is a filthy scandal raysed conserving her going to Eatreans."[77]

More common than these dramatic examples of named women drawing negative attention to the community and possibly perverting the Quaker message, there were various instances of "proud women" discussed. Anthony Pearson used this phrase in reference to a contingent of London preachers who could not be quieted in meetings.[78] Likewise, Edward Burrough and Francis Howgill stated in October of 1654 that "there are two women gone for France, th[ei]r obeydience will bee more than their service."[79] The Apostle Paul's commandment to be quiet reverberates throughout that statement. In a less patronizing manner, William Dewsbury told Fell in 1656 that there were some bad women causing trouble in Bedfordshire.[80] Lastly, in February of 1658, Hubberthorne related to Fox a problem in London concerning that "imprudent lasse that said shee was above the apostles & shee makes it her common practice to goe vpon the first dayse to the bull and mouth and to Woster house but heare is many great peaceable meetings in the citie."[81] Without mentioning her name, it is clear here that Hubberthorne and Fox, and possibly others, had communicated previously about this particular woman and her unwanted presence in the London Quaker community.

However, not every example of women mentioned in the letter record was laden with such negative sentiments. In the same missive in which Hubberthorne spoke against Agnes Vairy, he also noted that Elizabeth Leavens and Elizabeth Fletcher continued their good work in Wales.[82] Alexander Parker also praised the Elizabeths' efforts in May of 1655, saying they were of great service in Dublin.[83] In a likely reference to the same pair, Burroughs wrote to Fell that "but there are many pretious women, which euery weeke are stirreing abroad and getting meetings."[84] It seems that Fletcher and Leavens, unlike many of their female contemporaries, escaped the derision of their male counterparts.

In the end, it does not appear that Fell disagreed with preaching so much as she, like virtually all of her contemporaries, was prone to see the fault in women more easily than in men of the same occupation. In all of the instances mentioned above, the main complaints concerned the women's behavior rather than the content or delivery of their messages. Therefore, it seems that the problem was not so much with female preaching as it was with itinerancy. Even as progressive as the Quakers were for their time, they were still seventeenth-century people, judging one another by the standards of the day. Taking the positive comments of a few women who undertook this difficult task, none of those who were praised for their work garnered anything like the praise that Fell experienced from the comfort of Swarthmoor Hall.

This attitude also shaped her efforts to create an institutional memory, which was accomplished through the Committee on Sufferings. This committee determined what could be published based on whether or not it reflected Fell and Fox's agenda. Certainly by the Restoration, they knew that part of ensuring their position in the church involved manipulating the historical record. They endorsed letters to indicate that they were authentic, but also kept those that put Fox in a favorable light and tarnished the image or erased the memory of those who opposed his authority.[85] The most obvious examples include Nayler and Simmonds, but presumably others fell victim to the endorsement system. Of course there is no way to know for sure.[86]

Endorsed letters were preserved and were later utilized for histories written about the earliest period of Quakerism, such as Fox's journal, "The Great Book of Sufferings," and Joseph Besse's eighteenth-century martyrology, *A Collection of the Sufferings of People Call'd Quakers*. As discussed in Chapter 1, Fell and Fox biographers acknowledge the premeditated nature of this action and that it resulted in solidifying Fox's role as head of the church. Fell was keenly aware that preservation of

Interregnum letters would be important in memorializing certain aspects of the religious movement's origins. This point has not been emphasized enough in Quaker historiography—Fell possessed a great deal of power in her maintenance and manipulation of the letter record. Furthermore, while not a complete recounting of the 1650s, the letters are a better reflection of what actually occurred than Fox's selective memory reflected in his account of those years, which was not penned until the 1680s. Given that it was Fox's journal, and therefore recollections of his experiences, Fox plays a disproportionately significant role in the narrative he constructed. It is not surprising that he omitted some of the stories of others who were active in the movement; however, we have occasional glimpses of his opinions overshadowing his efforts to accurately capture the past when he diminishes those who, according to the letter record, were clearly significant. Fell outlived Fox (who by this point was her husband) by more than a decade; thus, she was able to continue to develop Fox's place in the institutional memory.

Ultimately it is insufficient to describe Fell as entirely traditional or progressive. Whether scholars thought of Fell as a passive supporter of Fox or a feminist ideal, they tend to reduce her role in ways that limit her true function in the Quaker movement. Focusing on her femininity or desire to break barriers misses the key function that she played in the religious community. Fell created and maintained the letter network that allowed the Quakers to survive. Without this network, no one would have remained informed of people's comings and goings and their suffering for the faith or kept abreast of the developing prominence of Fox in the church. Furthermore, without the letter network, there would not be a recorded memory of the early years, which she and Fox were later able to control in order to promote themselves and their brand of the faith. By focusing exclusively on either her maternal nature or later public life, the story of her role in the letter network has been largely overlooked. It may be the single most important aspect of the burgeoning faith—more than mystic preachers or martyred evangelists. Thus, reassessing Fell allows us to reassess the faith.

Notes

1. Judith Hayden, *In Search of Margaret Fell* (London: Quaker Books, 2002), 3.
2. MSS vol. 355/69. John Lawson to Margaret Fell: Chester, November 1653.
3. MSS vol. 354/171. Thomas Salthouse to Margaret Fell: Pardshaw, 1654.
4. MSS vol. 352/398. Anne Clayton to Margaret Fell: Lancaster, 1655.
5. MSS vol. S81/147. John Audland to Margaret Fell: Location unknown, July 1655.
6. MSS vol. S81/40. Thomas Salthouse and Myles Halhead to Margaret Fell: Location unknown, February 1656.
7. MSS vol. 352/313. William Caton to Margaret Fell: Launceston, July 23, 1656.
8. MSS vols. 323–24/57. Richard Waller to Margaret Fell: Waterford City Jail, August 10, 1657.

9. MSS vol. S81/52. Thomas Salthouse to Margaret Fell: Ilchester, February 20, 1658.
10. MSS vol. 352/369. Robert Salthouse to Margaret Fell: Dublin, August 9, 1658.
11. MSS vol. 352/321. Walter Clement to Margaret Fell: Olveston, June 10, 1660.
12. George Fox, *The Journal of George Fox*, ed. John L. Nickalls (Cambridge: Cambridge University Press, 1952), 114.
13. Ibid., Postscript written by Henry J. Cadbury, 714.
14. Braithwaite, *The Beginnings of Quakerism*, 162 and 185. "First Publishers of Truth" is a term that is used (often interchangeably with "The Valiant Sixty") to denote the leading Quaker itinerants of the 1650s.
15. Isabel Ross, *Margaret Fell, Mother of Quakerism* (London: Longmans, 1949).
16. Ross, *Margaret Fell, Mother of Quakerism*; and R. Tudor Jones, *Protestant Nonconformist Texts, Volume 1, 1550–1700* (Aldershot: Ashgate Publishing, 2007), 213. Jones uses this as an example of Fell's "formidable nature."
17. Kunze, *Margaret Fell and the Rise of Quakerism*.
18. MSS vol. 378/32. Margaret Fell to Isabel Gardner and Peter Moser: Swarthmoor Hall, 1653.
19. R. Tudor Jones, *Protestant Nonconformist Texts*, 214.
20. Phyllis Mack, *Visionary Women: Ecstatic Prophecy in Seventeenth-Century England* (Berkeley, CA: University of California Press, 1992), 288; and Su Fang Ng, "Marriage and Discipline: The Place of Women in Early Quaker Controversies," *The Seventeenth Century* 18.1 (2003): 124.
21. Margaret Hope Bacon, *Mothers of Feminism: The Story of Quaker Women in America* (Philadelphia: Friends General Conference, U.S., 1997).
22. Braithwaite, *The Beginnings of Quakerism*, 341.
23. Ibid.
24. Ng, "Marriage and Discipline," 119.
25. The Two Johns are mentioned above in reference to imprisonment in the 1650s.
26. Kunze, "'Poore and in Necessity': Margaret Fell and Quaker Female Philanthropy in Northwest England in the Late Seventeenth Century," *Albion* 21.4 (1989): 559.
27. Fox, *The Journal of George Fox*, ed. John L. Nickalls, 718.
28. Braithwaite, *The Second Period of Quakerism* (London: Macmillan, 1919), 296.
29. Ibid., 297.
30. Ibid., 298.
31. Patricia Crawford, *Women and Religion in England, 1500–1720*, 192.
32. Sally Bruyneel, *Margaret Fell and the End of Time: The Theology of the Mother of Quakerism* (Waco, TX: Baylor University Press, 2010), 19.
33. Ibid.
34. Ibid., 3.
35. In contrast to Anne G. Myles's excellent article "From Monster to Martyr: Re-Presenting Mary Dyer" in *Early American Literature* 36.1 (2001) in which she argues against the idea that Anne Hutchinson was exceptional among Puritan women, Fell did have a truly exceptional role in early Quakerism.
36. William Sewel, *The History of the Rise, Increase, and Progress, of the Christian People Called Quakers: Intermixed with Several Remarkable Occurrences. Written Originally in Low-Dutch, and Also Translated Into English* (London: J. Sowle, 1725), and Norman Penney's entry for Elizabeth Hooton in "Dictionary of Quaker Biography."

37. MSS vol. 378/9. Margaret Fell to The Friends of Grayrigg: 1653.
38. In a subsequent event in the 1670s, Fell admonished her former employee, Mary Taylor, for failing to carry herself in a proper manner that demonstrated subordination to Fox's leadership. There also appear to be issues concerning Fell's embarrassment from one of her household representing her mistress poorly in public.
39. Catie Gill, *Women in the Seventeenth-Century Quaker Community: A Literary Study of Public Identities* (London: Ashgate, 2005), 42.
40. Nuttall, *James Nayler: A Fresh Approach* (London: Friends' Historical Society, 1954), 12.
41. Braithwaite, *The Beginnings of Quakerism*, 247.
42. MSS vol. S81/116. Richard Hubberthorne to Margaret Fell: London, August 26, 1656.
43. MSS vol. 354/153. Richard Hubberthorne to Margaret Fell: Location unknown, September 16, 1656.
44. MSS vol. 354/195. George Fox to James Nayler: Location unknown, September 1656.
45. MSS vol. 351/181. Walter Clement to Margaret Fell: Olveston, October 4, 1656.
46. MSS vol. 354/193. George Fox to James Nayler: Reading, October 12, 1656.
47. MSS vol. 354/129. John Braithwaite to Margaret Fell: Christian Malford, August 3, 1657.
48. MSS vol. S81/123. Richard Hubberthorne to Margaret Fell: London, November 1657.
49. MSS vol. 378/38. Margaret Fell to James Nayler: Swarthmoor, October 15, 1656.
50. Ross, *Margaret Fell*, 98.
51. Ibid., 101.
52. MSS vols. 323–24/65. Francis Howgill to Margaret Fell: Location unknown, 1656.
53. Crawford, *Women and Religion in England,* 170, and Christine Trevett, *Quaker Women Prophets in England and Wales, 1650–1700* (London: Edwin Mellen Press, 2000), 244.
54. There are several examples of women being admonished for the way they preach or for other things, as in the case of Elizabeth Holme (nee Leavens) who was a "burden" to other Quakers since she was pregnant. It is important to note that both Fell and others maintained this position. The general attitude may have been that female preaching was acceptable, but that did not mean they were eager for it, or necessarily encouraging of it before "Women's Speaking Justified."
55. The Fifth Monarchy Men were a radical, militarized religious sect that anticipated the Second Coming and led an uprising against Charles II following the Restoration. According to their theology, Jesus's return would be followed by his rule as king of England. The Quaker Act was a law that targeted people who refused to take oaths and meetings of five or more sectarians.
56. Jane Couchman and Ann Crabb, "Form and Persuasion in Women's Letters, 1400–1700," in *Women's Letters across Europe, 1400–1700* (London: Ashgate, 2005), 15.
57. It would be a misrepresentation to state that Fell was an itinerant. She preached some and was imprisoned for her obstinacy but was never a traveling minister.
58. Luke 15:8–9.

59. Jeanne Shami, "Women and Sermons," in *The Oxford Handbook of Early Modern Sermons*, ed. Peter McCullough and Hugh Adlington (Oxford: Oxford University Press, 2011), 171.
60. Margaret Fell, "Women's Speaking Justified" (London: 1666).
61. Hilary Hinds, "Prophecy and Religious Polemic," in *The Cambridge Companion to Early Modern Women's Writing*, ed. Laura Lunger Knoppers (Cambridge: Cambridge University Press, 2009), 235.
62. 1 Cor. 14:34.
63. 1 Cor. 14:34 in MSS vol. 378/155. Margaret Fell "To Jeffrey Elletson, 1654," transcribed in *Undaunted Zeal*, Glines (ed.), 59.
64. Elizabeth Clarke, "Women in Church and in Devotional Spaces," in *The Cambridge Companion to Early Modern Women's Writing*, ed. Laura Lunger Knoppers (Cambridge: Cambridge University Press, 2009), 118.
65. Kunze, *Margaret Fell and the Rise of Quakerism*, 143.
66. Margaret Olofson Thickstun, "Writing the Spirit: Margaret Fell's Feminist Critique of Pauline Theology," *Journal of the American Academy of Religion* LXIII/2 (1995): 269–70.
67. Braithwaite, *The Beginnings of Quakerism*, 134.
68. Mack, *Visionary Women*, 245.
69. The most recent example is Ingle's *First among Friends*. In this work he relegates Fell to "helper" of the dynamic, charismatic Fox.
70. Braithwaite, *The Beginnings of Quakerism*, 345, and MSS vols 323–24/36. Edward Burrough to George Fox: London, February 12, 1657.
71. MSS vol. S81/74. Francis Howgill and Anthony Pearson to Margaret Fell: London, July 10, 1654.
72. MSS vol. 354/12. Thomas Rawlinson to Margaret Fell: Exeter, August 23, 1656.
73. The Dictionary of Quaker Biography is unclear on this point. Norman Penney and William Braithwaite state that Mary and Francis were siblings, but Geoffrey Nuttall doubts this claim.
74. MSS vol. 352/214. George Taylor to Margaret Fell: February 26, 1655.
75. MSS vol. 355/12. This letter also mentions a "wicked woman" who hindered Quaker progress in Amsterdam.
76. MSS vol. 355/89. Thomas Aldam to Margaret Fell: York, October 30, 1654.
77. MSS vol. 355/1. Richard Hubberthorne to George Fox: Frandley, Great Budworth, May 29, 1654.
78. MSS vol. 354/34. Anthony Pearson to George Fox: London, July 18, 1654.
79. MSS vol. S81/68. Edward Burrough and Francis Howgill to Margaret Fell: London, October 2, 1654.
80. MSS vol. S81/164. William Dewsbury to Margaret Fell: Essex, May 6, 1656.
81. MSS vol. 355/15. Richard Hubberthorne to George Fox: London, February 16, 1658.
82. MSS vol. 355/1. Richard Hubberthorne to George Fox: Frandley, Great Budworth, May 29, 1654.
83. MS vol. S81/92. Alexander Parker to Margaret Fell: London, May 29, 1655.
84. MS vol. S81/73. Edward Burrough to Margaret Fell: London, 1655.
85. *The Journal of George Fox* and Glines, *Undaunted Zeal*.
86. The "Two Johns," Christopher Atkinson, and George Keith from the 1670s are likely suspects but certainly not representative of everyone who fell out of favor with the Foxes.

4 Apostolic epistolary influences

Like many early Christian groups, Quakers sought advice from scripture as they searched for guidance in handling organizational and theological issues. It was natural that Quakers looked to the early church—particularly to the writings of Paul, champion for Protestants—to find answers to their theological and practical questions. As described in Chapter 2, Quakers, as an answer to Seekers' questions, provided a plausible example of Apostolic Christianity that was revered in the mid-seventeenth century by sectarians of various backgrounds. Like so many other religious communities facing persecution, Quakers looked back to the early Christians as a model of how to behave in times of crisis. Paul and other biblical figures provided examples for how one should stay strong when persecuted, how to spread information among distant congregations, and how to keep the faithful in line when they were challenged by authorities or struggling with internal strife. Furthermore, their early existence as an epistolary community gave them the basis of seeing themselves as the direct ancestors of Apostolic Christianity, since the first Christians operated in a similar manner.

This chapter explores the ways that Interregnum Quakers evoked Apostolic Christianity through appropriation of scripture in their letters. Quakers saw themselves as emulating early Christians because, like Jesus's immediate disciples, they had charismatic leaders with devoted followers. Furthermore, the Quakers' physical distance from each other that necessitated the letter network described in Chapter 2 was seen as a replication of early Christian communication techniques. But more than simply wanting to be like the first Christians, nascent Quakers actually functioned like them, too, in no small part due to the efforts of Margaret Fell. This again was in emulation of early church leaders, namely Paul. Fell, like Paul, maintained the network that brought cohesion to an otherwise disparate association of religious radicals. And although she was not always recognized for her efforts in this way—in fact, more often than not both she and others regarded Fox as assuming this role—Fell did in fact provide the stability needed for the movement to succeed. Therefore, in addition to using similar language and behaving in the manner they believed their ancestors to have done, Quakers called themselves Apostles and assigned ancient names to their contemporary brethren (Fox as Paul or Christ, Fell as Mary, etc.). By examining a wide array of letters, but particularly focusing on a case study of Margaret Fell's extant letters, we can see how this sort of language was utilized and how Quakers fashioned themselves to be the early modern reincarnation of Apostolic Christianity.[1] However, it is important to note that much must be inferred into Fell's choices when it comes to management of the letter record. She never explicitly stated her intentions regarding preservation of some missives over others; therefore, we must make assumptions regarding the extant scriptural examples, in both the letters penned by Fell and those written by others that she kept for posterity.

Return to Apostolic primitivism

The early Quakers had a complicated relationship with scripture despite their desire to imitate the first Christians. T.L. Underwood's excellent comparative study of early Quaker and Baptist theologies highlights the key issues concerning the Quakers' relationship to the Bible. In *Primitivism, Radicalism, and the Lamb's War: The Baptist-Quaker Conflict in Seventeenth-Century England*, Underwood states that the Quakers' primitivism, that is their belief that they alone were reviving the purity of the Apostolic church, is not only what formed the basis of their theology, but also what set them apart from so many of their contemporaries. "Primitivism, the emphasis in faith and practice on the first, was the earliest form or pattern as described in the New Testament that entailed efforts to recreate or imitate such a form in the present."[2] Unlike Baptists and other sectarian contemporaries, Quakers believed "they were the New Testament church," or as Underwood states, citing Mircea Eliade, this process can be described as the "recovery of the Great Time, illud tempus of 'the beginnings.'" This is what encouraged Quakers to stress the "immediate, inward, and spiritual qualities" of their faith. While not denying the historical Jesus, they focused on his divinity rather than his humanity. "The immediate experience of God by Quakers, like that enjoyed by New Testament Christians, placed the means of mediate inspiration, the Bible, in a secondary position. Consequently, Friends pleaded for the primacy of the authority of the Spirit above the Scripture."[3]

George Fox emphasized this idea in his journal, when stating that his purpose was to bring people away from archaic ceremonies and "men's inventions and windy doctrines" that resulted in their dissatisfaction and therefore "blowed the people about this way and the other way, from sect to sect."[4] Furthermore, Fox intended to help the faithful realize their own abilities to reach Christ without false "ministers of their own making" as well as steering them away "from all their images and crosses, and sprinkling of infants, with all their holy days (so called) and all their vain traditions, which they had gotten up since the apostles' days."[5]

This is a key insight into Quaker theology. Rather than strictly adhering to scripture like other sectarian groups, Jesus and his early followers were the basis of the Quakers' Apostolic nostalgia:

> Friends believed that primitive Christians had Christ as their authority since the New Testament had not yet been written, and that these

earliest Christians experienced their own spiritual resurrection and judgment, witnessed the beginning of the Lamb's War, practiced silence as well as quaking in worship, allowed the preaching of women, and advocated the disuse of outward baptism and the Lord's Supper.[6]

Thus it was their ideas about the emergent Christian community, rather than a strict interpretation of scripture, that inspired Quaker theology and some of their more notorious, outlandish behaviors. While early Quakers believed that their actions were aligned with their Apostolic Christian predecessors, they did not self-regulate to make sure that all of their behaviors adhered to a biblical precedent.

The significance of spirit over scripture as the basis of Quaker theology was that the early Christians were imparted with the Holy Spirit before the scriptures were ever recorded. Therefore anyone seeking to emulate the Apostolic Christians' behavior needed to evoke this more ephemeral quality of Christianity, the living spirit of Christ rather than what they called the "dead letters" on the page, like literalist Baptists and Presbyterians.[7] For Quakers, the Bible "had been inspired by the Spirit, and without the Spirit people could neither believe nor understand it. Surely, therefore, the Spirit, not the Bible, ought to be the rule of Christians."[8] Essentially this meant that Quakers believed that they should use the Spirit as a guide to reading the scripture in order to be as close as possible to Paul and the early Christians' standards. As Quaker historian Geoffrey Nuttall states:

> By Fox, and by early Friends generally, the Bible was constantly appealed to at every level: sometimes literally, as when Friends refused to take an oath—being given 'a booke to sweare on that commanded not to sweare at all', to quote the wry common-sense phrase that went around; more figuratively, as when in dispute with a Jesuit Fox posits that the words 'This is my body' are on par with the words 'I am the door', and equally metaphorical.[9]

To that point, Quaker itinerant minister Thomas Salthouse described scripture as "a witness with them of what they maintained and taught," which reiterated the idea that the Bible served as a "secondary guide" where Quaker doctrines could be further substantiated.[10] This did not negate the Bible's significance because the Spirit worked with, rather than against, it.[11]

Therefore, if Quakers demoted scripture in the development of their faith and practices, what role did it play for them? The fact remains that despite their emphasis of spirit over scripture, the Gospels and Acts of the Apostles remained the only source to understanding the behaviors of Paul and the other early church leaders, so they looked to the New Testament to find behaviors to imitate. By doing this, Quakers sought out scriptural references that justified their own actions. Therefore, we must complicate the general understanding of the Quakers' relationship to scripture in order to better understand its function in their early correspondence by examining the times that they used biblical references to justify their actions in contrast to the times that they ignored it.

Using scripture in letters

Understanding the role that scripture played in the development of Quaker theology and practices also addresses a key issue in determining what version of the Bible held authority for the early members of the faith. The lack of an orthodox faith in England during the Interregnum meant that people, particularly sectarians, had access to the wide array of biblical translations available due to the absence of censorship laws. By the mid-seventeenth century, the two most prevalent versions in the godly milieu were the King James Version and the Geneva Bible.[12] It is virtually impossible to know which one would have been considered more appropriate to early Quakers, but given the wide range of backgrounds founding members came from, it is reasonable to assume that they did not all use the same one. A Geneva Bible from the Friends House of London has been used for the passages used here.[13]

Arguably, the Quakers' approach to interpreting scripture was more important than the version of the Bible they used. As has been stated above, scripture played a diminished role in the development of Quaker beliefs and practices, therefore unlike many of their contemporaries, it is improbable that they argued, even among themselves, for a single, authoritative text. Underwood notes that by emphasizing the spirit, Quakers pointed "out certain weaknesses in the method of interpreting Scripture by itself." He attributes this to the numerous versions of Bibles in a variety of languages:

> William Penn wondered how a person could discern which was correct. Even when using the same translation, people could not agree on a common meaning. The former Baptist Samuel Fisher, learned in Greek and Hebrew, declared, "There's as many silly senses, misty meanings, and contradictory conceits in the minds of them that are ministers of it [Scripture], almost as they are Ministers of it."[14]

Given that the present work is a close study of several hundred Quaker letters from the 1650s, and not a single mention of a preferred version of the Bible is made, I feel confident stating that this was not a significant issue for the early Quakers.

Regardless of the version consulted, Quakers pulled from all areas of the Bible, both Old and New Testaments. Furthermore, certain patterns emerge when examining Fell's letters. Elsa F. Glines's *Undaunted Zeal: The Letters of Margaret Fell* shows that there are 166 extant letters written by

Fell. In this body of letters there are 155 Old Testament references and 343 New Testament references. Of those, 109 date from the period this study is concerned with, 1652–1660. Remarkably, most verses were only used once, demonstrating Fell's strong command of the Bible. However, there were some that were repeated over the years to various audiences. The vast majority of biblical books are referenced at least once, and of course it is possible that those omitted from discussion here were present in other letters that have failed to survive.[15] From the Old Testament, Fell used only two books more than 20 times: Psalms and Isaiah. However, from the New Testament, Fell referenced Matthew, John, Acts of the Apostles, Romans, 1 Corinthians, Hebrews, and Revelations 20 or more times. I am designating a "favorite" passage as one that she used a minimum of three times in the letters that have been preserved: Psalms 2:9, Song of Solomon 4:15, Isaiah 50:6, Isaiah 61:1, Daniel 2:45, Micah 6:8, Malachi 3:2, Matthew 5:48, Matthew 6:22, Matthew 15:14, John 1:5, John 1:9, John 8:12, Acts 9:5, Romans 14:23, 2 Corinthians 13:11, Ephesians 2:2, James 1:17, 2 Peter 2:3, and 1 John 1:5. Quaker historian Hugh Barbour states that most of the Quakers' "characteristic phrases" were biblical in origin and "in many Quaker tracts, letters, and even journals 70 per cent of the phrases are biblical quotations or paraphrases."[16]

Based on the passages borrowed for their letters, there is a clear correlation between the ways in which early Quakers used scripture and the messages that they sought to share. These methods were utilized both when writing amongst their brethren and in the messages they projected to their opponents or those in positions of authority whom they sought to influence. It is no surprise that the New Testament has a more pronounced presence than the Old Testament. However, it should be noted that while the Gospel of Matthew is referenced more often, the Gospel of John is often used with more vitriol than other biblical books. Given what Underwood has to say about Quakers' desires to recognize the "Great Time" of Apostolic Christianity, and their diminution of scripture to the Spirit, it is unsurprising that they focus on the Apostles' activities so much in their letters.

As this brief survey suggests, Fell's letters alone provide examples from nearly every book of the Bible. In her edition of Fell's correspondence, Glines identifies four categories of letters based on Fell's intended audience: petitions to those in authority such as Oliver Cromwell, Henrietta Maria, and local magistrates; polemical letters that attack non-believers on matters of doctrine; pastoral letters and epistles to members of the faith generally; and letters to those within the Quaker movement, often discussing religious business matters. Sixty-five are letters to friends and family (37 Interregnum letters), 40 are pastoral letters and epistles (31 Interregnum), there are 42 petitions to those in positions of authority (23 from the Interregnum), and all 16 polemical letters or epistles concerning doctrinal controversies come from the pre-1660 period. This wide variety of examples allows for a useful case study of scriptural references in Quaker letters.

98 *Apostolic epistolary influences*

And yet, even with these extensive records, we know that our understanding of Quakers' use of scripture in correspondence is limited by those letters that Fell elected to maintain. Close reading of the extant letters suggest that both she and her Quaker brethren favored some passages over others, but these alone cannot tell us the entirety of their beliefs and behaviors. Despite the spotty picture of what we have to work with, we can state that the abundance of scriptural references tells us that it was important to the first Quakers to demonstrate their ability to utilize the Bible when writing to one another and to those outside of the movement. This allows for a deeper understanding of the emergent Quaker faith and how they wanted to be perceived by the wider world. It also sheds light on Fell's sense of what it meant for her co-religionists to emulate Apostolic Christianity.

Borrowed beliefs

From this point forward, the chapter will examine a sample of the language that Fell and others borrowed from the scriptures. In emulating the early Christian fathers, Quakers demonstrated their biblical acumen, which they used as a retort to other godly sectarians who discounted Quaker theology for not emphasizing scriptures enough. In addition, by modeling their lives on those of the itinerant preachers of yore, Quakers claimed a legitimacy that many of their contemporaries could not: Quakers not only spoke like the Apostolic Christians, they also lived like them.

A variety of common phrases like "quaking," "the unmovable spirit," "for conscience sake," "truth" or "righteousness," and "names-sake" can be found in numerous letters. These terms signified some of the most important aspects of the development of early Quaker theology. As Elizabeth Clarke notes in her work on Renaissance religious verse, readers of religious poems "tend to remake their authors in their own image" and the Quakers also identified with what they wanted biblical passages to say about their own theological positions.[17] In a 1653 letter to Oliver Cromwell, Fell wrote, "All shall be as A plaine before him, and terrible and dreadfull is hee when he shall appar to shake terriblely the Earth, & he will be avenged of his enemies."[18] This passage comes from Isaiah 2:21: "feare of the Lorde, and from the glorie of his maiestie, when he shall rise to dstroy the earth."[19] While "quaking" was not evoked by members of the faith often, it became synonymous with the group and similar language evoking "shaking" may be found on occasion in their letters. One such example comes from Paul's letter to the Hebrews:

> Whose voice then shooke the earth, and nowe hath declared, saying, Yet once more will I shake, not the earth onley, but also heauen.
> And this [worde] Yet once more, signifieth the remouing of those things which are shaken, as of thinges which are made [with hands] that the things which are not shaken, may remaine,

Wherefore seeing we receiue a kingdom, which cannot be shae, let vs haue grace, whereby wee may so serue God, that we may please him with reuerence and feare.[20]

Fell used similar language when writing to Anthony Pearson in 1653. However, she inverted the meaning by saying Quakers were unmoved in contrast to the shakable non-believers: "Saying I shake not the earth only but heaven alsoe signyfieing the removeing of these things that are shaken, as of things that are made: that those things which cannot be shaken may remaine, but we have received A kingdome that cannot be moved."[21] In contrast to quaking, language concerning the immutability of their faith or of God's nature may be found throughout their letters. Similar language is present in 1655 when Fell wrote to William Dewsbury that she was his "deare sister in the unchangeable Truth."[22] Fell's steadfastness was something that her brethren often mentioned.

Another common trope was the idea of doing only what they could for their "conscience sake." The use of the conscience may be found repeatedly in scripture, such as in Acts 24:16, "And herein do I exercise myself, to have always a conscience voide of offense toward God, and toward men," when Fell wrote to Jeffrey Elletson in 1654 "therein doe I exercise myself to have all ways a Conscience voyd of offense towards god, and towards men."[23] Again, to Elletson, Fell said, "And the Apostle Sayd our rejoicing is this, the testimony of our conscience, that in simplicity, and godly Sincerity we have had our conversation amongst you in tyme past."[24] This time Fell quoted 2 Corinthians 1:12: "For our reioycing is this, the testimonie of our conscience, that in simplicitie and godly purenes."[25] Fell also evoked this passage from Paul's second letter to the Corinthians when writing to Justice John Sawrey: "For our rejoicing is in this the testimony of our Conscience that in simplicity & godly sinceritie, not with fleshly wisdom but by the grace of the lord we have had our conversation in the world."[26] Fell's contrast of Quakers, who lived according to their conscience as dictated by God, with foes like Elletson and Sawrey, who had no conscious at all, was clear by her use of strong language in these examples.

Even more often than the idea of the conscience, Quakers discussed the truth or their sense of righteousness in the face of all manner of opposition. John 14:17 states: "[Euen] the Spirit of trueth, whom the world cannot receiue, because it seeth him not, neither knoweth him: but ye knowe him: for hee dwelleth with you, and shalbe in you."[27] Once again writing to an opponent of the Quaker message, Fell said to Daniel Davis in 1657: "The Etarnall spirit whose Judgment shall stand condems thee and the pop together who hath shut thyselfe out from the spirit of truth."[28] Here Fell attributed Davis with the most offensive seventeenth-century insult for an English Protestant—to insinuate that he was aligned with the Pope.

Looking outside of Psalms, Quakers found their righteousness in the letters of the Apostles.[29] In Hebrews 1:8, it says: "But vnto the sonne [hee saith], O God, thy throne [is] for euer and euer: the septer of thy kingdome [is] a scepter of righteousnesse."[30] Fell praised both the Quaker mission and William Dewsbury when she wrote to him in 1655: "whos scepter is a scepter of Righteousness, of whose Kingdome there is no end, to whom bee everlasting glory & praise forevermore."[31] Righteousness is evoked again in Romans 10:6–8, which states, "But the righteousnes which is of faith, speaketh on this wise, Say not in thine heart, who shall ascend into heauen: (that is to bring Christ from aboue) Or, who shall descende into the deepe: (that is to bring Christ againe from the dead) But what saith it: The Worlde is neere thee, [euen] in thy mouth, and in thine heart. This is the worde of faith which we preach."[32] Fell utilized the idea of righteousness when writing to Henrietta Maria in November 1660: "We doe witness discending upon us, & manifesting himself in us & through us, & this is our testimony, the word of faith which we preach, which is nigh in the heart & in the mouth, which preacheth Rightesousnes, and saith neither ascend nor descend but the word is very nigh to hear it & doe it."[33] Here Fell attempted to win the queen's support by articulating, through use of scriptural passages that she assumed Henrietta Maria would be familiar with, that the Quaker faith was superior to its contemporaries. This was tricky for Fell to negotiate, given that she was not only trying to win support for her religious community, but also simultaneously denouncing the queen's Catholic faith. Similar phrases are repeated throughout Quaker correspondence.[34]

Despite the lack of biblical literalism in Quaker rhetoric, early letter writers did evoke scripture to justify their distinctive theological concepts. Having come from the puritan milieu, Fell and others claimed to have created a new covenant with God. This language is quite similar to that of their puritan contemporaries, but the grounds on which they claimed a new holy partnership were distinctly Quaker. In 1653, Fell wrote an open letter to Friends, stating: "And this is not the Letter without you, but this is the faithful Promise of God, which he hath promised to those who are taught of him, which is the substance of the New Covenant which he hath made; who hath said, I will put my Laws in their hearts, and write them in their inward parts."[35] This passage comes from Jeremiah: "But this shalbe the couenant that I will make with the house of Israel, After those daies, saith the Lord, I wil put my Law in their inward parts, and write it in their hearts, and will be their God, and they shalbe my people."[36] Seven years later, Fell wrote to King Charles II hoping to convince him of the Quaker truth by quoting Jeremiah 31: "Behold, the daies come, saith the Lord, that I will make a new couenat with the house of Israel, and with the house of Judah."[37] In 1660 Fell wrote to Charles II: "And this is the new Covenant which the Lord hath made with the house of Iasraell, & with the house of Judah, when the sin of the Iniquityes Shall be remembered noe more."[38] Perhaps Fell hoped to win Charles's support by suggesting he was ushering in a new age of Hebrew kings, although the Merry Monarch was probably not the most receptive audience for the godly message.

Language concerning the covenant was also pulled from a variety of books including Malachi. In 1654, Fell wrote an open letter to friends encouraging them to keep in mind the sacred task they had undertaken: "Remember that you have weryed the Lord with your words, but hee is sending his messengers to prepare the way before him, & the Lord whom yee seeke shall suddainly Come to his temple, even the messenger of the Covinent, behold hee will Come saith the Lord of hoasts."[39] Fell's letter is almost verbatim from Malachi 3:1.[40] From examples like this, we can infer that Fell had a profound knowledge of scripture but also a savvy approach to using it—direct quotations were employed when it served her purposes, but she was also able to paraphrase or have a looser approach. Like some of her contemporaries, Fell was not beholden to verbatim quotations because she thoroughly understood the text she employed.

Fell and other Quakers often utilized passages concerning the covenant, which they borrowed from the Old Testament; however, the most frequently evoked concept was the inner light, which was taken from numerous New Testament books. The Gospels of Matthew and John are inundated with references to the light. Chapter 5 of Matthew's Gospel states: "Ye are the light of the world. A citie that is set on an hill, can not be hid," and "Let your light so shine before men, that they may see your good works, & glorify your father which is in heaue."[41] Writing to Queen Mother Henrietta Maria in 1660, Fell stated: "Who is to let their Light shine forth before men that they may see their good works & Glorify their father which is in heaven."[42] Again we see Fell forgiving the queen's Catholicism when given the opportunity to win favor (or lessen persecution) of her brethren—even if it meant acknowledging that Henrietta Maria may possess the light in her, as well.

One of Fell's most oft-used phrases comes from a cobbled together passage of John 1:4 and 1:9, "In it was life, & the life was the light of men ... That was the true light, which lighteth euery man that commeth into the world."[43] She evoked these passages repeatedly in her letters. To Jeffrey Elletson in 1654, Fell stated, "For that which may be knowne of god is made manifest in them, for god is light."[44] Again in 1654, Fell wrote to Judge Hugh Wyndham stating, "& the scripture is fulfilled upon thee, the saying of John, Light shines in darknes & darknes doth not Comprehend it."[45] Later in 1655, to Francis Benson, Fell stated: "and this is the condemnation, that light is come into the world, & men love darknes rather than light because their deeds are evil, for every one that doth evill hateth the light, neither cometh to the light least his deeds should bee reproved."[46] But these examples are merely a sample. Numerous additional examples from John can be found below.[47]

Similar to the use of "light," Fell often conjures the "spirit." Acknowledgement of the spirit was tantamount to the inner light—the central tenet of Quaker theology. Therefore, discussion of the spirit can be found throughout Quaker epistles. Unlike covenant or light, references for spirit may be found in both the Old and New Testaments. Isaiah 42:1, "mine elect, [in whom] my soule delighteth: I have put my Spirit upon him: he shall bring forth iudgement to the Gentiles," is evoked in a letter from Fell "To the World, Priests, and People" in 1654: "And the Prophet Isaiah, who prophesied of Christ, saith I the Lord have called thee in Righteousness and will hold thine hand, and will keep thee, and give thee for a Covenant to the people, and a Light unto the Gentiles."[48] As we see here, whenever possible, Fell would indicate to her reader (particularly when writing to Quaker opponents) that she not only knew scripture, but also could guide others in their reading of it by specifically mentioning books or chapters of verse.[49]

Seemingly interchangeably with light and spirit, Fell applies the idea of the living word or life in general, which may be found in Quakers versus the dead word, or more generally death that pertains to all other forms of worship. In 1653, Fell wrote to future Quaker Justice Anthony Pearson, "For our god is not the god of the dead but of the living," which comes from Matthew 22:32: "I am the God of Abraham, and the God of Isaac, and the God of Iacob? God is not the God of the dead, but of the liuing."[50] Then in 1655, Fell pulled from John 1:4, "In it was life, & the life was the light of men," when she told Francis Benson, "for in him is life and his life is the light of men."[51] The "him" Fell refers to is no doubt Fox. In this one passage, Fell was able to simultaneously show off her scriptural prowess to an opponent and exalt Fox. Further, her maintenance of the letter network allowed for her perception of Fox to be spread among the Quaker movement, thus elevating his status.

However, she only utilized Protestants' most used biblical passage, John 3:16, once in all of her extant letters: "For God so loued the worlde, that he hath giuen his onely begotten sonne, that whosoeuer beleaeth in him, should not perish, but haue euerlasting life."[52] This is in response to a series of questions that had been proposed by James Cave in 1656. He asked how men should obey the light within them. She spiritedly replied, "O thou darke ignorant Infidell, hath not God sent his only begotten sonne into the world, that whosoever believes in him should not perish but have everlasting life."[53] But as stated above, these are only a small sample of Quaker attempts to replicate biblical references to life over death.[54]

In part, Fell and others sought to convey that through acceptance of the inner light—incorporation of the Spirit into the self—people could achieve perfection. This was done both when writing inside and outside of the Quaker community. Underwood identifies this as a key difference between Quakers and their sectarian contemporaries, particularly the Baptists. Quaker critics and polemicists saw this as the basis of one form of blasphemy, yet Fell stated that if those who denounced them knew scripture well, they would not make such damning accusations. Apparently Fell's favorite passage with which to make this point came from Matthew 5:48, "Ye shall therefore be perfite, as your Father which is in heaven, is perfit."[55] She referenced this passage no less than three times in the 1650s. The first was in an epistle clearly meant for publication addressed to "the World, Priests and People" in 1654: "And so they plead for Sin, and against Christ Jesus, and against the Apostles and Prophets, and all the Holy Men of God; for Christ saith, Be ye perfect, as your Heavenly Father is perfect."[56] Then in 1655 she wrote to Philip Bennett, "his doctrine saith be yee perfect as your heavenly father is perfect," indicating that this "hireling" did not understand the scripture, or perhaps was unfamiliar with it due to lack of reading.[57] Finally in 1657, she wrote to another adversary, Daniel Davis, stating: "the appostell saith he that sinns of the Divell: in thyne thou saith chrirst Jesus hath affinity with the Pop; who saith be yee perfecte as your hevenly Father is Parfecte."[58] Once again, this is not the only passage that emphasized the Quaker ability to achieve perfection like God—numerous additional examples may be found below.[59]

As these examples show, early Quakers shaped their theology by writing to one another with examples from the Bible to illustrate their meanings. By doing so, they utilized familiar references that gave the movement a sound foundation and legitimized their efforts as a renewal of ancient beliefs and practices. As Margaret Fell's exchanges with puritan ministers demonstrate, their use of biblical references allowed Quakers to communicate with adversarial contemporaries, as well as with one another. Furthermore, Fell's position in creating and maintaining the letter network allowed her ideas, which promoted Fox, to be circulated, and they eventually became the accepted version of Quaker orthodoxy in the early movement.

Fighting the Lamb's War and suffering for salvation

Spreading the Quaker message was not an easy effort. For Fell and the other early Quakers, their perfection or acceptance of the inner light was evidence of being on the right side of the Lamb's War, which they continued to fight, just as the Apostles had before them. When evoking combative language, the Book of Revelations provided the most justification for waging war. References come from Revelations 14:4, 14:10–11, 17:14, and 21:27. Revelations 14:10–11 is the most frequently quoted: "The same shall drink of the wine of the wrath of God, which is poured out without mixture into the cup of his indignation; and he shall be tormented with fire and brimstone in the presence of the holy angels, and in the presence of the Lamb."[60] Fell evoked this passage in response to Daniel Davis in 1657: "Daniell Davis: thou hast opened thy mouth as blasphemy against the lambe & his folowers: which is a trew marke of the Beast. Which is in thy forhead And the wine of the wrath of god shall thou drinke which is pouered out with mixteuer into the copp of his indignation."[61] Fell and other Quakers used images like this to promote the Quakers' sense of purpose while suffering through the trials of itinerancy. They were God's representatives in the Lamb's War and repeated reminders of the dignity of their efforts served to strengthen the troops. As Fell spread news of courageous efforts throughout the network, devotion to the Quaker cause strengthened and at times even won over new adherents.

Here we see how Fell and her fellow Quakers juxtaposed themselves as lambs against their enemies using phrases like dragon, devil, serpent, and Antichrist virtually interchangeably in both their letters to and about adversaries. Summoning the serpent, Fell took from Matthew 10:16: "Beholde, I sende you as sheepe in the middes of wolues: be yee therefore wise as serpents, and innocent as doues."[62] Writing to William Knipe in 1656, Fell stated: "And wheras thou broughtest that scripture where Christ sayd be wyse as serpents, that was when Christ sent forth his disciples as lambs amongst the woolfesh natures as men"[63] Never missing an opportunity to demonstrate her superior knowledge over her ignorant adversaries, Fell illustrated here that the simplistic form of educating through parable may be required when speaking to non-Quakers. In another instance, Fell set the Quaker angel against the devil as described in Jude 1:8–9: "Likewise notwithstanding these dreamers also defile the flesh, and despite gouernement, and speak euill of them that are in authortie. Yet Michael the Archangel, when hee stroue against the devil, and disputed about the bodie of Moses, durst to blame him with cursed speaking, but said, The Lord rebuke thee." This passage was used to defend her position in a dispute at Manchester in 1656: "and soe thus you are in your contention, and striving about the body of Jesus, as the Divell did about the body of moses."[64] This time Fell employed a more direct method of explaining basic aspects of biblical information to a letter recipient who presumably was familiar with Jesus and Moses but fell short of Fell's standards of comprehension.

Similarly, the oft mentioned dragon of Revelations appeared in her missives, as well: "And there appeared a great wonder in heauen: A woman clothed with & sunne, and the moone was vnder her feete, and vpon her head a crowne of twelue stares."[65] This passage spurred a sarcastic response to a series of questions posed by Reverend Thomas Shaw:

> Q:3:4:5:6: Thou asketh what do you understand by the Dragon? 4: what by his heads? 5: what by his hornes? 6: what by his 7: Crownes? Answ: Wee doe understand & knowe assuredly & affirme, that the pope ___ (who houlds your Catholique Church and thou, and all you who have your ground & ordination from the pope, are the Dragon: And with your Seven heads & 10 hornes and 7: Crownes (which thou speakes of) are you Standing before the woman, who is ready to be delivered, for to devoure her Child as Soone as he is borne.[66]

The letter exchange between Fell and Shaw was unusual in that he asked her questions, clearly intending to highlight her and more generally Quakers' ignorance of scripture, and she responded in kind. Each equated the other with the dragon—undoubtedly neither was convinced that he or she was the embodiment of the devil. Fell proved herself capable of taking a male opponent to task and was regarded as an opponent, albeit in a condescending manner. This example contrasts sharply with Fell's manner of writing to likeminded Quaker men. She certainly deferred to Fox, but she only took a sharp tone with those outside of the faith or those who had fallen out with the religious community, and occassionally Quaker women.

In addition to engaging in a war of words with Quaker detractors, Fell also communicated via the letter network to loved ones about the need to defeat the enemy.[67] Throughout the Interregnum, Quakers felt like they were under siege from all sides; therefore, it is no wonder that Fell encouraged her co-religionists to be alert to threats to the faith. They were waging the Lamb's War, after all. Writing to an indeterminate group of Quakers about the enemy, Fell used Revelations 20:8: "And shall go out onto deceiue the people, which are in the foure quarters of the eart: [euen] Gog and Magog, to gather them together to battell, whose number [is] as the land of the sea," when she wrote in 1654: "this is the day of the Lords battle, & this is the day of the deceivers of the nations, which are in the foure Corners of the earth, Gog and Magog are gathering together in battle, to Compass the saints and the beloved City, but fire is coming down from god to devoure them."[68] This cryptic language, one they were not only familiar with but also identified with, no doubt served as the rallying cry Fell hoped for. As Elizabeth Clarke has noted in her discussion of the Song of Songs, seventeenth-century readers would have had a greater familiarity with various biblical passages "and understood its arcane imagery in a manner entirely divorced from its literal reading."[69] Numerous letter authors from this period urged recipients to embrace the virtue of their mission and their inevitable victory over their theological enemies.

Almost as frequently as they utilized these derogatory monikers, Fell and her brethren also positioned themselves vis-à-vis the sinful multitude who resided in the wilderness. A classic example, and one utilized multiple times, came from Psalms 7:9: "Oh let the malice of the wicked come to an ende: but guide thou the iust: for the righteous God trieth the hearts and reigns."[70] Once to Henrietta Maria in 1660 Fell wrote: "who knows it? & the answer is, this Light that shines in the heart, knows the heart and the secrets of it, & searcheth the heart & tryes the Reins."[71] In a completely contrasting example, Fell vividly evoked Jeremiah 17:9—"The heart is deceitfull and wicked aboue all things, who can knowe it?"—when she wrote to John Garnet in 1655: "Thou who art turned with the dogs to the vomit, into thy drunkennesse and filthynesse, from the light of christ-Jesus which hee hath enlightened thee withal, which if thou were obeydient to it, it would show thee thy decietfull hart."[72] While Fell could be compelled to insult her letter recipient, as evidenced here, she had the wherewithal to refrain from such acerbic language to the queen mother.

As they preached and wrote to one another about their experiences trying to convince the masses, Quakers felt vindicated given their excessive sufferings because they were examples of how God wanted the word spread, rather than examples of "hirelings" or "professors" like so many of their contemporaries. There is Old and New Testament support for their position on this matter. The Gospel according to Matthew proved to be quite a fruitful source when chastising paid priests. Matthew 7:29, 12:24, and 23:34 were all used to make this claim. The last of these may be the most illustrative: "Wherefore beholde, I sende unto you Prophetes, and wise men, and Scribes, and of them ye shall kill & crucifie: and of them shall ye scourge in your Synagogues, and persecute from citie to citie."[73] Fell once again suggested that her foe, William Knipe, may not be familiar with scripture when she wrote in 1656: "Ried Mathew the 23 wher for I send unto you profits and wise men and som of them you shall kill and crusifi and som of them you shall scourg in your sinagogues and persecute them from sitti to sitti."[74] Here Fell not only insinuated that Knipe had not read or understood Matthew 23, but also that as a persecutor of Quakers, Knipe was like those who crucified Christ.

Naturally, Quakers felt defensive due to what they perceived as a constant state of unjust persecution. As a result, they sought biblical support for their stances on the law. Matthew 5:18 states: "For truly I say unto you, Till heauen and earth perish, one fote, or one title of the lawe shall not reape, till all thinges be fulfilled."[75] Fell wrote to "Brethren and Sisters" in 1658: "& how you Can beare witnesse in your measures to the truth of these things, for not one jot nor tittle of the Law shall passe away till all be fulfilled."[76] The Apostle Paul wrote about law in Romans 8:3–4: "That the righteousnes of the law might be fulfilled in vs, which walke not after the flesh, but after the Spirit."[77] Fell was able to liken Quakers to Apostles and claim scriptural support when writing to Philip Bennett in 1655: "And the Apostle saith god sent forth his sonne in the likeness of sinfull flesh, & for sin condemned Sin in the flesh, and that the righteousness of the Law might be fulfilled in us."[78] Fell evoked a similar idea with Paul's first letter to the Corinthians 11:2–3: "Nowe, brethren, I commend you, that ye remember all my things and keepe the ordinances, as I deliuered them to you."[79] Fell then said: "And the Apostle exhorted them to keepe the ordinances & he delivered them to them & he saith that the head of every man is xt. This is the ordinance which is ordeyned of god for Salvation."[80] As will be discussed in Chapter 5, Quakers had a peculiar approach to the law. In this passage, Paul compelled the Corinthians to "keep the ordinances." When Fell told her recipient, "the professor" to do the same, it was not to suggest that he had broken English law, but that he had offended God's law. While Quakers did not regularly adhere to man's law, they perceived themselves as devotees of holy ordinances.

Both the earliest Christians and seventeenth-century Quakers referred to themselves as "prisoner(s) of God." This title was a source of pride to the individual and signaled respect of the greater community. Paul called himself a prisoner of God in Ephesians 3:1: "For this cause, I Paul [am] the prisoner of Jesus Christ for you Gentiles"; a prisoner of Christ Jesus in Philemon 9–10: "[Yet] for loues sake I rather beseech thee, though I bee as I am, euen Paul aged, and euen now a prisoner for Jesus Christ I beseech thee for my Sonne Duelimus, whom I haue begotten in my bondes"; and a prisoner for the Lord's sake in Ephesians 4:1: "Therefore, being prisoner in the Lord, pray you that ye walke worthy of the vocation on whereunto ye are called."[81] Similar phrasing can be found throughout Quaker manuscripts. In 1655, Thomas Salthouse signed a letter to Margaret Fell: "T.S. now prisoner of the Lord in the Comon Goale in Exon."[82] Also in 1655, Richard Hubberthorne and George Whitehead separately signed the same letter as "prisoner of the lord in norwich Castle" and "prisoner off the Lord in the same Jaol in Norwhich with James Lancaster," respectively.[83] Richard Hubberthorne again signed a letter to Fell as "Prisoner of the Lord in Norwich Castle," denoting both his allegiance and his place of imprisonment. Similar sentiments were expressed when James Myers signed a letter from the Launceston jail as "A prisoner for the ware,"[84] and when Hubberthorne called himself "A prisonor for rightousnes sake."[85] In the early Quaker mindset, working for the Lord and his war were demonstrations of righteousness, which were the same for Paul and the early Christians as they were for those working for the truth in the seventeenth century. It is worth noting that there are no letters from Fell of this kind because she did not endure imprisonment during the Interregnum. However, subsequent Fell letters include signatures like these once she was jailed during the Restoration.[86]

Like Paul's encouragement to withstand imprisonment bravely, Quaker authors raised and answered both theological and practical questions. This was particularly the case in examples concerning the Quakers' positions on sufferings. Issues over why one suffers and encouragement for others to suffer well and to embrace their imprisonment were based on Paul's correspondence. Just as the early Quakers were divided on the meaning of sufferings, Paul's letters reflect the lack of a unified position on the subject among early Christians. Paul said in Romans 5:3–5 that one suffers to demonstrate his endurance for the benefit of the church, which gives hope to other believers: "Neither that onely, but also we reioyce in tribulations, knowing that tribulation bringeth forth patience, And patience experience, and experience hope, And hope maketh not ashamed, because the loue of God is shed abroade in our heartes by the holy Ghost, which is giuen vnto vs."[87] Similarly, Quakers Thomas Salthouse and Myles Halhead stated that one suffers for God's glory: "to the will of our Father we give vp to do or to suffer, that he may be honoured and glorified."[88] Later in Romans 8:16–18, Paul states that one shares Christ's suffering by glorifying him:

> The same Spirit beareth witness with our spirit, that we are the children of God. If [we be] children, [we are] also heires, euen the heires of God, and heires annexed with Christ, if so be that we suffer with him, that we may also be glorified with him. For I count that the afflictions of this present time [are] not worthie of the glory, which shalbe shewed vnto vs.[89]

Again, Paul states in 2 Thessalonians 1:4 that worthiness is determined by devotion through suffering: "So that we our selues reioyce of you in the

Churches of God, because of your pacience and faith in all your persecutions & tribulations that ye suffer."[90] Paul, like the Quakers, let his readers know that suffering not only glorified one to God but resulted in fame and respect among other believers.

Another thread of discussion surrounding suffering focused on its results. In Philippians 1:11, Paul states that suffering is part of Christians' righteous plan: "Filled with the fruites of righteousnesse, which are by Iesus Christ vnto the glorie and praise of God."[91] In this passage, Paul claimed that doing God's work encourages others to be faithful and to suffer in kind. This sentiment was often echoed in Quaker ideas concerning the importance of encouraging others to suffer based on the demonstration of suffering and imprisonment of leading members of the community. In Colossians 1:24, Paul states that suffering is what constitutes the church: "Nowe reioyce I in my sufferings for you, and fulfill the rest of the afflictions of Christ in m flesh, for his bodyes sake, which is the Church."[92] These points come together to describe the church as those people who were dedicated to "Christ's cause" and demonstrate their dedication by willingly suffering. This dovetails with the notion of the Quaker covenant with God that was present throughout the manuscript letters. Early Quakers adopted their puritan predecessors' covenant with God, but altered its meaning to focus strictly on suffering in exchange for salvation. In 1655, Thomas Salthouse and Myles Halhead stated that the Christian accepted the burden of suffering in order to receive God's salvation and truth:

> In the Eternall onenesse of the Spirit doe wee injoy thee as present bonds cannot breake our vnion, as wee abide in that which leades out of time, and from under the dark power into the pure freedome w[hi]ch is purchased for us by the blood of the euerlasting Covenant; and through sufferinges is our way, but faithfull is hee that hath called not only to beleeve but to suffer with him, that wee may alsoe reign with him, when the Lambes testimony is finished.[93]

Here Salthouse and Halhead clearly linked the necessary experience of suffering to continuing God's work. Quakers could rest easy knowing that their suffering went toward a specific goal that would further their efforts as a community.

Furthermore, both early Christians and Quakers believed that it was a privilege to suffer for God. In Philippians 1:7, Paul said: "As it becommeth me so to iudge of you all, because I haue you in rememberance that both in my bandes, and in [my] defence, and confirmation of the Gospell you all were partakers of my grace."[94] Again, in Philippians 1:28-29 Paul said: "And in nothing feare your aduersaries, which is to them a token of perdition, and to you of saluation, and that of God. For vnto you it is the giuen for Christ, that not onely ye should beleeue in him, but also suffer for his sake."[95] The early Christians saw suffering as the mark of salvation, and

Paul wrote to fellow believers throughout the ancient world to notify them of others' trials and to encourage them to suffer, as well. Likewise, Henry Fell wrote to an imprisoned friend, Thomas Rawlinson, to encourage him to embrace the honor to suffer for God: "I heare that thou art in prison in Excetor. In it rejoyce that thou art found worthy not only to beleeve on his name, but alsoe to suffer for his sake."[96] Perhaps such comments could abate the fears of the imprisoned, embolden them to remain strong in their suffering, and encourage others in the community to adopt a similar attitude when it was their turn to suffer.

The letter network, as demonstrated here, was instrumental in maintaining early Quakers' emphasis on suffering. Edward Burrough stressed the honor associated with suffering when he said, "though it be wholly a Crosse, to us both to be separated, his is the lesser burthen who is in the prison."[97] Another example of suffering as an honor was demonstrated in a letter from Thomas Salthouse and Myles Halhead to Margaret Fell in 1656, in which they used vehement language to stress the reason one suffers: "Soe in the will of God we stand chusseing rather to suffer imprisonment or banishment out of the Land then to purchasse outward freedome by making a Covenant with death and soe bring our selves into inward bondage."[98] While "imprisonment," "suffer," "death," and "bondage" may not be words that warm the hearts of modern readers, they were awe-inspiring commitments to their faith for early modern Quakers. This was not always the case, though, as seen in Ann Audland's letter to Fox in 1654 when she wrote, "I can haue no ease till thou ease me; here is very great service, reach to me th[a]t I may haue strength; my Crosse was never so, as it is now; pray for me that I faint not till I see thee."[99] Thus, not everyone welcomed suffering with elation; however, Fell clearly felt that the sufferer's experience needed to be preserved. She chose to keep a wide array of suffering accounts because they proved to be essential to the future of the Quaker identity.

While clearly influenced by Paul's ideas, some Quaker letters appear less confident than others about their mission. This may be because they often reported their suffering rather than their being called to arms in the manner that Paul employs in his epistles. Could this be because Paul felt a direct (or at least more direct) connection to Jesus compared to those who were further removed in Greece, Rome, and the rest of the Mediterranean? Was there a similar effect to those would-be Quakers who were closest to the center of the movement (i.e., close to or converted by Fox, Nayler, etc.), who may have seen their role as special like Paul's? If so, there was never a sense at the beginning of the movement that all people were equal in importance—there was a hierarchy from the start, and they only had to look to the early Christians to see their model. This example still allowed them to separate themselves from hierarchical church organizations such as the Catholics, then defunct Anglicans, and other contemporary churches (even the Presbyterian synod system), but also gave them a sense of who was most important in the group and to whom to turn when in need of help and guidance. Therefore, everyone who participated in the Quaker movement would have had a sense of purpose in belonging to the group—some were meant to lead, like Fell and Fox, whereas others were meant to follow. Looking to the early Christians for inspiration, the inchoate Quakers would have found a relevant model and therefore felt justified in assuming the roles they held in their religious organization.

A final poignant example of welcoming suffering comes from Paul's letter to the Galatians: "But the fruite of the Spirite is loue, ioye, peace, long suffering, gentlenesse, goodnesse, faith, Meekenesse, temperancie: against such there is no Lawe."[100] Fell used this reference to muster support from Colonel William West in 1656: "And against those who are guided by this & bring forth the fruite of the spirit the apostle saith there is no Law And soe under the Lawes of man, which is made in the will of man, wee cannot Come, nor stoop to that Law which is made by the Carnall mind, which the Apostle saith is not subject to the Law of god."[101] Here Fell allowed herself a wide interpretation of Paul's message to the Galatians. She inserted the Quaker idea of separating man's law from God's law into a scriptural passage, thereby attempting to diminish any question of their authority. Given that she was writing to a friend of the Quakers, she must have felt reasonably assured that her intention would be understood.

As will be argued in Chapter 5, Quakers suffered and experienced imprisonment often, so it is no wonder that they looked to scripture for justification of the behavior that put them there. The commonly quoted passage from Isaiah 61 was used repeatedly:

> The Spirit of the Lord God [is] upon me, therefore hath the Lord anoynted mee: hee hath sent me to preache good tidinges unto the poore, to binde up the broken hearted, to preach libertie to the captiues, and to them that are bounde, the opening of the prison, To preach the acceptable yeere of the Lorde, and the day of vengeance of our God, to comfort all that mourne.[102]

The first example came from an epistle to friends in 1653, which implored them to listen to their leader and teacher in righteousness, which "speakes to the Spirits in Prison" because without guidance, they cannot find "liberty to the Captives is come." It is repeated to "All Friends, Brethren and Sisters" in 1655: "liberty to the Captive and prisoner" and yet again to Francis Howgill and Thomas Robertson on June 21, 1657: "My soule longs after, your publishing the glad tideings to the poore, Liberty to the Captive, that the prisoner might have his Liberty."[103] It is interesting that they repeatedly sought "liberty to the captive," when nearly all letters from prison stated that they were free in conscience, so their "outward" imprisonment did not bother them.

Fell cautioned enemies with similar language, as well. Using John 5:37–38: "And his worde haue yee not abiding in you: for whom he hath sent, him ye beleeue not," Fell admonished John Ravel in 1654, quoting this passage almost verbatim: "& yee have not his word abiding in you for him whome he hath sent him yee believed not saith xt."[104] She used Acts 5:19, "But the Angel of the Lord, by night opened the prison doors, and brought them forth," to speak against William Knipe in 1656: "Read the 4 and 5 of the acts and after wardes when the Lord sent his Engles to deliver the aposiles out of prison the Capten of the Temple."[105] This gave Fell the teaching opportunity that she so relished when chastising a less knowledgeable hireling in her midst. And apparently Fell's favorite passage for enemies was Acts 9:5: "And he sayd, who art thou, Lord: And the Lord said, I am Jesus whom thou persecuted: it is hard for thee to kicke against prickes." This passage was used at least three times. First, it appeared in a letter to Judge John Archer in 1653: "& thou kickes against the prickes & strives with thy maker therefore is thy portion." And later she wrote to John Ravel in 1654: "& I bid thee give over persecuting of Jesus, it is hard for thee to kicke against the Pricks." And she used it a third time when writing to George Braithwaite in 1656: "its hard for thee to kick against the pricks."[106] This scriptural reference equates "hireling" priests with a physical obstacle for Quakers to maneuver around, or more specifically, to kick against. Thus the Lamb's War remained an important part of the Quakers' epistolary exchanges throughout the Interregnum and, thanks to Fell's archival efforts, an essential aspect of the ways in which they subsequently remembered their early years as a faith.

Quaker idiosyncrasies

Much like their position that preaching was for those who were awakened to the inner light rather than those with formal educations who were paid for their work, Fell sought biblical support for the more uniquely Quaker behaviors, such as going naked as a sign, their resistance to water baptism, and opposition to taking oaths. The activities that often got them into the most trouble, such as refusing hat honors or the use of thee and thou, were not justified by scripture. This is not to say that they would not have utilized a biblical justification if it were available, but presumably neither the Old nor the New Testament says much on the seventeenth-century practices of respecting one's social betters by removing hats or using informal Jacobean language.

With regards to public nakedness, Fell—who apparently never did this herself—makes strange use of scripture. Here she used one biblical passage in a variety of ways. Isaiah 20:3 says: "And the Lord said, Like as my seruant Isaiah hath walked naked, and barefoote three yeeres, as a signe and wonder vpon Egypt, and Ethiopia."[107] Fell utilized this passage when writing to Gabriel Camelford in 1654 stating, "thou goes about by all meanes thou canst to make the truth odious, & bringes in the going naked, who is as the profett Is saith was set for signes & wonders amongst the generation of dispisers."[108] What is curious about this usage is not this specific reference, but that she did not go on to use the rest of Isaiah 20, which provides considerable detail about nakedness as a sign. Should we assume that this was the only portion of the biblical book that she recalled and did not have a copy handy to reference? Or was there some aspect of this particular verse that spoke to her, whereas the rest of the book did not? It is impossible to know, but it seems like a missed opportunity. A more likely explanation is that there was an assumed common knowledge so she did not believe the passage needed to be quoted in its entirety.

However, unlike the reference to nakedness, there were more opportunities for Quakers to justify their position on baptism. They saw water baptism as a papist remnant that played no part in salvation. Most of Fell's correspondence on baptism is found in a letter to Jeffrey Elletson from 1654. Here she evoked Matthew 3:11: "In deede I baptize you with water to amendment of life, but he that commeth after me, is mightier then I, whose shoes I am not worthie to beare: hee will baptize you with the holy Ghost, and with fire." This passage was repeated in the following manner: "For the Baptisme of repentance, which washeth away the filth of the flesh, thou art not yet come too."[109] It is worth noting that Fell omitted all mention of water in her letter. Also to Elletson, Fell used Paul's first letter to the Corinthians 12:13, "For by one Spirit are we all baptized into one bodie, whether [wee bee] Jewes or Grecians, whether [wee bee] bond, or free, and haue beene all made to drinke into one Spirit," when she said: "And if ever thou know the true & livinge God, thou must owne us, for god is but one, and the way one, the faith but one, & the Baptisme one by one Spirit into one body."[110] Again, there is no mention of water, but the intention has shifted to the role of the Spirit in salvation. In yet another example, Fell took the following from 1 Peter 3: "Whereof the baptisme that nowe is, answering that figure, (which is not a putting away of the filth of the flesh, but a confident demaunding which a good conscience maketh to God) saueth vs also by the resurrection of Iesus Christ."[111] This is used later in the letter to Elletson when she said: "And when he spoke of Noahs preaching to the Spiritts in prison, to them which were sometimes disobeydient he tould them they had the like figure whereunto even Baptisme doth allsoe Save u not puttinge away the filth of the flesh; but the answeare of a good conscience towards god by the resurrection of Jesus xt."[112] Even when mentioning a biblical figure synonymous with water like Noah, Fell omitted all mention of water when discussing baptism as it was contrary to the Quaker concept of baptism in light.

Like their stance on nakedness as a sign, there are few passages used to defend Quakers' stance on oaths; however, these passages are evoked much more often, as Quakers were punished for refusal to swear more often than they were for going naked as a sign. Both Matthew 5:34, "But I say unto you, Sweare not at all, neither by heauen, for it is the throne of God," and James 5:12, "But before al things, my brethren, sweare not, neither by heauen, nor by earth, nor by any other othe: but let your yea, be yea, and [your] nay, nay, least ye fall into condemnation" were frequently found in letters.[113] Fell wrote

Apostolic epistolary influences 113

to Philip Bennett about why no one, neither Quakers nor others, should take oaths: "And the Apostle James saith above all things my Bretheren Sweare not at all nether by heaven nor by Earth neither by any other Oath but let your yea be yea, & your nay, nay, lest you fall into Condemnation and thou saith that an oath is lawfull."[114] For a religious community that was fairly liberal with its biblical literalism, Quakers took a hard line on the one issue of oaths. The fact that they did not adopt a similar position on baptism must have dismayed their sectarian contemporaries. While it is important to discuss how Quakers saw themselves in relation to the Apostolic predecessors, most of the topics discussed in this chapter are hardly surprising. That they would seek to emulate those before them through the use of biblical language makes them quite similar to many of their contemporaries.

Emulating the apostles

Perhaps the most important uses of scripture were the comparisons drawn between early Quaker leaders and Apostolic Christians; therefore, their letters reflect a return to early Christian forms, particularly to Paul's epistles as the model for their own correspondence. Fell and Fox looked to Paul's letters for help with particular problems that the early Christians also faced, which provided recommendations for how local communities should organize and disseminate information. Paul was also a model for Fox as a leader, who often compared himself to the apostle in his journal.[115] In *The Beginnings of Quakerism*, Braithwaite repeatedly compares Fox to Paul. Historian of dissent Michael Watts further states: "What was distinctive about Fox was not his opinions but the sense of spiritual power, the depth of insight, and the profound conviction of the reality of his own experience which he conveyed to other men."[116] To that end, Fell references Paul in two major ways: one, as an apostle and therefore a model for all Quakers, and two, as sources of comparison with Fox. Regarding the role of the apostle, Fell naturally used passages from the Acts of the Apostles. Acts 13:50 states: "But the Iewes stirred certaine deuoute and honourable women, and the chiefe men of the citie, and raised persecution against Paul and Barnabas, and expelled them out of their coastes."[117] Fell evoked this passage when writing to William Knipe in 1656:

> And what did they doe unto paule at Antioch when hee went into the innogogue of the sabeth day and preached unto them the Law & the prophit & ministrasion of John and allsoe of Christ death & his resurrection & of Those that heard him Contredickted him & blasfeameed and sterod up the people to persicuision against paule & barnebas & expelled them out of there Coste acts the 13.[118]

Here Fell reminded her reader of Quaker suffering in comparison to Paul's persecution. In another passage in the same letter to Knipe, Fell said "& also of masadony, where Paule & Silas preached serten dayes the multitude Rose up against them, & the magistrate Rent of there Close & commanded them to bee beatten & when they had leyd many stripes upon them they Cast them into prison acts 16."[119] This came from Acts 16:22–23, which states: "Then there came certaine Iewes from Antiochia and Iconium, which when they had persuaded the people, stoned Paul, and drewe him out of the citie, supposing he had bene dead."[120] These examples could be used for a variety of circumstances as Paul served as a model for all good Christians.

Yet Fell utilized Paul most explicitly as an example to Fox. This statement may seem to contradict a main tenet of this book, which is that Fell served in a Pauline manner for the emergent Quakers. Yet it does not because Fell did not argue for that position for herself. In her own lifetime, Fell was first and foremost a champion for Fox, therefore she would have been loath to draw comparison to herself with the most evangelical of the apostles, while Fox was apparently quite comfortable with the comparison.[121] There are numerous examples to illustrate this point, a few of which follow. From Acts 9:22, Fell used this passage: "But Saul increased the more in strength, and confounded the Jewes which dwelt at Damascus, confirming, that this was the Christ."[122] Fell used it to liken Fox to Paul, stating, "& how they goe with paule when hee preached Christ att Damascus and perceved that hee was the very Christ."[123] This passage references the times that Fox was accused of calling himself the son of God. She conjured similar ideas when using Romans 1:4–5: "And declared mightily [to be] the Sonne of God, touching the Spirit of sanctification by the resurrection from the dead) By whom we haue receiued grace and Apostleship (that obedience might be giuen vnto the faith) in his Name among all the Gentiles."[124] The comparison was quite stark in her 1656 letter to George Braithwaite using Romans 1:

> And againe mark thy ignorance of the scripture, who sayest wee are in the covenant of works because wee teach obedience to the light, wheras the Apostle saith in his epistle which hee wrote to the Romuns who was an Apostle separated unto the gospel of god Jesus and whom hee declared to bee the son of god according to the spirit of holiness by whom wee have received grace and Apostleship for obedience to the faith & this thou callest works.[125]

Here Fox, as apostle, wrote to spread Jesus's gospel. Fell encouraged the recipient of her letter to maintain his obedience to Fox as the leader of their community.

Perhaps the most interesting comparison comes when Fell reproved those who failed to follow Fox/Paul's commands. From the first letter to the Corinthians 1:12: "Nowe this I say, that euery one of you saith, I am Pauls, and I am Apollos, and I am Cephas, and I am Christes."[126] While she did not say explicitly that those who considered leaving Fox's fold were wrong, she did suggest it when saying: "And you know few or none in the life as you ought to know them, but you are Even Jeless of all, and redy to Question all, and dare hardly Joy to any, except I be these that are one with the Spirit that is head in you, and Soe yee be come one for Paule and one for Apallow, & one for Cephes."[127] This passage was also used by London Quakers in 1656 in the midst of the Nayler Affair, who claimed "I am of James" or "I am of Francis and Edward."[128] Thus, even in times of difficulty and potential schism, the Quakers sought validation in the early Christian church.

Fell's use of biblical language echoed throughout Quaker letters written by numerous ministers. The early Quakers used Paul's letters as the basis of their organization's structure and the names that they called themselves in the first decade. For all Quaker authors, Paul's ideas influenced the format of letters, the shape of the network, and the names they used, such as the Children of Light and Friends. Concerning the format of letters, Quakers looked to Romans 1:1 for the ending: "Paul a seruant of Jesus Christ, called [to be] an Apostle, put apart [to preach] the Gospel of God."[129] Quakers also offered greetings to a large group of both known and unknown people, such as in Romans 16:2–16 where salutations are offered to a long list of recipients who are among the faithful in that community.[130] Of course, neither Paul and the early Christians nor Fell and the early Quakers knew everyone who received their messages. The vagueness of terms like these allowed for a wider, ever-growing community to be included in their messages.

Other monikers were only used by a few members of the community. Fell did not use the phrase "Children of Light" as much as contemporary itinerants. An obvious reason for this omission may be that she did not join the movement until it had transformed into something else in 1652, and the term was on its way out by that time. The names that this amorphous group of people employed were based on the names that Paul used in letters to early Christians. In 1 Thessalonians 5:5, Paul said: "Yee are all the children of light."[131] Thomas Barcroft noted that it was commonplace for sects to be called "Grindletonians, Antinomians, Heretiets, Sectaries, and such like names of reproach, as in these days by the men of the Same generation of Cain that a murderer, The Children of Light are in scorn called Quakers."[132] While not around much for the use of Children of Light to describe the group, Fell was present for the rise of the term "Friend," and there is no shortage of examples of its use. John 15:14, "Ye are my friends, if ye do whatsoeuer I command you," was written to Brethren and Sisters in 1658: "Yee are my friends saith Christ, if you doe whatsoever I command you, so dwelling in the light, there is the Commaund of the Lord received, there is the will of the Lord done."[133] Fell used the next verse, John 15:15, as well: "Henceforth, call I you not seruantes: for the seruant knoweth not what his master doeth: but I haue called you friendes."[134] This time she was writing to Samuel Fisher in 1656: "But friends, for the sarvant knoweth not what his Lord doth yee are my friends when you doe what soe ever I commaund you."[135] Clearly the use of "friend" takes on a different connotation given the recipient.

Perhaps the most compelling biblical example of "friend" comes from James 2:23: "And the Scripture was fulfilled which sayeth, Abraham beleeued God, and it was imputed vnto him for righteousnesse: and hee was called the friende of God." The earliest Quaker reference to the term "friends" came in 1652 when Thomas Aldam said that news should be passed along to others in the movement: "I am free to make knowne to thee; some thinge Concerneinge: our Beinge Amongst vs, that thou may th[a]t make knowne to frends, least Gealozize; & troubles Arise Amongst them: as Concerneinge vs."[136] Later in the same letter, Aldam stated that inchoate Quakers lamented that "noe freedome to come amongst any frends verye litle," indicating that there existed a recognition of those who were part of the movement and that, early on, some felt isolation from others within the group.[137] Subsequent use of the term "friend" can be found throughout the letters. One example comes from Richard Hubberthorne to Friends at Swarthmoor Hall in 1654 when he requested that his letter be sent to "Swarthmore and friends abroad"[138] or in 1656 when Richard Hunter implored fellow Quakers to comment on the publication of a paper he had written:

> Therefore I say if thou and other freinds see it conveniant that I should cause the thing to be published to the world th[a]t see hereafter, there mouthes might be Stoped from vttering such false reports as is before mentioned, and after the publiclcation there of to take her to wife before friends; now if this be thought conveniant by thee and thereoff of friends I shall, if the lord permit Do so the same; for my one perticelour I am free other to publish it to the world, before it be don; or after: whether way soe euer it may be most to the keeping the truth cleare: but if this be contrary to thy freedome and the rest of freinds I desire thee let me know; th[a]t soe I may bee nothing th[a]t may cause our vnion to be broken.[139]

These examples demonstrate the use of "friend" to indicate people known personally by the author, as indicated by the Aldam letter, but the moniker was also employed to designate interested parties as described by Hubberthorne and Hunter. Such broad use of the term was similar to the ways that the early Christians used it. Geoffrey Nuttall states that the early use of this term was imbued with "rich overtones: the dawning of the gospel day, and of the new kingdom, is what it points to, at least as much as to light within the soul."[140]

As this chapter has attempted to show, scriptural references can be found throughout Interregnum letters, but a close reading of those written by Fell can provide a case study for in-depth inquiry. In Fell's letters, there are errors of citation of biblical passages—sometimes she had the chapter or verse correct, but sometimes the other is wrong, which Glines corrects in the text. I mention this not to quibble at Fell's ability to recollect scripture readily, but rather to note that her basic understanding of scripture was so well developed that she could get the meaning right and invert numbers or make slight errors when writing them down. This suggests that she was familiar with scripture and that she did not look passages up when noting them in letters, even when writing to those whom she admonished.

Early Quakers sought to compare themselves with the early Christians, and while they did not believe that scripture held the key to understanding Christ and his followers, they did use the information available about the Apostolic period to illuminate their own activities. Rather than seeing the scripture as the basis of their understanding of truth, it is better to see them as using a language that the audience could understand. The early Quakers spoke the language of the early church, but in order to communicate with their contemporaries, they had to use the Bible as shorthand for disseminating their beliefs effectively. In both her own letters and in those written by other Quakers that she preserved, Fell ensured that the movement remained accessible to the godly milieu of the English Interregnum.

The early modern Quakers were a religious movement much like the early Christians. The church was comprised of disparate communities of strangers scattered throughout the ancient world, communicating through letters and infrequent visits from leaders of the emerging establishment, persecuted often with imprisonment but also with more severe punishments. Quakers modeled themselves on the early Christian example. They saw local meetings and collections of Quakers to be like the early congregations of the new Christian faith. While they were divided by space, they were united in faith, and they kept abreast of news through letters written by leaders of the movement. When Quaker authors quoted and paraphrased scripture they did so to validate their theology and religious practices. Moreover, Fell and others likened both individual leaders, as well as the ministry as a whole, to early Christian leadership. Thus by borrowing from scripture in their letters, Quakers and specifically Fell, in her maintenance of their correspondence, made a compelling argument that they facilitated a return to the primitivism of Apostolic Christianity.

Notes

1. Much debt is owed in this particular chapter to Glines's *Undaunted Zeal: The Letters of Margaret Fell*, an edited volume of Fell's letters.
2. Underwood, *Primitivism, Radicalism, and the Lamb's War*, 3.
3. Ibid., 4.
4. Fox, *The Journal of George Fox*, ed. John L. Nickalls, 36.
5. Ibid.
6. Underwood, 6.
7. Ibid., 21.
8. Ibid., 24.
9. Geoffrey Nuttall, "'Nothing Else Would Do': Early Friends and the Bible," *Friends Quarterly* 22, no. 10 (April 1982): 652.

10. Underwood, 24.
11. Ibid., 28.
12. Gerald Hammond states that "probably every literate Elizabethan owned and read the Geneva Bible, making it the single most influential English book ever published. First printed in 1560, soon after Elizabeth's accession, it ran through multiple editions right into the 1640s." Hammond, "Translations of the Bible," in *A Companion to English Renaissance Literature and Culture*, ed. Michael Hattaway (London: Blackwell, 2002), 166.
13. The Friends House library in London has an internal document with the header "BIBLE as used by George Fox and Margaret Fell." While it provides immensely helpful information about the types of Bibles available to seventeenth-century Quakers, it does not give a definitive determination on which one was used most often. George Fox's personal Bible, known as the Treacle Bible, is housed at Swarthmoor Hall where it is on display to visitors, but not intended to be used for scholarly research.
14. Underwood, *Primitivism, Radicalism, and the Lamb's War*, 30.
15. The following books were referenced the following number of times: Gen., 11; Exod., 3; Lev., 1; Num., 1; Deut., 9; Josh., 1; 1 Sam., 2; 2 Sam., 2; 1 Kings, 1; 1 Chron., 2; Job, 3; Ps., 31; Prov., 14; Song of Sol., 3; Isa., 40; Jer., 16; Ezek., 8; Dan., 6; Hosea, 1; Joel, 2; Amos, 3; Jon., 1; Mic., 4; Zeph., 5; Mal., 7; Matt., 74; Mark, 9; Luke, 15; John, 54; Acts, 23; Rom., 26; 1 Cor., 27; 2 Cor., 18; Gal., 5; Eph., 14; Phil., 3; Colo., 8; 1 Thess., 1; 2 Thess., 6; 1 Tim., 7; 2 Tim., 9; Titus, 1; Heb., 26; James, 8; 1 Pet., 11; 2 Pet., 8; 1 John, 13; 2 John, 2; Jude, 2; Rev., 41.
16. Hugh Barbour, *The Quakers in Puritan England* (New Haven: Yale University Press, 1964), 157. Barbour identifies the following terms and their scriptural basis as the most common in Quaker correspondence and publications: "On the leading of the Spirit see Matt 4:1; Acts 2:4, 4:8, 8:29, 39; 10:19; 11:12; 11:28; 13:2; 4; 16:6; 20:23; 21:11; 23:8. From the Book of Revelation came 'The Great Beast,' 'the Lamb,' 'the Harlot,' 'The Mystery of Iniquity,' 'the eternal gospel,' and 'plagues' in a symbolic sense, the Quaker apocalyptic ideas in general. For other beloved passages see John 1:1–19; 3:19–21; 15–19; 26; I Cor. 2:5; 10–16; II Cor. 3:6; 10:3–4; 1 Tim. 1:19; 4:2; II Tim. 3:1–4; Titus 1:11; James 4:1–3; 5:12; I John 2:15–17; 3:9; 4:1; 6. Surprisingly few are from the Synoptic Gospels." 157 note 104.
17. Elizabeth Clarke, "Religious Verse," in *A Companion to English Renaissance Literature and Culture*, ed. Michael Hattaway (London: Blackwell, 2002), 404.
18. MSS Spence 3/90. Margaret Fell "To Oliver Cromwell, 1653," transcribed in Glines, 37.
19. Isa. 2:21.
20. Heb. 12:26–28.
21. MSS vol. 378/28. Margaret Fell "To Justice Anthony Pearson," transcribed in Glines, 22.
22. MSS York 14, from *Journal of Friends Historical Society Supplement* 22 (1948). MSS York 14. Margaret Fell "To William Dewsbury, August 14, 1655," transcribed in Glines, 140.
23. Acts 24:16. In MSS vol. 387/156. Margaret Fell "To Jeffrey Elletson, 1654," transcribed in Glines, 62. Another verse used was 1 Cor. 10:27: "If any of them

that believe not bid you to a feast, and ye be disposed to go; whatsoever is set before you, eat, asking no question for conscience sake."
24. MSS vol. 378/156. Margaret Fell "To Jeffrey Elletson, 1654," transcribed in Glines, 62.
25. 2 Cor. 1:12.
26. MSS vol. 378/145. Margaret Fell "To Justice John Sawrey, 1653," transcribed in Glines, 39.
27. John 14:17.
28. MSS vol. 378/163–64. Margaret Fell "To Daniel Davis, 1657?," transcribed in Glines, 227. Also in Psalms 1:1, it reads, "Blessed is the man that walketh not in the counsel of the ungodly, nor standeth in the way of sinners, nor sitteth in the seat of the scornful." Fell evoked this in 1655 writing to adversary Philip Bennett: "For David saith blessed is the man that walketh not in the Counsell of the ungodly, and he saith the ungodly is liketh the Chaffe which the winde driveth away." MSS vol. 378/142–43. Margaret Fell "To James Cave, a Minister, Probably 1656," transcribed in Glines, 157.
29. "I have chosen the way of truth: thy judgments have I laid before me." Psalms 119:30. MSS vol. 378/145. Margaret Fell "To Justice John Sawrey, 1653," transcribed in Glines, 39.
30. Heb. 1:8.
31. MSS York 14 from *Journal of Friends Historical Society Supplement* 22 (1948), 34–35. Margaret Fell "To William Dewsbury, August 14, 1655," transcribed in Glines, 140.
32. Rom. 10:6–8.
33. MSS vol. 378/101. Margaret Fell "To Henrietta Maria, Queen Mother, November 1660," transcribed in Glines, 320.
34. Ps. 119:30 in MSS vol. 378/145. Margaret Fell "To Justice John Sawrey, 1653," transcribed in Glines, 39; Ps. 7:9 in MSS vol. 378/101. Margaret Fell "To Henrietta Maria, Queen Mother, November 1660," transcribed in Glines, 319; Mal. 3:2 in MSS vol. 378/29–30. Margaret Fell "To Colonel William West, 1653," transcribed in Glines, 28; MSS vol. 378/51. Margaret Fell "To John Moore, 1657," transcribed in Glines, 240; Matt. 5:6 in MSS vol. 378/13–14. Margaret Fell "To the Saints, Brethren, and Sisters, 1659," transcribed in Glines, 267; Matt. 6:33 in Historical Society of PA, Etting Papers, 46. Margaret Fell "To Friends in Prison, with a postscript by Henry Fell, March 5, 1661," transcribed in Glines, 340; Mark 13:22. MSS vol. 378/125–26. Margaret Fell "To Gabriel Camelford, a Minister, 1654," transcribed in Glines, 66; Rom. 5:19 and 6:16 in MSS vol. 378/151–52. Margaret Fell "To George Braithwaite, 1656," transcribed in Glines, 204; Rom. 10:6–8 in MSS vol. 378/101. Margaret Fell "To Henrietta Maria, Queen Mother, November 1660," transcribed in Glines, 320; Rom. 14:17 in MSS vol. 378/28. Margaret Fell "To Justice Anthony Pearson, 1653," transcribed in Glines, 21.
35. Margaret Fell "An Epistle to Friends, 1653," transcribed in Glines, 53.
36. Jer. 31:33.
37. Jer. 31:31.
38. MSS vol. 378/109. Margaret Fell "To King Charles II, Probably May 1660," transcribed in Glines, 277.
39. Tapper MSS Box C:4:23. Margaret Fell "To Friends, Concerning Tithes, 1654," transcribed in Glines, 87.

120 *Apostolic epistolary influences*

40. Mal. 3:1: "Beholde, I will send my messenger, and hee shall prepare the way before mee: and the Lord whom ye seeke, shall speedily come to his Temple: euen the messenger of the couenat whom ye desire: beholde, hee shall come, saith the Lord of hostes."
41. Matthew 5:13–14 and 5:16.
42. "Soe they are the Salte of the Earth & the light of the world, and A Citty Set in a hill, which judgeth the World yea Angels." MSS vol. 378/13–14. Margaret Fell "To the Saints, Brethren and Sisters, 1659," transcribed in Glines, 267; MSS vol. 378/101. Margaret Fell "To Henrietta Maria, Queen Mother, November 1660," transcribed in Glines, 318.
43. John 1:4 and 1:9.
44. MSS vol. 378/156. Margaret Fell "To Jeffrey Elletson, 1654," transcribed in Glines, 61.
45. MSS vol. 378/131. Margaret Fell "To Judge Hugh Wyndham, 1654," transcribed in Glines, 108.
46. MSS vol. 378/33–34. Margaret Fell "To Francis Benson, 1655," transcribed in Glines, 131.
47. John 1:6–9 in Margaret Fell "An Epistle to Friends, 1653," transcribed in Glines, 52, and MSS vol. 378/101. Margaret Fell "To Henrietta Maria, Queen Mother, November 1653," transcribed in Glines, 319; John 3:19–20 in MSS vol. 378/93–94. Margaret Fell "To Oliver Cromwell, 1654," transcribed in Glines, 115, and MSS vol. 378/163–64. Margaret Fell "To Daniel Davis, 1657," transcribed in Glines, 230; John 8:12 in MSS vol. 378/125–26. Margaret Fell "To Gabriel Camelford, a Minister, 1654," transcribed in Glines, 65, Margaret Fell "To the World, Priests and People, 1654," transcribed in Glines, 100, MSS vol. 378/93–94. Margaret Fell "To Oliver Cromwell, 1654," transcribed in Glines, 114, MSS vol. 378/33–34. Margaret Fell "To Francis Benson, 1655," transcribed in Glines, 131, and MSS 378/142–43. Margaret Fell "To James Cave, a Minister, 1656," transcribed in Glines, 159; John 9:4 in Fell "To All Friends, Brethren and Sisters, 1655," transcribed in Glines, 124; John 9:5 in MSS vol. 378/8. Margaret Fell "To Gabriel Camelford, a Minister, 1654," transcribed in Glines, 65; John 12:46 in MSS vol. 378/125–26. Margaret Fell "To Gabriel Camelford, a Minister, 1654," transcribed in Glines, 65; 2 Cor. 4:6 in MSS vol. 378/163–64. Margaret Fell "To Daniel Davis, 1657," transcribed in Glines, 230; James 1:17 in MSS vol. 364/1. Margaret Fell "To Judge Thomas Fell, February 18 1653," transcribed in Glines, 18, MSS vol. 378/28. Margaret Fell "To Justice Anthony Pearson, 1653," transcribed in Glines, 21, Margaret Fell "To the World, Priests and People, 1654," transcribed in Glines, 106, and MSS vol. 378/109. Margaret Fell "To King Charles II, 1660," transcribed in Glines, 277; 2 Pet. 3:10 in MSS Tapper Box C:4:23. Margaret Fell "To Friends Concerning Tithes, 1654," transcribed in Glines, 86; 1 John 1:15 in MSS vol. 378/125–26. Margaret Fell "To Gabriel Camelford, a Minister, 1654," transcribed in Glines, 65, and MSS vol. 378/8. Margaret Fell "To All Friends, Brethren and Sisters, 1655," transcribed in Glines, 124; 1 John 1:7 in MSS vol. S81/1:60–66. Margaret Fell "To Friends, Brethren and Sisters, 1656," transcribed in Glines, 211, and MSS vol. 378/101. Margaret Fell "To Henrietta Maria November, 1660," transcribed in Glines, 319.
48. Isa. 42 in Margaret Fell "To the World, Priests and People, 1654," transcribed in Glines, 100.

49. And yet again in John 3:8: "The winde bloweth where it lysteth, and thou hearest the sounde thereof, but canst not tell whence it commeth, and whither it goeth: so is euery man that is borne of the Spirit," which is repeated to John Hall in 1657: "soe beware of that temptation for thou knows not, what the lord might manifest to thee, the wind bloweth where it listeth." MSS vol. 378/52. Margaret Fell "To John Hall, April 16, 1657," transcribed in Glines, 217. These examples continue. Fell wrote to minister Philip Bennett in 1655, imploring him to read Romans: "And the Apostle saith god sent forth his sonne in the linkeness of sinfull flesh, & for sin condemned Sin in the flesh, and that the righteousness of the Law might be fulfilled," which was taken from Rom. 8:3–4: "For (that that was impossible to the lawe, in as much as it was weake because of the flesh) God sending his owne Sonne, in the similitude of sinful flesh, and for sinne, condemned sinne in the flesh, That the righteousnes of the law might be fulfilled in vs, which walke not after the flesh, but after the Spirit," Glines, 155. And yet another example comes from Revelations: "He that hath an ear, let him hear what the Spirit saith unto the churches: To him that overcometh will I give to eat of the hidden manna, and will give him a white stone, and in the stone a new name written, which no man knoweth saving he that receiveth it." This passage is repeated to Quaker brethren and sisters in 1657 when Fell writes, "but theres none that knows this Name but hee that hath it, the whit stone Reed & understand." Rev. 2:17 in MSS vol. 378/11–12. Margaret Fell "To Brethren and Sisters, 1657," transcribed in Glines, 239. See also: John 4:24 in MSS vol. 378/90. Margaret Fell "To Oliver Cromwell, 1653," transcribed in Glines, 37; John 14:17 in MSS vol. 378/163–64. Margaret Fell "To Daniel Davis, 1657," transcribed in Glines, 227; Acts 2:17–18 in MSS vol. 378/101. Margaret Fell "To Henrietta Maria, 1660," transcribed in Glines, 319; 1 Cor. 6:20 in MSS vol. 378/31. Margaret Fell "To Col William West, 1653," transcribed in Glines, 33. 1 Cor. 12:13 in MSS vol. 378/155. Margaret Fell "To Jeffrey Elletson, 1654," transcribed in Glines, 59; 2 Cor. 7:1 in Margaret Fell "To the World, Priests and People, 1654," transcribed in Glines, 106, and MSS vol. 378/163–64. Margaret Fell "To Daniel Davis, 1657," transcribed in Glines, 229; Eph. 2:2 in MSS vol. 378/146–47. Margaret Fell "To Justice John Sawrey, 1653," transcribed in Glines, 46, MSS vol. 378/125–26. Margaret Fell "To Gabriel Camelford A minister, 1654," transcribed in Glines, 65, and MSS vol. 378/142–43. Margaret Fell "To James Cave, 1656," transcribed in Glines, 162; Eph. 4:3 in MSS vol. 378/11–12. Margaret Fell "To Brethren and Sisters, 1657," transcribed in Glines, 237; Heb. 9:14 in MSS vol. 378/157. Margaret Fell "To Jeffrey Elletson, 1657," transcribed in Glines, 243; 1 Pet. 2:5 in MSS Box C41/1. Margaret Fell "To Brethren and Sisters, 1658," transcribed in Glines, 259; 1 John 4:1 in Margaret Fell "To the World, Priests and People, 1654," transcribed in Glines, 101; 1 John 4:2 in Margaret Fell "To the World, Priests and People, 1654," transcribed in Glines, 101; 1 John 4:6 in MSS vol. 378/163–64. Margaret Fell "To Daniel Davis, 1657," transcribed in Glines, 227.
50. Matt. 23:32 in MSS vol. 378/28. Margaret Fell "To Justice Anthony Pearson, 1653," transcribed in Glines, 21.
51. John 1:4, 1:9 in MSS vol. 378/33–34. Margaret Fell "To Francis Benson, 1655," transcribed in Glines, 131.
52. John 3:16.

53. MSS vol. 378/142–43. Margaret Fell "To James Cave, A Minister, Probably 1656," transcribed in Glines, 162.
54. John 11:25 in MSS vol. 378/11–12. Margaret Fell "To Brethren and Sisters 1657," transcribed in Glines, 239; 1 Cor. 15:16–17 in MSS vol. 378/163–64. Margaret Fell "To Daniel Davis, 1657," transcribed in Glines, 229; Colo. 3:3 in MSS vol. 378/28. Margaret Fell "To Anthony Pearson, 1653," transcribed in Glines, 22; Rev. 2:10 in MSS vol. 364/1. Margaret Fell "To Judge Thomas Fell, Feb 18 1653," transcribed in Glines, 18.
55. Matt. 5:48.
56. Margaret Fell "To the World, Priests and People, 1654," transcribed in Glines, 105.
57. MSS vol. 378/140–41. Margaret Fell "To Philip Bennett, A Minister, 1655?," transcribed in Glines, 154.
58. MSS vol. 378/163–64. Margaret Fell "To Daniel Davis, 1657?," transcribed in Glines, 228.
59. Gen. 17:1 in Margaret Fell "To the World, Priests and People 1654," transcribed in Glines, 105; Ps. 19:7 in MSS vol. 378/145. Margaret Fell "To John Sawrey, 1653," transcribed in Glines, 39; Ps. 101:6 in MSS Box C41/1. Margaret Fell "To Brethren and Sisters, 1658," transcribed in Glines, 261; Prov. 2:21 in Margaret Fell "To the World, Priests and People, 1654," transcribed in Glines, 105; Prov. 11:5 in Margaret Fell "To the World, Priests and People, 1654," transcribed in Glines, 105; Acts 3:16 in MSS vol. 378/149–50. Margaret Fell "To William Knipe, 1656," transcribed in Glines, 207; 2 Cor. 7:1 in Margaret Fell "To the World, Priests and People, 1654," transcribed in Glines, 106, and MSS vol. 378/163–64. Margaret Fell "To Daniel Davis, 1657?," transcribed in Glines, 229; 2 Cor. 12:9 in MSS vol. 378/140–41. Margaret Fell "To Philip Bennett, 1655," transcribed in Glines, 154; Eph. 4:13 in Margaret Fell "To the World, Priests and People, 1654," transcribed in Glines, 105; 1 Thes. 3:10 in Margaret Fell "To the World, Priests and People, 1654," transcribed in Glines, 105; Heb. 9:9 in MSS vol. 378/157. Margaret Fell "To Jeffery Elletson, 1657," transcribed in Glines, 243; James 1:4 in Margaret Fell "To Daniel Davis, 1657?," transcribed in Glines, 228; 1 John 2:5 in Margaret Fell "To Daniel Davis, 1657?," transcribed in Glines, 228.
60. "These are they, which are not defiled with women: for they are virgins: these followe the Lame whither so euer hee goeth: these are bought from men, being the first fruites vnto God, and to the Lambe." (Rev. 14:4). "And this is our Joy and our peace to follow the Lambe where ever he goes, throrow reproaches, whippings stockings, Imprisonment." MSS vol. 378/31. Margaret Fell "To Col William West, 1653," transcribed in Glines, 33; "These shall fight with the Lambe, and the Lambe shall ouercome them: for he is Lorde of Lords, and King of Kings: and they that are on his side, called, and chosen and faithfull." (Rev. 17:14). "The war is begun Michall and his Angells, and the Drangon & his Angells: is feightinge But the lamb shall overcome." Glines, 32; "And there shall enter into it none uncleane thing, neither whatsoeuer worketh abomination or lies: but they which are written in the Lambes Booke of life." (Rev. 21:27). "The world knows us not where the mistery of the Fellowshipp is, where noe vullenous eyes nor venomous beasts can come, neither anything enter that defileth, nethr whatsoever worketh abomination or maketh a lye, but they which are written in the Lambs booke of life" MSS vol. 378/144.

Margaret Fell "To All Friends, Brethren and Sisters, 1655," transcribed in Glines, xx.
61. MSS vol. 378/163–64. Margaret Fell "To Daniel Davis, 1657?," transcribed in Glines, 226. Also Response to James Cave in 1656: "object: 6 then God is in every Creature. Yea, in the Divells, for they are Creatures & doe live. Answ: This Testimony thou may beare for they live in thee, and the Divell is thy God But when Saw thou them that thou saith, they are Creatures or what shape have they? Thou beares his Image & his marck in thy forehead, & thou shalt be sure to drinke of the wine of the wrath of god, which is powered out without mixture." MSS vol. 378/142–43. Margaret Fell "To James Cave, a Minister, Probably 1656," transcribed in Glines, 161.
62. Matt. 10:16.
63. MSS vol. 378/149–150. Margaret Fell "To William Knipe, 1656," transcribed in Glines, 208.
64. Jude 1:8–9 in MSS vol. 378/160. Margaret Fell "Concerning a Dispute at Manchester, 1656," transcribed in Glines, 201.
65. Rev. 12:1.
66. Rev. 12:3–5 in MSS vol. 378/137–39. Margaret Fell "To Thomas Shaw, a Minister, 1654," transcribed in Glines, 78.
67. For example, she wrote to her husband in 1653 utilizing yet another passage from Rev. 2:10: "Feare none of those things, which thou shalt suffer: behold, it shall come to passe, that the Devill shall cast some of you into prison, that ye may be tried, and ye shal haue tribulation ten dayes: be thou faithfull vnto the death, and I will giue thee the crowne of life," which appears in her own words as: "therefore be faithful: unto death and he will give thee Crowne of life, and stand firme and close to the lord and bee not afraid of man." MSS vol. 364/1. Margaret Fell "To Judge Thomas Fell, February 18, 1653," transcribed in Glines, 18.
68. Rev. 20:8 in MSS Box C:4:23. Margaret Fell "To Friends Concerning Tithes, 1654," transcribed in Glines, 86. Also see: 2 Cor. 12:7 in MSS 378/137–39. Margaret Fell "To Thomas Shaw, 1654," transcribed in Glines, 77; 2 John 1:7 in MSS vol. 378/125–26. Margaret Fell "To Gabriel Camelford, 1654," transcribed in Glines, 67; Rev. 12:7 in MSS vol. 378/31. Margaret Fell "To Col William West, 1653," transcribed in Glines, 32, and MSS vol. 378/137–39. Margaret Fell "To Thomas Shaw, 1654," transcribed in Glines, 79; Rev. 12:15–16 in MSS vol. 378/137–39. Margaret Fell "To Thomas Shaw, 1654," transcribed in Glines, 78; Rev. 13:1–2 in MSS vol. 378/137–39. Margaret Fell "To Thomas Shaw, 1654," transcribed in Glines, 78; Rev. 13:11 in MSS vol. 378/137–39. Margaret Fell "To Thomas Shaw, 1654," transcribed in Glines, 79; Rev. 16:12–13 in MSS vol. 378/137–39. Margaret Fell "To Thomas Shaw, 1654," transcribed in Glines, 77, 176; Rev. 19:20 in MSS vol. 378/31. Margaret Fell "To Col William West, 1652." transcribed in Glines, 33.
69. Elizabeth Clarke, *Politics, Religion, and the Song of Songs in Seventeenth-Century England* (London: Palgrave, 2011), 1.
70. Ps. 7:9.
71. In an earlier letter to John Stubbs in 1656, she wrote "and an highway shall be there, and a way, and it shall be called the way of holiness; the unclean shall not pass over it; but it shall be for those: the wayfaring men, the fools." Ps. 7:9 in MSS vol. 378/101. Margaret Fell "To Henrietta Maria, Queen Mother, November

124 *Apostolic epistolary influences*

1660," transcribed in Glines, 319, and MSS vol. 378/40. Margaret Fell "To John Stubbs, 1656," transcribed in Glines, 185; Isa. 35:8 in Margaret Fell "To John Stubbs, 1656," transcribed in Glines, 185, and MSS vol. 378/11–12. Margaret Fell "To Brethren and Sisters, 1657," transcribed in Glines, 237. Isa. 35:8 is also repeated multiple times, again to John Stubbs in 1656 amongst a list of questions to the "teachers and rabbis" and again to brethren and sisters in 1657: "and the one Soule, where ther is noe Devition, but the puer path of Life is knowne the way of holiness, whence the uncleane Cannot pass."

72. Jer. 17:9 in MSS vol. 378/4. Margaret Fell "To John Garnet, 1655," transcribed in Glines, 121.
73. Matt. 23:34.
74. MSS vol. 378/149–50. Margaret Fell "To William Knipe, 1656," transcribed in Glines, 206. See also John 10:12–13 in MSS vol. 378/137–39. Margaret Fell "To Thomas Shaw, 1654," transcribed in Glines, 82.
75. Matt. 5:18.
76. MSS Box C41/1. Margaret Fell "To Brethren and Sisters, 1658," transcribed in Glines, 260.
77. Rom. 8:3–4.
78. MSS vol. 378/140–41. Margaret Fell "To Philip Bennett," transcribed in Glines, 155.
79. 1 Cor. 11:2–3.
80. MSS vol. 378/158–59. Margaret Fell "To a Professor, 1655," transcribed in Glines, 167.
81. Eph. 3:1, Philem. 9–10, and Eph. 4:1.
82. MSS vol. S81/38. Thomas Salthouse to Margaret Fell: Exeter, 1655.
83. MSS vol. 352/345. Richard Hubberthorne and Others to Margaret Fell: Norwich, January 17, 1655.
84. MSS vol. 352/360. James Myers to Friends: Launceston, April 14, 1656.
85. MSS vol. 352/339. Richard Hubberthorne to Margaret Fell: Chester, December 4, 1653.
86. See Chapter 5 for further discussion of Fell's personal suffering in contrast to other Quakers' imprisonments.
87. Rom. 5:3–5.
88. MSS vol. S81/42. Thomas Salthouse and Myles Halhead to Margaret Fell: Bridewell, July 1655.
89. Rom. 8:16–18.
90. 2 Thess., 1:4–9.
91. Phil. 1:11.
92. Col. 1:24.
93. MSS vol. S81/44. Thomas Salthouse and Myles Halhead to Margaret Fell: Exeter, February 9, 1655.
94. Phil. 1:7.
95. Phil. 1:28–29.
96. MSS vol. 352/42. Henry Fell to Thomas Rawlinson: Bristol, August 19, 1656.
97. MS Box P2/15/20. Edward Burrough to George Fox: Location unknown, 1653.
98. MSS vol. S81/44. Thomas Salthouse and Myles Hallhead to Margaret Fell: Exeter, February 9, 1655/56.
99. MS Box P2/15/23, Ann Audland to George Fox: Location unknown, 1654.

Apostolic epistolary influences 125

100. Gal. 5:22–23.
101. MSS vol. 378/43–44. Margaret Fell "To Colonel William West, 1656," transcribed in Glines, 190. See also: Eph. 2:15 in MSS vol. 378/8. Margaret Fell "To All Friends, Brethren and Sisters, 1655?," transcribed in Glines, 124; Col. 2:20–22 in MSS vol. 378/8. Margaret Fell "To a Professor, 1655," transcribed in Glines, 167. And concerning witness/suffering/persecution/prison/bondage: Exod. 1:11 in MSS vol. 378/28. Margaret Fell "To Justice Anthony Pearson, 1653," transcribed in Glines, 21; Ps. 14:7 in MSS vol. 378/11–12. Margaret Fell "To Brethren and Sisters, 1657," transcribed in Glines, 238; Ps. 16:10 in "MSS at Swarthmore College Library" Margaret Fell "To John Ravell, 1654," transcribed in Glines, 71; Isa. 58:6 in MSS York 14 from *Journal of Friends Historical Society Supplement* 22 (1948). Margaret Fell "To William Dewsbury, August 14 1655," transcribed in Glines, 140; Jon. 2:2 in "MSS at Swarthmore College Library." Margaret Fell "To John Ravell, 1654," transcribed in Glines, 72; Matt. 23:13 in MSS vol. 378/148. Margaret Fell "To Judge John Archer, 1653," transcribed in Glines, 49; John 5:37–38 in "MSS at Swarthmore College Library." Margaret Fell "To John Ravel, 1654," transcribed in Glines, 71; Acts 5:19 in MSS vol. 378/149–50. Margaret Fell "To William Knipe, 1656," transcribed in Glines, 207; Acts 16:22–23 in MSS vol. 378/149–50. Margaret Fell "To William Knipe, 1656," transcribed in Glines, 207; Rom. 8:21 in MSS vol. 378/11–12. Margaret Fell "To Brethren and Sisters, 1657," and MSS vol. 378/149–50. Margaret Fell "To William Knipe, 1656," transcribed in Glines, 237; 1 Cor. 13:7 in MSS vol. 378/163–64. Margaret Fell "To Daniel Davis, 1657?," transcribed in Glines, 229; Eph. 4:1 in MSS vol. 378/27. "To James Nayler and Francis Howgill, 1653," transcribed in Glines, 23; 2 Tim. 2:12 in MSS vol. 378/109. Margaret Fell "To King Charles II, Probably May 1660," transcribed in Glines, 278; Heb. 2:10 in MSS vol. 378/19–20. Margaret Fell "To William and John Edmondson, November 25, 1661," transcribed in Glines, 350.
102. Isa. 61:1–2.
103. Margaret Fell "An Epistle to Friends, 1653," transcribed in Glines, 53; MSS vol. 378/8. Margaret Fell "To All Friends, Brethren and Sisters, 1655," transcribed in Glines, 126; MSS vol. 378/48. Margaret Fell "To Francis Howgill and Thomas Robertson, 1657," transcribed in Glines, 221.
104. John 5:37–38 in "MSS at Swarthmore College Library." Margaret Fell "To John Ravel, 1654," transcribed in Glines, 71.
105. Acts 5:19 in MSS vol. 378/149–50. Margaret Fell "To William Knipe, 1656," transcribed in Glines, 207.
106. Acts 9:5 in MSS vol. 378/148. Margaret Fell "To Judge John Archer, 1653," transcribed in Glines, 50, "MSS at Swarthmore College Library." Margaret Fell "To John Ravel, 1654," transcribed in Glines, 71, and MSS vol. 3.151–52. Margaret Fell "To George Braithwaite, 1656," transcribed in Glines, 205. See also: Heb. 13:3 in MSS vol. 378/8. Margaret Fell "To All Friends, Brethren and Sisters, 1655?," transcribed in Glines, 125.
107. Isa. 20:3.
108. MSS vol. 378/125–26. Margaret Fell "To Gabriel Camelford, a Minister, 1654," transcribed in Glines, 68.
109. Matt. 3:11 in MSS vol. 378/155. Margaret Fell "To Jeffrey Elletson, 1654," transcribed in Glines, 59, and MSS vol. 378/33–34. Margaret Fell "To Francis Benson, 1655," transcribed in Glines, 131.

126 *Apostolic epistolary influences*

110. 1 Cor. 12:13 in MSS vol. 378/155. Margaret Fell "To Jeffrey Elletson, 1654," transcribed in Glines, 59.
111. 1 Pet. 3.
112. MSS vol. 378/156. Margaret Fell "To Jeffrey Elletson, 1654," transcribed in Glines, 63.
113. Matt. 5:34 and James 5:12. The only reference to the passage from Matthew is after the Interregnum, which may indicate that Fell didn't relate to this passage as much until she was jailed after 1660. This reference may be found in MSS Box P2. Margaret Fell "Exceprts from the Trials at Lancaster and Letter to the Magistrates and People of England, June 7, 1664," transcribed in Glines, 370.
114. MSS vol. 378/140–41. Margaret Fell "To Philip Bennett, A Minister," transcribed in Glines, 153.
115. Fox, *The Journal of George Fox*, ed. John L. Nickalls, 89.
116. Watts, *The Dissenters*, 192.
117. Acts 13:50.
118. MSS vol. 378/149–50. Margaret Fell "To William Knipe, 1656," transcribed in Glines, 206.
119. MSS vol. 378/149–50. Margaret Fell "To William Knipe, 1656," transcribed in Glines, 207. See also Acts 23:3 in MSS vol. 378/148. Margaret Fell "Judge John Archer, 1653," and MSS vol. 378/149–50. Margaret Fell "To William Knipe, 1656," transcribed in Glines, 50.
120. Acts 16:22–23.
121. Fox, *The Journal of George Fox*, 89.
122. Acts 9:22.
123. MSS vol. 378/149–50. Margaret Fell "To William Knipe, 1656," transcribed in Glines, 207.
124. Rom. 1:4–5.
125. MSS vol. 378/151–52. Margaret Fell "To George Braithwaite, 1656," transcribed in Glines, 204. See also: 1 Cor. 16:1 in MSS vol. 378/8. Margaret Fell "To All Friends, Brethren and Sisters, 1655?," transcribed in Glines, 126; 2 Cor. 11:13 in MSS vol. 378/145. Margaret Fell "To Justice John Sawrey, 1653," transcribed in Glines, 40; 2 Thess. 1:10 in MSS vol. 378/29–30. Margaret Fell "To Colonel William West, 1653," transcribed in Glines, 27. Concerning Son of God/Son of Man: Ezek. 5:1 in MSS vol. 378/125–26. Margaret Fell "To Gabriel Camelford, a Minister, 1654," transcribed in Glines, 68; Matt. 10:23 in MSS vol. 378/149–50. Margaret Fell "To William Knipe," transcribed in Glines, 208; Matt. 11:17–19 in MSS vol. 378/149–50. Margaret Fell "To William Knipe," transcribed in Glines, 206; Luke 6:22–23 in MSS Box C:4:23. Margaret Fell "To Friends, Concerning Tithes, 1654," MSS vol. 378/149–50. Margaret Fell "To William Knipe," transcribed in Glines, 88, and MSS vol. 378/101. Margaret Fell "To Henrietta Maria, 1660," transcribed in Glines, 319; John 3:18–20 in MSS vol. 378/33–34. Margaret Fell "To Francis Benson, 1655," transcribed in Glines, 131; John 5:18 in "MSS at Swarthmore College Library." Margaret Fell "To John Ravell, 1654," transcribed in Glines, 70; Rom. 1:4–5 in MSS vol. 378/151–52. Margaret Fell "To George Braithwaite, 1656," transcribed in Glines, 204; Rom. 8:19 in MSS vol. 378/48. Margaret Fell "To Francis Howgill and Thomas Robertson, June 21, 1657," transcribed in Glines, 221.
126. 1 Cor. 1:12.

127. MSS vol. 378/29–30. Margaret Fell "To Colonel William West," transcribed in Glines, 26.
128. MSS vol. 354/131. Richard Roper to Fell: Woburn, October 20, 1656.
129. Rom. 1:1.
130. Rom. 16:2–16.
131. 1 Thess., 5:5.
132. MSS vol. 352/174. Footnote in Braithwaite also references this citation.
133. John 15:14 in MSS Box C41/1. Margaret Fell "To Brethren and Sisters, 1658," transcribed in Glines, 261.
134. John 15:15.
135. MSS vol. 378/37. Margaret Fell "To Samuel Fisher, March 17, 1656," transcribed in Glines, 173.
136. MSS vol. 354/40. Thomas Aldam to Friends: York, November 1652. Also see Braithwaite, 73, for additional information on the first use of "Friends." This letter discusses a schism or at least a separation emerging in the jail among Friends—see Nuttall's calendar.
137. Ibid.
138. MSS vol. 355/6. Richard Hubberthorne to Friends at Swarthmoor Hall: Norwich, December 28, 1654.
139. MSS vol. 352/357. Richard Hunter to Margaret Fell: Bickerstaffe, 1656.
140. Geoffrey Nuttall, *To the Refreshing of the Children of Light*. Pendle Hill pamphlet no. 101 (1951), 5–11.

5 Suffering, prison, and the law in the Quaker tradition

Quakers were among many groups persecuted in the Interregnum, but they were uncommon in their understanding and utilization of suffering to promote an identity as martyrs. Early Quaker letters are riddled with examples of punishments at the hands of the state, religious authorities, and neighbors. Various actions incurred the wrath of the authorities. Some of the most frequently prosecuted behaviors included refusal to pay tithes, negation of hat honors and other avoidances of social differentiation such as the use of "thee" and "thou," disturbing the peace, interruption of church services, blasphemy, and vagrancy. These actions were met with a variety of punishments, including fines, confiscation of goods, and rare occasions of corporal punishments such as branding, boxing of ears, boring tongues, and even death. The most common punishment, singularly or in conjunction with another, was imprisonment.[1]

This chapter examines Quaker approaches to law during the Interregnum and the arguments they used to justify their behavior. Further, it looks into the ways that prison, as the most common punishment early Quakers experienced, helped cultivate an inner circle of itinerant preachers who formed the leadership and base of the new religious group. From Swarthmoor Hall, Margaret Fell managed communication amongst these itinerants and served as a model of suffering and martyrdom for the network. This chapter will also address the importance of suffering to the inchoate Quakers and how its various meanings helped shape their early identity as martyrs, which will be discussed in greater detail in Chapter 6.

Quakers and the law

The earliest Quakers were outlaws.[2] The methods they used to evangelize violated a variety of mid-seventeenth century legislation. They perceived themselves as quite literally above the law, existing on a plane that was superior to the system they scorned. Furthermore, they did this while claiming to be good citizens of the English commonwealth because they broke only those laws that were immoral and defied God's higher law. Regardless of how they perceived their own actions, they often found themselves in conflict with local and national authorities who punished them for their illegal behavior. Beverly Adams argues that Quakers were "active sufferers" and used their troubled relationship with "spiritual and civil" authorities to create two distinct identities, which "drove a wedge into the brittle synthesis of religious and political duty."[3] The religious and political instability of the time gave the Quakers freedom to negotiate not only their theology, but also their relationship to the state and attitudes toward non-Quakers. Their struggles with the legal system echoed the difficulty they faced when trying to create a unified religious community in the Restoration and in subsequent decades.

Quakers saw that their travels and confrontations with local religious and secular authorities demanded that they negotiate a relationship with the law. This was because two common characteristics of early Quaker identity were that they were the bearers of "truth" and that they suffered. Those who suffered believed what they endured was the fulfillment of their covenant with God. Itinerants often wrote to Margaret Fell to express this belief, such as when in 1659, prisoner Henry Fell wrote about his desire for Fell to "Let thy prayers bee for mee that I may bee kept in his Couenant vnto the end., soe shall I neuer be ashamed."[4]

Some members of the early community believed that their commitment to God was often tested by a cruel, unjust legal system that sought to undermine their spiritual righteousness. However, there was no clear foe in the Quaker struggle against unjust laws because the Interregnum was a politically and legally tumultuous period. The source of authority was unclear on both the national and local levels, making it uncertain what laws or powers religious radicals like the Quakers stood against. The Interregnum was further complicated by the absence of church courts. Civil authority replaced church authority and in so doing brought religious radicals into secular courts for religious crimes. What constituted a religious infraction was often unclear because there was no central, orthodox church against which Quakers and other radicals rebelled. Instead the Quakers' presence in English society emphasized the instability of the period.

There was no shortage of reasons Quakers were constantly in trouble with the law. Like Baptists, Quakers saw the forced payment of tithes and licensing of preachers as persecution at the hands of an unchristian state.[5] For example, they were often accused of violating laws that predated the Interregnum, such as the Marian statute against interrupting sermons, which also provided punishments to those who did not attend Sunday mass.[6] Tom Webster has recently identified the irony that despite the fact that this law was outdated given that England had not been Catholic since 1558, Puritan authorities evoked it throughout the subsequent century.[7] Given the longevity of the Marian policies, and the persistent use of such claims against dissenters, Quakers should have been fully aware that they repeatedly broke the law, even as new legislation was introduced. While both local Interregnum officials and Parliament attempted to police the radical consequences of religious pluralism in a society not ready for full toleration, the political and legal confusion of the era resulted in inconsistent application and enforcement of new policies like the Blasphemy Act of 1650 and the Humble Petition and Advice. Furthermore, while there was often discussion in early letters as to how to avoid being caught breaking laws seen as ungodly and contradictory to the Quaker perception of God's plan, they never encouraged the faithful to obey laws. Hence, leading itinerant ministers actively participated in the shaping of the group's image as subversive and cultivated their identity as outlaws.

Quakers viewed divine law as superior to the manmade English law. Even more so, there were times in which the English legal system was perceived as anathema to God's law, such as when Thomas Salthouse stated, "our parsecuters haue noe Law but their wills to stay us by, but in the will of God doe wee patiently waite."[8] This was because Quakers saw that fulfillment of their covenant with God required committing crimes against the everchanging English state. Therefore, when accused of illegal behavior, they argued that it was their duty to break one law in order to live according to another. When Ann Audland described the grounds for her imprisonment in 1655, she demonstrated the inherent conflict between these legal systems. When accused of blasphemy, she wrote, "I answered that they were out of the doctrine of Christ, all they spoke was untruth ... so they made a mittimus for me, and said I was accused of blasphemy and I must either put in bond or goe to prison, and I said I had broke no law, neither had I done wrong to any and would put in no bond so they sent me away to prison."[9] She denied the accusation of wrongdoing on several grounds: first, she stated that they incorrectly evoked Christ's doctrine; second, she said that she did not commit the crime she was accused of committing; and third, by refusing their authority to issue sentence, she would not bargain for her freedom. Others who made this claim often supported it with the assertion that their foes were "full of deceit" and jealous of Quakers (jealous of what they never clearly articulated, but presumably of their covenant with God). English authorities did not recognize the validity of Quaker legal arguments; therefore, this convoluted discourse demonstrates the inherent problem of the inability of each side to understand the other on a fundamental level.

One must assume, however, that Quakers were not correct in their assessment of the conflict, that they were not accused of crimes because everyone else was jealous of their relationship with God or because the authorities refused to accept God's law. As Adrian Davies notes, both Puritan and religiously moderate neighbors were quite likely to see Quakers as subversive, thus explaining widespread negative reactions to them.[10] It is quite reasonable to assume that when Quakers were disruptive, but not breaking the law, claims of illegality may have been invented to get rid of them but not for the reasons that Quakers claimed. They were often accused of vagrancy although they did not beg or attempt to benefit from the charity of communities they visited. Local authorities may have feared further disruption to their communities from the presence of Quaker instigations. Richard

Hubberthorne speculated about his persecution in 1654 when he said: "This is the ground of my Imprisonment; not because I am guilty of the breach of any Law, but least we should Increase."[11] Furthermore in 1655, itinerants Thomas Salthouse and Myles Halhead wrote to Margaret Fell from Bridewell that "some of the magistrates say if wee goe on and have liberty wee will overthrowe both law and ordinances and seduce the whole country and for preventing this spread of it they have given order to the soldiers that keep [us]."[12] These examples suggest that their "stranger status" caused Quakers to be suspect in the eyes of those they met through itinerancy. Thus, being a nuisance or foreigner aroused suspicion, which may have led to unfair accusations against itinerant Quakers that they then interpreted as persecution due to others' jealousy of the Quakers' relationship with God.

Quaker conflicts with legal and political authorities were shaped by the inconsistency of rule due to reforms in government. Keith Thomas highlights the significance of religious laws moving from ecclesiastical to secular courts in the mid-seventeenth century.[13] But as Blair Worden notes, debates concerning the nature of the rule of law were not new to the Interregnum period. What changed, however, were MPs attitudes toward law reform given that their "case in the civil war rested largely on a claim to defend the common law."[14] Debates in Parliament ensued from 1649–1650, but little was accomplished because "MPs were unlikely to display enthusiasm for aggressive criticism of that law" because the Rump was embarrassed by its constitutional illegitimacy.[15]

For Worden, the resulting effect was that MPs were able to distance their personal religious beliefs from the political state. As theology became "a hobby of increasing fascination," some began to "prefer private to public worship, attending services at a wide variety of churches" but spending "Sundays at home in devotions" with their families.[16] Therefore, throughout the 1650s, "tolerance and radicalism increasingly went separate ways."[17] In contrast, John Morrill focuses on the corrupt nature of Cromwell's rule and his willingness to abuse his power (as well as abuses by the Parliament that supported him) in order to attain God's will in the future. Ultimately, this would cause "Englishmen to lose faith in paper constitutions and in shuffling sovereign power between the executive and legislative branches of government."[18]

Regardless of the legitimacy of accusations against them, early Quakers used a variety of methods to justify their illegal behavior. R.M. Rogers defines the "Quaker law code" as adherence to the "Law of God" that "within the individual and constituting the immediate and final source of justice and measure of conduct in worldly matters."[19] They believed that God's law "could not be 'made' (because God implanted it in the consciences of all people) and that it never varied throughout history." Its constancy meant that neither the changeable English law nor the standard by which Quakers lived was superior. "The Law of God was 'activated' or received in the conscience after the individual had been 'convinced of the truth' and touched by the 'inner light of Christ," according to Rogers. This tells us that convincement of Quaker truth was required to fully understand the law of God. Since non-Quakers did not understand or accept the law, they could not apply it properly either, which gave Quakers the right to choose to ignore those that were not divinely inspired. Rogers states that "this amounted to a legal anarchy ... just as the spiritual anarchy of the 'inner light' by-passed the clergy and established religion."[20] This understanding of the law was the Quakers' most commonly evoked legal argument. When accused of breaking English law, Quakers would respond by stating that their behavior was justified because they were doing God's work and therefore fulfilling all legal and moral obligations.

Interestingly, it was often their interpretation of God's law rather than English law that kept them in prison. York Castle prisoner Christopher Moore wrote to George Fox in 1658:

> I was moved of the Lord to goe to speake to them caled Justices and had time to speake a pretie whyle & they weare silent & when they had noething wherewith to acuse me for what I spoke they said I might p[ro]vide bond for good behaviour and said I was a disturber of thee pease, and caried my selve contemptuously in ther courtt because I stood with my hatt on and because I stood in the well of god and could not give bond they sent me to Iaole where I am now at present praises be to god.[21]

In this passage, Moore demonstrated that his imprisonment was his choice as he was given the opportunity to post bond and give assurance to the local authorities that he would avoid future legal trouble. Moore refused because he did not feel responsible to secular magistrates and could not know what God may direct him to do in the future. It is curious that while some complained about suffering, Quakers often refused the leniency offered by secular officials, thus problematizing their meaning of suffering. Furthermore, submission to God's directives was not limited to where an itinerant could go, but also included behaviors, such as going naked as a sign. Ann Nicholson was commanded by the Lord to go naked, which resulted in her imprisonment in York in 1653.[22] Subsequently, both male and female ministers were arrested for going naked as a sign throughout the Interregnum. Elizabeth Fletcher was whipped in Oxford in June 1654 for nakedness; prior to James Parnell's lengthy imprisonment in Cambridge, he was arrested for going naked in Littleport in September 1654, and Thomas Holme was jailed in August 1655 for nakedness in Chester, followed shortly after by Richard Sale in October for the same offense.

In addition to divine law, Quakers demonstrated an understanding of the English legal system. When accused of blasphemy, Quakers responded by stating that they were accused of committing invalid crimes, such as the aforementioned outdated Marian laws. This was a rather sophisticated claim; it demonstrated that they were aware of the evolution of laws even in the legislative confusion of the Interregnum. John Miller notes that "while offensive," Quakers' speaking in church was "not necessarily illegal," given that "after 1650 there was no law requiring attendance at church or forbidding meetings outside the church."[23] Itinerant minister Ann Blacklaine was charged in Cambridgeshire in 1654 under the Marian statute for interrupting a sermon:

> Then An Blaicklaine was called, And charged with disturbeing the minister, And by Queen Maryes Act they proued their Law, then An spoke freely to them, and denyed him to be any Minister of god, And said they might all be ashamed to vphold there Law by A popish Law, then the Recorder said she hath suffered her time let her haue her Lyberty, but they putt her againe into prison, contrary to their owne order.[24]

As this letter demonstrates, Blacklaine compared the Cambridgeshire magistrates to Queen Mary and her Catholic administration, a comparison certainly not lost by seventeenth-century authorities. While this line of argument did not prevent Quakers from being charged, it may have intimidated their accusers who feared being likened to Catholics more than they feared the threat of Quakerism. More importantly it strengthened the resolve of Quakers communicating with one another that they were standing firm in opposition to false religions and to the state that oppressed them.

Writing to Colonel William West in 1653, Fell articulated this hypocrisy:

> O how dare you professe reformation when cruelty and tyranny rules in the land, O looke backe & see if ever there was the like in all the kings or Bishops time since Queen Mary dayes that slew the marters, that soe many Goalls was furnished with prisoners meeerly for conscience sake, or was ther ever any that suffered for conscience, that was put among theeves and murderers, or scares ever was there any except it was papish preiste or Jesuits that ever was kept in prison but they ever spoke treason againe Kinge or State.[25]

And Fell again reminded Oliver Cromwell of his hypocrisy when she wrote:

> And if thou hold up A Law to guard and protect Antichrist against the power of christ, which speakes in his servants, as many here can wittnesse, who suffers by that Law, which was made in Maryes dayes, though they spake against popery, but that is all they have to guard their ministry withal, and to protect them in their pullpitts, which was an Act made by her dayes which makes them manifest they are Antichrist, and not of Christ, And severall prisoners have suffered in these northern parts, and doth suffer Imprisonment, both at Carlile

Kendal Lancaster and Yorke, which is at this time imprisoned by that Act, others because they cannot pay tythes, contrary to that in their conscience, which if they doe, they must deny christ come in the flesh, And whosoever doth that is an Antichrist.[26]

Fell clearly understood the complexity of the Quaker situation, and perhaps given her proximity to legal authorities in both her household and through social relationships, she was aware of legal arguments. It is interesting that she, rather than male members of the movement, seemed better versed on the particulars of the Marian Act.

However, early Quakers were conflicted over the role of sufferings in their lives. While some did not embrace their suffering enthusiastically, many more claimed that it was their obligation to suffer in order to demonstrate their covenant with God. They often wrote to one another stating that they "want nothing for the outward," or that they only needed communion with the community and their brethren's prayers rather than physical comforts.[27] By refusing provisions, or outward comforts, imprisoned Quakers suffered greater hardships, rather than lessening their pains. However, if this were consistently true, then they would not have required the assistance of legal experts, upon whom they called from time to time. Most early Quakers lacked legal expertise; however, there were a few influential allies amongst them. Margaret Fell's husband, Judge Thomas Fell, was sympathetic to his wife's religion but was not convinced of the Quaker message. He often provided legal advice to George Fox and other itinerants.

Justices Anthony Pearson and Gervase Benson were faithful Quakers and constant sources of legal advice for those in particularly difficult situations. James Nayler, writing to Margaret Fell in 1655, sang Benson's praises as a useful legal resource to Quakers who found themselves in trouble. "G: Benson is a faithfull man, and of much service amongst the judges and lawyers: he stands above the deceipt and prospers great is our god blessed for euermore."[28] Again in 1657, Benson inquired on Thomas Taylor's behalf to see the grounds of his presentment at the Appleby Assizes.[29] For religious radicals living outside mainstream Interregnum England, well-connected Friends were often welcomed.[30] To that point, in 1656 Robert Widder wrote to Fell asking that her husband (Judge Fell), Col. William West, or Anthony Pearson intercede on his and his fellow prisoners' behalf: "It would be better that thy husband William west or Anthony Pearson or some of them might take the warrant & goe to the jealor & take course in it, better then wee our selves, soe as thou seest in thee light which way may be likest I would haue thee write to mee, & speake to thy husband or william west if hee be with thee."[31]

These examples of early Quaker responses to legal problems reflect the absence of a coherent point of view. Some early Quakers opted for any argument that suited their needs at a particular point in time. When a given law was questionable because of its papist overtones, they attacked the validity of the law. Quakers claimed to be above English law; however, when legal savvy was needed, they called on Friends with knowledge of the law to provide them with loopholes and to rely on political connections. This was not a cogent legal argument, but it was consistent with the nascent nature of Quakerism in the 1650s.

Imprisoned Quakers

Richard Baxter stated in 1659 that "many turned Quakers, because the Quakers kept their meetings openly, and went to prison for it cheerfully."[32] Imprisonment was an important form of punishment because it allowed both the authorities and early Quakers to single out individuals for their behavior. For authorities, it was an effective, efficient way to isolate troublemakers from the rest of society. For Quakers, prison provided the religious organization with heroes who were willing to sacrifice themselves for the greater good of the propagation of the word of God.

Interregnum prisons were full of people who broke the ever-changing laws of the constantly fluctuating governments of the 1650s, the height of Quaker confinement being during the Interregnum, only to be rivaled by persecutions of nonconformists during the 1680s.[33] Catie Gill notes that approximately 2,000 people suffered imprisonment or "public punishment (such as whipping or stocking)" in the 1650s.[34] Early Quakers were a widely identifiable, national problem and could be found in prisons throughout England; they thus had the power to evoke hatred or sympathy on a national level. It is important to consider both how those in power wishing to quash a Quaker presence throughout the country and Quakers hoping to engender a positive response to their efforts would have understood Quaker imprisonment.

One way to better understand this is through examination of prison letters, which provide a unique insight into how Quakers perceived their own suffering. In many letters, Quakers castigated authorities for inflicting undue punishments. Will Caton wrote to Fell in 1655 concerning the corruption of local authorities and the harsh treatment he endured in the local prison: "Theire persecution daily in creaseth they will not suffer any friend nor any other to come into the prison to me."[35] Caton went on to say that "these have more liberty" than he, suggesting that Quakers in Norwich received undue punishments at the hands of unjust jailers. Likewise, in 1657, Ann Dewsbury wrote to Margaret Fell of the deplorable prison conditions that she endured because of the unkindness of her captors: "I was had againe to prison and the mittymus giuen to men to haue me away the next day I was not to take any foode, much of the tyme I lay on the prison flowar w[i]thout straw or any thinge."[36] Some prisons became notorious in the Quaker community, such as the "hole of rock" mentioned by former Chester prison inmate, Richard Sale.[37] In contrast to the horrors of being jailed, letters like these also demonstrate a keen understanding of the beneficial side effects of imprisonment. These positive effects included having central figures stand out as martyrs for local Quakers and potential believers to rally behind. The longer Quaker leaders endured their punishment, the greater respect and support they could hope to achieve.

Following seventeenth-century standards of imprisonment and punishment, Quakers were often afforded means of communication with the outside world. Generally they were allowed visitors and writing implements and were not required to stay inside the prison at all times. Thus, rare cases like James Nayler's jailing after the episode in Bristol in which he was refused both writing implements and visitors was perceived as especially harsh given the severity of the case. Of course there were few instances that elicited Parliament's involvement to the extent that the Nayler Affair did; this event forced a Parliamentary discussion on the extent of religious toleration to be afforded in the Commonwealth. Blair Worden states that the division between conservatives and Cromwellians came to a head during the Second Protectorate Parliament, and John Morrill argues that this episode signaled to Cromwell's critics that his rule was more arbitrary than Charles I's.[38] John Marshall notes that Nayler's blasphemy was likened to leprosy and deemed "infectious and contagious."[39] However, most tales of imprisonment were not as extreme as Nayler's. In 1656, Myles Halhead and Thomas Salthouse wrote to Margaret Fell of a generous jailer who was "glad of it with all his hart" to house and keep them and was generally very kind to them.[40] Also in 1656, Thomas Robertson wrote to George Fox from Horsham about Thomas Seacoke's relatively pleasant imprisonment: "The goaler is prty loueing & his wife more. & we are well glory to the lord god, who hath made his mighty power knowne among his seruants."[41]

But not all Quakers were so generous toward their captors. On a few occasions, itinerants described the meanness of their guards, such as when Will Caton wrote to Fell that the room that he and other Friends were kept in was cold without blankets, "And the men were so cruell and hard-harted toward us that they would not giue us soe much as A bitt of A saile cloath to lye under or aboue us, but for the most part of the time were laid vpon the boarde which ascended vp the Chimney."[42] A much worse circumstance arose when, in 1653, a group of female itinerants experienced harsh treatment at the hands of a jailer's wife:

> And presently after the goalers Wife came in & shut us Down the Stayrs, and gott a Rocke in her hand, & beat us with it till she was weary; & then she got a staffe, & beat us with, and ran violently against the body of her that was naked, as she would haue run it into her body; but the Lord did preserue her that it did not enter; but it hath pierced upon her body, & hath made many sore plates, which is weared Standing red as Blood to be seene, The prints of the staffe, which she beat us with stands wearing with blood; but Eternall

praise & Glory, be to his Name for ever, who hath preserved us, & glorifyed his own Name in us & ours, & our glorying & rejoycing is in his Crosse that he hath counted us worthy to suffer.[43]

However, even in these conditions, Quakers were quick to articulate their spiritual freedom as bearers of the truth despite physical constraints. Likewise, when Richard Hubberthorne wrote to Margaret Fell in 1655, "I am set free from outward bondes," he both meant that he had been freed from jail, but also distinguished his body or "outward" condition from his soul or "inward" state.[44]

Hubberthorne's peace of mind remained intact while imprisoned because he was doing God's work by losing his personal freedom. Therefore, loss of outward freedom was a means of demonstrating one's inward liberty that came with acceptance of the truth. While the early Quakers were certainly aware of the practical benefits of suffering, it is also true that they possessed a genuinely pious compulsion to suffer for the faith. True freedom was spiritual, not physical, an idea that is demonstrated in their correspondence time and again. In 1655, Thomas Salthouse and Myles Halhead wrote to Fell stating, "we want nothing for the outward," and again later in October of the same year they said "wee are well and for the outward have noo want."[45] The strongest expression of Quaker resolve also came from Salthouse and Halhead in 1656 when they stated, "Soe in the will of God we stand chusseing rather to suffer imprisonment or banishment out of the Land then to purchasse outward freedome by making a Covenant with death and soe bring our selves into inward bondage."[46] Here the idea of life as suffering versus death in freedom is clearly stated.

Despite the prevalence of Quakers in prison, their first decade was wrought with inconsistent notions of what this particular form of suffering meant. Furthermore, it is not clear that all incarcerated Friends understood their experiences in the same way. As described in Chapter 4, letters were often signed "Prisoner of the Lord," echoing Apostolic Christianity, which had larger implications than simply suffering for God. Thomas Holme signed a letter to Thomas Willan in 1654 as "a prisner of the lord in Cheshure."[47] Such a description could suggest that one was jailed while serving God, but it could also mean that ascribing to the faith made one God's prisoner. The latter was rife with theological implications, particularly that God's presence is a prison unto itself. However, similar phrases provide better clues into the authors' intentions. In 1654, John Lawson wrote to Margaret Fell that he was a "prisoner for the testimony of the truth at Chester."[48] This example suggests that imprisonment was part of the itinerant minister's job; he was jailed for preaching his faith. Thus, the variety of descriptions of prison demonstrate that experiencing outward imprisonment was less important when one acknowledged that the individual self was no longer free to act of its own will.[49]

Sacrificing personal freedom for the "truth's sake" was meant to garner compassion for Quakers. However, sympathy for suffering could not create a sustained religion on its own. While Quakers appreciated the utility of imprisonment to the furtherance of the movement, they were also aware of the necessity of freedom to travel around the country spreading the word. In 1655, Francis Howgill wrote to Margaret Fell that freedom was hard to come by and that the Quakers needed to make the most of it whenever possible: "I should meet him this weeke at Elys Ile but G.F. is hardy free I should goe least our Lyberty should be hindred, for its of great value now in the seruice."[50] He went on to describe how many leaders of the community were "in cheins" while he and a few others were free to preach throughout the countryside. Prisoners included George Fox in Ely and Myles Halhead and Thomas Salthouse who were confined in Exeter. However, others including John Stubbs, Will Caton, and Edward Burrough were free, at least for the moment. When writing this letter, Howgill was not sure where the Spirit would move him to go, but he clearly stated that he and others must take advantage of freedom while it was available. He was pessimistic about the possibility of freedom lasting long, as it was likely that they would all be imprisoned again soon.[51]

There was a common belief among Interregnum Quakers that those who suffered the most and under the worst conditions best exemplified commitment to God and their cause. The most pragmatic argument for demonstrably suffering was that it helped convince others of the truth. John Wilkinson and John Story wrote in 1655 that "though the hethen rage: our Kinge reaignes & the seed growes notwithstandinge all the suferinges more still is conuinced by it."[52] Both the community and the individual sacrificed themselves for the benefit of saving souls. The argument was that even "heathens" could appreciate their suffering, which was meant to be a demonstration of godliness. According to the early members of the faith, when non-believers saw Quakers persecuted in the streets or jailed for dubious reasons, and did so without complaint, they would see God in the suffering Quakers' actions and then be convinced themselves. Caton wrote to Fell in 1656 that magistrates kept him and his fellow itinerants for about a week, "in which time seuerall priests and many people came to us," which gave them opportunities "to clear our Consciences to them."[53] Caton wrote again to Fell in 1657 that Quakers in Steyning were greatly persecuted by "rude people" who later were convinced of the validity of the Quakers' beliefs:

> Vpon that day called Shroudtuseday I had A meetting closse by A markett Towne where there had neuer bene any of Friendes before, And they bett a drom in the Towne togathe the Barbarous rude people together, and when they were come together they Come marching vp to the house Like men ready for battle in A most desperate rude manner as though they would haue pulled the house downe ouer our heades, And I spoke something to them out at A winddow, and afterwardes was moved to goe out to them, and spoke to them & asked them what they wantted they said Quakeres I told them I was one

w[i]th seuerall other wordes, and presently their Countenance fell and fear surprised them, and they with drew / with shame and Confussion vpon their faces, not haueing power to harme A haire of our heads, praised be the Lord.[54]

Fell circulated such statements because they were useful tools to encourage other itinerants to suffer as a way of evangelizing; however, there is no way to measure how non-Quakers interpreted these outward expressions of faith. While Quaker letters are a poor source for assessing the effects of imprisonment as a tool of conversion, they do provide insights into the conversation and arguments for the benefit of outward suffering.

Imprisonment could also be an effective tool for encouraging other Quakers throughout the letter network to sustain themselves through their own suffering. They were clearly aware of the power of their suffering, which Quaker prisoners used to motivate their brethren jailed elsewhere. In 1658, Richard Hubberthorne wrote to the prisoners of Chester to tell them that their suffering was powerful and that they needed to continue on in the fight for the faith.[55] As a leader of the itinerant movement writing to lesser-known Friends enduring a similar punishment, Hubberthorne's words must have served as a great motivator to continue their sufferings. The modern reader can almost hear a collective rallying cry from the Chester prisoners as their suffering was acknowledged. Letters like this one also demonstrate the awareness of Quakers throughout England, imprisoned and free, of the activities of the movement's members. News was shared to keep people abreast of changes in the group's progress in spreading their beliefs but also to show the similarities of experiences everywhere. Thus, being in jail did not necessarily isolate one from the greater world.

A letter from Myles Halhead to Margaret Fell discussed the utility of convincement from prison: "One of the friends that came from Plimouth" came to visit Friends in prison, and the combination of suffering in jail and commitment to downtrodden Friends from free people helped convince the other prisoners of the "Truth":

> There are great desires begotten in the hartes of many after the truth, and some of them are eternally convinced that have been with us in prison and they did receive our friend in much love: the eternall living truth spreads exceedingly convinced, his wife and family, he hath bene made to wone us openly in the greatest persecution and is very servicible to us, and many are convinced that dare not confess it openly, the rage is soe great.[56]

This passage shows both the compelling nature of the Quaker plea for conversion and also the varying levels of commitment among Friends. The new Quakers "dare not confess it openly" because "the rage is soe great," but the author does not seem deterred by this level of conversion. Perhaps no one expected that newly initiated members would be willing to put themselves in harm's way for their recently acquired faith, but the idea that they could now be counted amongst the faithful was enough for Halhead. Regardless of their commitment, the author seems satisfied that additional souls had been won.

This was a judicious approach to seeking new members in prison. Many newly initiated would likely find themselves in conflict with the law in the future (especially those who had already been imprisoned for unrelated offenses). Thomas Salthouse and Myles Halhead wrote to Margaret Fell from Exeter prison in 1655 stating that locals who visited and showed support to imprisoned Quakers were in turn imprisoned themselves: "My friends that come to us may have more liberty than formerly was allowed, for wee are not locked up so strongly as we were at the first; and the keeper of the ward his famelly are loving and many of the soldiers convinced of their errour in keeping our friends from us by a guard contrary to law."[57] That people were willing to come into a religious community even though doing so might have immediate repercussions demonstrated that prison was a powerful tool utilized by early Quakers. Prison had the power to transform people either by conversion resulting in imprisonment or by witnessing others' suffering and going out into the community to spread the word.

The phenomenon of imprisoned Quakers claiming to be able to convince others beyond the confines of the jailhouse illuminates an important process in heterodox conversion. In the aforementioned letter, Salthouse and Halhead articulated a process that others could replicate, essentially stating that if one suffers, those who witness the suffering will convert. In the eyes of the jailed Friend, the process looked something like this: Preaching would almost always be followed by persecution, which, if approached correctly could lead to sympathy from those who heard about the suffering or witnessed it themselves in the community or in jail. Sympathy resulted in a larger, stronger community that was united in a sense of the truth of the faith due to unjust treatment at the hands of corrupt leaders. Those who were convinced by this behavior would in turn act out in a demonstration of their faith, which would result in further persecution. And thus the cycle continued.

Hence, the underlying importance of this process: Margaret Fell's efforts to keep Quakers aware of others' sufferings were increasingly important as members of the faith were imprisoned. Prison greatly reduced the number of itinerants who were available for proselytizing at any given moment. The sheer number of Quakers in prison as reflected in the letters did not leave many itinerant ministers to travel around the countryside. Furthermore, few of the convinced were actually traveling and spreading the word of God. Prison was a necessary means of transmitting ideas when itinerants were unable to bring their message to the people—people would come to them. Especially in cases when Quakers were jailed in small communities, it must have been quite the scene to have a nationally renowned heretic in the town jail. Godly people would have been repulsed or intrigued by his or her presence, and a Quaker would have been exciting for the townspeople in general. Beyond the fact that strangers would visit due to intrigue or genuine interest in the religious message, Quakers could use their imprisonment as a means to garner publicity. The punishment that authorities thought would diminish Quakers among the local townsfolk may have had the opposite effect and made people sympathetic to or excited by the prisoner's presence.

Not all suffering Quakers had the strength to keep up the good fight without encouragement. As the Chester prisoners show, help from fellow believers was often necessary, and many letters contain pleas for prayers and help from those on the outside to make them strong enough to sustain the hardships that came with renown for suffering. This is in part because their imprisonment was largely within their power to escape. Quakers were often given the choice between imprisonment and other harsh treatments if they were unwilling to leave town. In 1654, Ann Audland wrote to Margaret Fell that she refused freedom when it was offered:

> Dear hart I am A prisoner in bondes at Banbery in Oxfordshire; I can say little how long I stay here, but in the Counsell & will of god I waite to be guided I am in great seruice & keepes meetings often: I shall open my hart into thy bosome when the Lord orders us to meett Dear hart after I had refussed to put in bond and was Committed to prison Friendes of the Towne went to the magistrates & made A bond, and then the magistrates sent for mee to come before them and said there was two men that had bound themselves for my Appearance at the Sessions, and asked mee, if I was willing and said nay I was not willing then they asked the men if they were willing, and they said they were, And then they said it was noe matter for me, & soe they put me forth.[58]

Here, Audland not only refused to provide a bond, but she would not allow anyone to take her place in prison. She stated that she was bound to do what God directed her to do, and apparently he directed her to stay in prison. The Quaker sentiment is concisely stated by fellow dissenter, John Bunyan, who said that regardless of the trials of jail, his obligation was to do God's bidding: "the good will of God, to do with me as he pleaseth ... they can do no more, nor go no farther than God permits them."[59] Leaving town was an admission of guilt that Quakers refused to make. Thomas Salthouse and Myles Halhead stated that exchanging "outward freedom" at the expense of following God's command would destroy their souls: "So in the will of God we stand chussing rather to suffer imprisonment than to purchase outward freedom by making a covenant with death and so bring ourselves into inward bondage."[60] In virtually every case they refused freedom, claiming that God directed them to go to that place and therefore they could not leave.

One example of a Quaker opting for freedom is James Parnell who subsequently died during another imprisonment. When offered the choice between prison and leaving Cambridge in 1655, Parnell left stating:

> I was put into the low gaole among the Theives & an the next day justice Blackley, sent his warrant, & set mee free from the Tirantes bondes but I was made very willing to Remane, if it had beene the Lordes will, but in his Large wisdom hee ordered it according to his good will & pleasure for I did not motion it unto Blackley but hee did it of his owne accord & the next day I went to a meeting.

Parnell summed up the situation by stating, "but according to the good will of god bee it, as it standes to his glory I am content wheth[e]r in bondes or out of bondes."[61] It seems that this one exception may prove the rule rather than being a guiding principle. Of course, there is the possibility that others may have accepted freedom when faced with imprisonment, but the letter records are overwhelmingly in favor of prison over freedom. Moreover, Fell chose to only keep the records that reflected this sentiment because it furthered the Quaker cause. This example, like others that differ from it, is couched in the Quaker's compulsion to go where God demands he be. Parnell must have been directed elsewhere at this time, but it seems that when confronted by secular authorities, generally Quakers did not flinch. Loss of personal freedom was generally believed to be God's preference for the faithful.

Meanings of suffering

Given their predilection to suffer, the Quakers were arguably the most persecuted Protestant sect of the Interregnum. Their beliefs were seen as both religiously and socially insidious amongst virtually everyone from the godly to conformists and attracted the attention of local and national authorities. From the early 1650s when they started being persecuted for their beliefs, it became clear that suffering was a problem that many Friends faced. Margaret Fell and others at the center of the movement realized the benefit of embracing and putting a positive spin on persecution. Early Quakers were not unique in their attitude toward suffering, but they appreciated better than their contemporaries the value of recording their persecution. Thus, the slightest insult to or grievance suffered by a Quaker was designated a form of suffering and worth recording. Nothing was left out of the suffering records, and all forms of persecution—from branding, to fines, to imprisonment—were recorded equally in letters. Despite the consistent view that all persecution should be memorialized, neither contemporaries nor subsequent historians have been able to agree on the meaning of Quaker suffering.

From the beginning, suffering was not simply the experience of punishment for committing a crime—it was also perceived by some as the contractual obligation of the Quaker for having received the truth from God. In Quaker letters there is a clear understanding that suffering had both temporal and ephemeral qualities, but the meaning of the spiritual type of suffering was inconsistent. In 1655, Thomas Salthouse and Myles Halhead stated in a letter to Margaret Fell that suffering glorified both them and God: "To the will of our Father we giue vp to doe or to suffer, that hee may be honoured and glorified by us and all deceite Confounded, that he may Reign to whom all honour and glory doth belong for euermore."[62] As in many other Protestant sects, some Quakers understood salvation to be a reward for receiving God's truth, but it did not come without a cost. Quakers were required to continuously demonstrate their devotion to God. But just as legal arguments and prison experiences varied, so did the ultimate meaning of suffering.

Early Quakers appeared unified in the belief that suffering was an essential aspect of their faith as God directed. William Dewsbury wrote to Margaret Fell from Leicester in 1655 that suffering showed one's devotion to God:

> The euerlasting God of power giue thee dominion, in the power of his spirit to rull ouer all deceite, it to breake downe & under; bring to the pure liueing Liueing life it to raise vp to rull to the praise of god ouer all blessed for euer: who cleares the Innocent and hath the enemyes of his truth Confounded in this place, to the shame & confusion of their faces before many people, that their names stinkes, and shall rott and perish: but the name of our god hee hath exalted in keeping his babes in his mighty power in their measure faithfull to finish their testimony in sufferinges in this place.[63]

J.C. Davis articulates this notion, stating: "The pilgrim's progress through [life] had to be guided every step of the way by God."[64] Despite a general acceptance of this underlying idea, it was more difficult for them to agree upon the exact meaning of suffering and what that obligation entailed. In 1658, Richard Hubberthorne said: "When the lord comanded me out of the town I should goe but I was not at his comand soe he Caried me to prison wheare I am cept in my fathers loue knowinge it is for his seruice."[65]

While Hubberthorne's statement that he would have to defer to God for knowledge of his future travels may have been a trope claimed by many Quakers in the Interregnum, one cannot assume that suffering meant the same thing to everyone. In 1656 Lancelot Wardell wrote to Margaret Fell about the potential problem of so many ideas on suffering existing within the group. Some leaders, such as Anthony Pearson and Joseph Langstaffe, believed that it was better for some to "suffer quietly" because drawing attention to persecution "would butt stirr up more strife in the minde of those whom it concernes," while unnamed others sought to publish accounts of their persecution to help promote the Quaker cause.[66] Wardell did not resolve the matter, but rather he acknowledged an area of debate within the emergent faith.

In contrast, Will Caton was quite sure of the purpose and meaning of sufferings. He stated that suffering was to "serve for a tryall of our faith," suggesting that doing the work of the faith was a form of suffering and that one had to demonstrate his willingness to suffer for his work to be worthy of God.[67] It is an important distinction between God as one who causes suffering and for whom one suffers. Suffering then echoed the Quakers' Puritan roots of passing tests for God's favor. It was a choice made by the individual who sought to prove himself. Furthermore, Quakers echoed godly speech when saying that suffering was part of the covenant with God. In 1655, Thomas Salthouse and Myles Halhead wrote to Margaret Fell describing their contractual obligation to suffer:

> In the eternall oneness of the spirit doo wee enjoy thee present bonds cannot break our union, as wee abide in that which leads out of time, and from under the dark power into the pure freedom is purchased for us by the blood of the everlasting Covenant; and through sufferings is our way, but faithfull is hee that hath called not only to believe but to suffer with him, that wee may alsoe reign with him, when the Lambes testimony is finished.[68]

Halhead and Salthouse anticipated God's favor for their willingness to sacrifice "with him." Their freedom "purchased by the blood" was granted in exchange for their suffering. They wrote about the inward freedom that they gained by losing their outward liberty. Thus this explanation of suffering described an even trade in which both Quakers and God participated.

In yet another example, Thomas Salthouse stated in a letter that God called one to suffer. These different points of view centered on a debate over whether the individual chose or was chosen to do God's work. It further addresses the issue of who was called. According to Salthouse's argument, all Quakers (i.e., all those called by God to witness his truth) were obligated to suffer for him. This is a mandate beyond acknowledging God's law or living by a particular religious code, rather it was a form of worship. Suffering would thus mean something part and parcel of belief. Therefore, those who did not suffer were bad Quakers. Suffering was not only the obligation of itinerants like Salthouse, but rather all believers had to outwardly demonstrate their devotion. Such a claim seems to be a response to differing opinions of suffering during the Interregnum.[69] Whether suffering was a choice made by the individual, a requirement made by God, or acceptance to obey God's requirement, it was a way to glorify their Lord. "To the will of our father we give up to do or to suffer, that he may be honoured and glorified."[70] And elsewhere Myles Halhead stated, "to suffer for his namesake" would be a fulfillment of the Quaker's obligation.[71]

The sense of suffering as an obligation was often echoed in letters when imprisoned Friends asked others to pray for them because they felt unsure of their ability to withstand the suffering. Implicit in such a statement is the expectation or requirement to continue to suffer, such as when Thomas Salthouse and Myles Halhead spoke of their indefinite imprisonment.[72] Salthouse repeatedly asked Margaret Fell to pray for him. In 1655 he pled, "Deare Sister as thou art moved pray for us that we may bee kept faithfull to the end to finish our testimony of sufferinges that the eternall truth may be exalted and Deceite trampled vpon and Confounded."[73] Later, in 1657, Salthouse said, "Oh my deare & tender harted Mo: pray for me (as the liuinge _ giues vtterance) that I may be kept in patience & Cfert peace my testimony to finish in the feare of god."[74] Yet again, he said that suffering was not supposed to be seen as a negative experience. Not only were those in prison celebrated, but also those who wrote to them expressed sentiments approaching envy that some were able to suffer for God, while they could not.[75]

Suffering could also be experienced by those who were removed from physical danger but suffered in absentia in order to promote a sort of camaraderie through communication with those in dire situations. Early in the movement, Anthony Pearson wrote to Edward Burrough that some were unable to take on a ministry, despite their desires to do so. In this passage he described the difficulty to travel even short distances to hear Fox speak: "There are divers friends would come with me but since thru being subkect to parents and masters cannot get so far as Lancashire and therefore would meet him at the nearest."[76] In general, unnamed Quakers who were unable to make more of a mark on the development of the faith are largely ignored in the letter record.

However, Margaret Fell may best exemplify this type of ephemeral suffering, and her suffering is well known. She lived a very comfortable life by seventeenth-century standards and was far removed from the legal and physical troubles of itinerant ministers of the period, yet she was considered to have suffered greatly. Few early Quakers were treated with as much respect as Margaret Fell, and letters both to and from her reflect how difficult her situation was understood to be as architect of the early movement. This is not to confuse her later imprisonment with that of the early years—from the beginning she was understood to be among those who suffered the most due to her devotion to God and the movement (not to mention her devotion to George Fox). In subsequent decades, after she and Fox married, she drew large crowds to her public engagements and endured punishments in a manner similar to those of the early itinerants, but from the very earliest years, she suffered despite not traveling or experiencing physical discomfort.[77] Alexander Parker writing to Margaret Fell stated that he knew that her pain was with those who suffer and that she rejoiced with those who rejoice. Her suffering was stationary and physically comfortable but spiritually difficult: "Deare Sister knowing thy tender care ower the flock of God and joy, to hear of the florishing of Truth that thou dost suffer with them that suffer, and reioice with them th[a]t doe rejoice & in the Lord."[78] This is compelling because one must assume that as those in prison wrote to her and gave her their sympathies, her experiences were considered as akin to other forms of suffering like imprisonment.

This idea is echoed by Edward Burrough writing to George Fox when he stated that while Friends inside and outside of prison had many burdens, those outside had greater ones. This argument seems counterintuitive because imprisoned Quakers sacrificed their personal freedom for the sake of the group, but Burrough appeals to the sense of longing that isolated Quakers must have felt. Quakers in prison would often have one another's company and also a great sense of importance of their role in the movement. Those outside might suffer silently or away from a great number of Friends. Fame from imprisonment could provide consolation for a suffering Quaker, which could serve as positive reinforcement for those enduring persecution.

But not all suffering leaders maintained such a magnanimous attitude toward their free brethren. Edward Burrough and Francis Howgill wavered on their feelings about the group experience of suffering. In one instance they describe suffering as a group effort, felt by everyone, whether one personally experienced pain or suffered by supporting imprisoned Friends.[79] However, in a letter written two years earlier, the pair appeared to resent their role as leaders and therefore sufferers, while some quietly worshiped at home. "It may be others may water and another may reap in the will of god,"[80] Burrough and Howgill wrote with affection to Margaret Fell, and it may be that there was an understood exception for Fell given her devotion to the movement and her suffering in quiet—private comfort was given a pass because of all of her other efforts. But as these two express, this was not a sentiment that was universally felt for all members of the flock.

What, then, did suffering mean to inchoate Quakers? One could argue that physical sacrifice was the ultimate form of suffering, especially as the early itinerants were great sufferers and many endured pain and loss of freedom. However, one could also argue that it was simply setting oneself apart from non-believers, therefore dealing with the inevitable ramifications of financial, social, and political losses. But what of suffering as a testament to God? All that was required was loss of the self to the greater good of Quakerism, or more simply put by the early Quakers, as submission to the truth. Thus someone like Margaret Fell could qualify as an ideal sufferer because she devoted her life to the movement without enduring any physical discomfort. Fell was in a unique position to suffer from afar because of her responsibilities as a woman of her socio-economic status. Of course there were female preachers in the inchoate movement, but even in this relatively open religious community, their role was far from straightforward, as was argued in Chapter 3. Yet, it is clear that while there was no one understanding of Quakerism, all of these views contributed to Quaker suffering and highlight why their efforts to make themselves into martyrs confounded neighbors and authorities. In the eighteenth century, martyrologist Joseph Besse saw the early Quakers as reviving the "primitive Spirit of

Protestantism" he found in the first English reformers, familiar from John Foxe's pages, who "went through the fiery Trial." These embattled Quakers belonged to another kind of heroic age, given definition by what Besse characterized as "the sufferings of a plain, honest, and conscientious people."[81]

How Quakers understood their own experiences with suffering and wrote to one another about those experiences translated into a new sense of martyrdom that was quite different from that which most previous Christians had meant. For Quakers, imprisonment was one of many ways in which one could suffer, but the time that one spent in jail was also a sacrifice akin to martyrdom because the self was given up for the good of the cause. Thus, other forms of suffering also could count in the number of persons who were martyrs for Quakerism, not merely only those few in New England who died for the cause.[82] A more traditional view of martyrdom may be generous enough to include those who died in or shortly after having experienced particularly grueling imprisonment or physical injury, but Quakers went even further than that. All suffering, physical, economic, social, political, mental, spiritual, etc., equated to sacrifice, therefore counted as suffering and thus meant that one was "martyred" for the faith. While sentiments like "the Laying Downe of our lives if it bee Required" were frequently expressed in the letters that circulated throughout the network, no Quakers in England ever found themselves before an executioner.[83] These concepts of sacrificing the self for the greater good and the various early modern meanings of martyrdom are explored in Chapter 6. It was only after the age of martyrs was over, and Quakerism was effectively no longer under assault, that a process of remembering the early years of sacrifice was systematically achieved.

Notes

1. C.W. Horle, *The Quakers and the English Legal System, 1660–1688* (Philadelphia: University of Pennsylvania Press, 1988), 151.
2. Geoffrey Nuttall, *The Puritan Spirit: Essays and Addresses* (London: Epworth, 1967), 288–303.
3. Beverly Adams, "The Experience of Defeat Revisited: Suffering, Identity and the Politics of Obedience among Hertford Quakers, 1655–65," in *Religion in Revolutionary England*, ed. Christopher Durston and Judith Maltby (Manchester: Manchester University Press, 2007), 249–50.
4. MSS vol. S81/82. Henry Fell to Margaret Fell: Barbados, May 8, 1659.
5. Mark Bell, "Freedom to Form: The Development of Baptist Movements during the English Revolution," in *Religion in Revolutionary England*, ed. Christopher Durston and Judith Maltby, (Manchester: Manchester University Press, 2007), 185.
6. More information on the Marian Statute can be found in: R.M. Rogers, "Quakerism and the Law in Revolutionary England," *Canadian Journal of History* 22 (1987); John Morrill, *The Nature of the English Revolution* (London and New York: Longman, 1993), 388; and Chapter 3 of Barry Reay, *The Quakers and the English Revolution* (New York: St. Martin's Press, 1985).

7. Tom Webster, "Preaching and Parliament, 1640–1659," in *The Oxford Handbook of the Early Modern Sermon*, ed. Peter McCullough, Hugh Adlington, and Emma Rhatigan (Oxford: Oxford University Press, 2011), 417.
8. MSS vol. S81/38. Thomas Salthouse to Margaret Fell: Exeter, 1655 or 1656.
9. MS Box P2/15/23. Ann Audland to George Fox: Location unknown, February 1655.
10. Davies, *The Quakers in English Society*, 182.
11. MSS vol. S81/108. Richard Hubberthorne to Margaret Fell: Cambridge, August 25, 1654.
12. MSS vol. S81/42. Thomas Salthouse and Myles Halhead to Margaret Fell: Bridewell, July 1655.
13. Keith Thomas. "Puritans and Adultery: the Act of 1650 Reconsidered," in *Puritans and Revolutionaries: Essays in Seventeenth-Century History Presented to Christopher Hill*, ed. Donald Pennington and Keith Thomas (Oxford: Clarendon Press, 1978), 265.
14. Blair Worden, *The Rump Parliament, 1648–1653* (Cambridge: Cambridge University Press, 1974), 106.
15. Ibid., 116.
16. Ibid.,132.
17. Ibid.,116.
18. Morrill, *The Nature of the English Revolution*, 398.
19. Rogers, "Quakerism and the Law in Revolutionary England," 150.
20. Ibid., 151.
21. MSS vol. 351/24. Christopher Moore to George Fox: York, January 27, 1658.
22. MS Box P2/15/1. Agnes Wilkinson, Barbara Pattison, and Ann Nicholson to Unknown: York on Ouse Bridge, 1653.
23. John Miller, "'A Suffering People': English Quakers and Their Neighbors c. 1650–1700," *Past and Present*, no. 188 (August 2005): 77.
24. MSS vol. S81/109. Richard Hubberthrone and James Parnell to Margaret Fell: Oakington Cambridgeshire, September 28, 1654.
25. MSS vol. 378/29–30. Margaret Fell to Colonel William West: Swarthmoor, 1653.
26. MSS vol. 378/93–94. Margaret Fell to Oliver Cromwell: Swarthmoor, date unknown.
27. MSS vol. S81/41. Thomas Salthouse and Myles Halhead to Margaret Fell: Location unknown, 1655.
28. MSS vol. 354/80. James Nayler to Margaret Fell: London, November 3, 1655.
29. MSS vol. 354/27. Thomas Taylor to Margaret Fell: Appleby, 1657.
30. Adams, "The Experience of Defeat Revisited," 249.
31. MSS vol. 355/102. Robert Widder to Margaret Fell: Location unknown, 1656.
32. Richard Baxter, "Autobiography," in *Calendar of the Correspondence of Richard Baxter, Volume One: 1638–1660*, ed. Geoffrey Nuttall (Oxford: Oxford University Press, 1991), 190.
33. Davies, *The Quakers in English Society*, 183.
34. Gill, *Women in the Seventeenth-Century Quaker Community*, 42.
35. MSS vol. S81/9. Alexander Parker and Will Caton to Margaret Fell: Location unknown, 1655.
36. MSS vol. 355/145. Ann Dewsbury to Margaret Fell: Wakefield, 1657.
37. MSS vol. 355/114. Richard Sale to Margaret Fell: Chester, March 11, 1657.

38. Worden, *The Rump Parliament*, 116, and Morrill, *The Nature of the English Revolution*, 398.
39. John Marshall, "Defining and Redefining Heresy up to Locke's *Letters Concerning Toleration*," in *Heresy, Literature, and Politics in Early Modern English Culture*, ed. David Loewenstein and John Marshall (Cambridge: Cambridge University Press, 2006), 262.
40. MSS vol. S81/49. Myles Halhead and Thomas Salthouse to Margaret Fell: Exeter, 1656.
41. MSS vol. 355/200. Thomas Robertson to George Fox: Horsham, 1656.
42. MSS vol. S81/3. William Caton to Margaret Fell: Holland, November 1656.
43. MS Box P2/15/1. Agnes Wilkinson, Barbara Pattison, and Ann Nicholson to Unknown: York, 1653.
44. MSS vol. S81/110. Richard Hubberthorne to Margaret Fell: Location unknown, 1655.
45. MSS vol. S81/41. Thomas Salthouse and Myles Halhead to Margaret Fell: Location unknown, 1655; MSS vol. S81/43. Thomas Salthouse and Myles Halhead to Margaret Fell: Exeter, October 26, 1655.
46. MSS vol. S81/44. Thomas Salthouse and Myles Halhead to Margaret Fell: Exeter, February 9, 1656.
47. MSS vol. 355/248. Thomas Holme to Thomas Willan: Location unknown, 1654.
48. MSS vol. 355/68. John Lawson to Margaret Fell: Location unknown, 1654.
49. "Thine in my measure of the eternall light & life of god. T. S. now prisoner of the Lord in the Comon Goale in Exon." MSS vol. S81/38. Thomas Salthouse to Margaret Fell: Exeter, 1655.
50. MSS vol. S81/72. Francis Howgill to Margaret Fell: London, March 1655.
51. Ibid.
52. MSS vols. 323–24/162. John Wilkinson and John Story to Francis Howgill and Edward Burrough: Bristol, 1655.
53. MSS vol. S81/3. William Caton to Margaret Fell: Swarthmoor, November 1656.
54. MSS vol. 352/315. William Caton to Margaret Fell: Steyning, February 13, 1657.
55. MSS vol. 352/342. Richard Hubberthorne to the Prisoners at Chester: Congleton, July 19, 1658.
56. MSS vol. S81/47. Myles Halhead to Margaret Fell: No date or location provided.
57. MSS vol. S81/42. Thomas Salthouse and Myles Halhead to Margaret Fell: Exeter, 1655.
58. MSS vol. S81/140. Ann Audland to Margaret Fell: Location unknown, 1654.
59. John Bunyan, *The Pilgrim's Progress*, ed. Roger Pooley (New York: Penguin Classics, 2009).
60. MSS vol. S81/44. Thomas Salthouse and Myles Halhead to Margaret Fell: Exeter, February 9, 1655.
61. MSS vols. 323–24/29. James Parnell to Edward Burrough and Francis Howgill: Cambridge, May 1655.
62. MSS vol. S81/42. Thomas Salthouse and Myles Halhead to Margaret Fell: Bridewell, July 1655.
63. MSS vol. S81/163. William Dewsbury to Margaret Fell: Leicester, January 25, 1655.

64. J.C. Davis, "Living with the Living God: Radical Religion and the English Revolution," in *Religion in Revolutionary England*, ed. Christopher Durston and Judith Maltby (Manchester: Manchester University Press, 2006), 33.
65. MSS vol. 352/342. Richard Hubberthorne to the Prisoners at Chester: Location unknown, July 19, 1658.
66. MSS vol. 352/277. Lancelot Wardell to Margaret Fell: Sunderland, July 18, 1656.
67. MSS vol. S81/9. William Caton to Margaret Fell: Location unknown, 1655.
68. MSS vol. S81/44. Thomas Salthouse and Myles Halhead to Margaret Fell: Exeter, February 1655.
69. MSS vol. S81/40. Thomas Salthouse to Margaret Fell: Location unknown, February 1655.
70. MSS vol. S81/42. Thomas Salthouse and Myles Halhead to Margaret Fell: Bridewell, July 1655.
71. MSS vol. S81/47. Myles Halhead to Margaret Fell: No date or location provided.
72. MSS vol. S81/43. Thomas Salthouse and Myles Halhead to Margaret Fell: Exeter, October 1655.
73. MSS vol. S81/43. Thomas Salthouse and Myles Halhead to Margaret Fell: Exeter, 1655.
74. MSS vol. S81/52. Thomas Salthouse to Margaret Fell: Ilchester, Feb 20, 1657.
75. MSS vol. 351/42. Henry Fell to Thomas Rawlinson: Bristol, August 19, 1656. It should be noted that while Henry Fell celebrated others' suffering, he bordered on whining when it was his turn in Barbados and the North American colonies.
76. MSS vol. 354/35. Anthony Pearson to Edward Burrough: Location unknown, February 21, 1654.
77. MSS vol. 355/19. Richard Hubberthorne to George Fox: London, July 24, 1660.
78. MSS vol. 351/166. Alexander Parker to Margaret Fell: Tregangeeves (St. Austell), August 19, 1656.
79. MSS vol. S81/61. Francis Howgill and Edward Burrough to Margaret Fell: London, August 1656.
80. MSS vol. S81/62. Edward Burrough and Francis Howgill to Margaret Fell: London, August 1654.
81. Besse quoted in John Knott, *Discourses of Martyrdom in English Literature, 1563–1694* (Cambridge: Cambridge University Press, 1993), 219.
82. Pestana, "The Quaker Executions as Myth and History."
83. MSS vol. S81/47. Myles Halhead to Margaret Fell: No date or location provided.

6 The afterlife of the movement

The first Quakers believed that their mission was to reestablish the Apostolic purity of Christianity, and they were willing, even eager, to sacrifice themselves in pursuit of that goal. The purpose of this chapter is to show how suffering, an integral part of the story of early Quakerism, became the central feature of the eighteenth-century memory of the inchoate period. In earlier chapters, it has been argued that George Fox's emergence as sole leader resulted from Margaret Fell's active role in shaping the memory of these early years with the publication of his journal, creation of the Meeting on Sufferings, and editing of manuscript records like the letters housed in Swarthmoor Hall that became known as the Original Records of Sufferings.[1] Fox did this with Fell's help by reorganizing extant letters, signing his approval for those to be kept, and possibly eliminating those that detracted from his approved narrative of early Quakerism. This chapter shows what happened to Quaker suffering and ideas of martyrdom in the century following the Restoration in order to examine the devolution of the religious sect and development of the church. Those efforts, while attributed to Fox, were the result of Margaret Fell's work to solidify Fox's position and the institutional memory of his leadership role in the community.

The main work that encapsulated these ideas and promoted the legacy of a Quaker image as sufferers was Joseph Besse's martyrology, *A Collection of Sufferings of the People Call'd Quakers*, which sealed the notion of the Quakers' place in a line of Protestant persecuted peoples. While Besse shifted the focus of the group's formation away from the central leaders of the movement to everyone who participated and suffered in the early years, some individuals, notably George Fox, remained as dominant examples of suffering. This resulted in a changing meaning of suffering for Quakers that expanded beyond a few prominent individuals to all Quakers who sacrificed for the church's sake. Besse emulated early modern hagiographers, but most of all, John Foxe's *Acts and Monuments*; in so doing, he placed the Quakers in line with sixteenth-century Protestant martyrs and even the earliest Christians. John Knott states that Quakers incorporated Foxe into their sense of themselves as a movement long before the publication of Besse's *Collection*:

It formed part of the effort of Quaker leaders to justify their resistance to persecution by placing themselves in a tradition of martyrdom whose origins they found in the Bible. Foxe's *Acts and Monuments* was a mirror in which the early Quakers saw what they looked for, among other things a faith defined by the refusal to swear oaths.[2]

The first in the long line of Quakers appropriating Besse was Ellis Hookes, who "drew heavily upon Foxe" for the examples in his seventeenth-century works. Furthermore, Knott identifies the Quaker willingness to see themselves as part of a line of persecution that included Waldensians, in addition to the Marian martyrs highlighted in Foxe. As Knott describes it, "Hookes praises the Waldensians for refusing oaths and quotes extensively from the examinations of various martyrs reprinted by Foxe to make a similar point."[3] Similar work could be found even earlier in William Penn's *No Cross, No Crown* from 1682 and *Primitive Christianity Revived* from 1696, as well as Isaac Pennington's *Concerning Persecution* as early as 1661. As a result of these works and the foundation they laid for Besse, by the mid-eighteenth century, Quakers no longer saw themselves as uniquely outside of the context of Protestant suffering, but rather once they no longer feared persecution, they argued for their place in a larger Protestant Christian narrative.

As discussed in Chapter 1, the period from roughly 1646–1652 was a time in which the leadership of Quaker faith came together and began the initial negotiation of what it meant to be a member of the community. From 1652 to 1656, a consensus began to build based on a few individuals who were singled out (or who alternately singled themselves out) as the center of the group, largely due to Fell's efforts to highlight their roles in the community. The Nayler Affair and a growing sense of national irritation with radical dissenters caused a shift in the internal focus of this religious community.[4] Quakerism went from being expansive and experimental to closing off avenues for initiative within the faith and instead began to focus on establishing a single cohesive orthodox belief system. By the end of the Interregnum, while Quakers continued to be persecuted at times, Fell and Fox had solidly codified the structure and dogma of the church, thus demonstrating the transition from a flimsy religious movement to an established religion.

Chapter 5 explored the meaning of suffering for the inchoate Quakers. While there was a period of enhanced suffering at points throughout Charles II's reign and subsequently leading up to the Act of Toleration in 1688, by the end of the seventeenth century, Quakers experienced a sense of freedom to worship that they had not known before. This was the result of their surviving beyond the initial period of persecution and Fell and others' clever practice of incorporating suffering as a key characteristic of the Quaker identity. Restoration legislation like the Clarendon Code's Five Mile Act and Conventicle Act, not to mention the Quaker Act, targeted dissenters like the Quakers. Enforcement of these new anti-nonconformist laws resulted in increased numbers of imprisoned Quakers. However, despite these temporary spikes of years of persecution, by the mid-eighteenth century, Quakers lived rather peaceably among their English neighbors and they were neither threatened nor considered the threat that they once had been. They were able to practice their faith openly without fear of undue harm. It was during this period that the most comprehensive and accessible work on Quaker sufferings was created—Besse's *A Collection of the Sufferings of the People Call'd Quakers*.

The question one must ask is why was the book commissioned at this point, when the Quakers were no longer fearful of suppression? The answer, in large part, is due to the success of Fell's systematic maintenance of records during the earliest years of Quakerism, thus allowing subsequent hagiographic histories to be written. Essentially, Besse's *Collection* was the fulfillment of Fell's Interregnum work by formally memorializing the concept of Quakers as suffering peoples, an image she had preserved in the letters.

The Quaker meaning of martyrdom

In the early years of the Quaker movement, there was no single definition of any aspect of the faith. Just as Quakers had conflicting meanings of the legal system and suffering, so too did they argue over the meaning of martyrdom. A likely cause for these inconsistencies can be found in the wide and varied antecedents to this emergent faith. As described in previous chapters, many would-be Quakers migrated from other dissenting faiths, such as Familists in previous generations, as well as other radical groups like Independents, Baptists, and other seeking sorts in the seventeenth century. The early group did not have a single, coherent system of organization or belief, and its members looked to others for answers.

The application of this inconsistency can be seen in their use of terms associated with suffering. Despite the infrequent use of the term "martyr," the implication is clear when Quakers suggested willingness to die for the cause. Carla Pestana states that "once condemned to die, the missionaries saw themselves as literal martyrs."[5] While certainly true, the letters show that the association with martyrdom was applied subsequent to or even without a death sentence. In 1656, Thomas Salthouse and Myles Halhead wrote to Margaret Fell: "Soe in the will of God we stand chusseing rather to suffer imprisonment or banishment out of the Land then to purchasse outward freedome by making a Couenant with death and soe bring our selves into inward bondage."[6] Here, the meaning of life and death are inverted.[7] In this instance, physical death would equate to life or a spiritual living; however, for the Quakers, living outside of the church was equated to death. In another instance, Myles Halhead wrote to Margaret Fell that the covenant required one "not only to beleeve but alsoe to suffer for his namesake that wee may finish our testimony with joy and Rejoiceing to the Laying Downe of our lives if it bee Required."[8] Again, while the word "martyr" is not used, its meaning cannot be missed. Nowhere in this letter does Halhead suggest that any ministers' lives were in danger, but he states the idea that one should sacrifice his life if necessary. No Quakers were executed in England despite periods of intense persecution. The only person who could arguably fall under the standard definition of "martyr" during the Interregnum was James Parnell. His death due to poor prison conditions is arguably a better case of martyrdom than the likes of the most famous sufferers, even Fox or Nayler, much less Fell.

While the term "martyr" was not used frequently in early records, its use to describe mundane events along with extraordinary examples of suffering demonstrates two things: first that not everyone used the term in the same way, thus illustrating the lack of a cohesive concept of suffering and martyrdom, and second that all forms of suffering were considered equal. Some suffered greatly for the cause, while others did not, thus demonstrating the egalitarian application of the term martyr—all of those people who suffered and held up their end of the covenant were equally serving God as martyrs for their faith. As Pestana notes, "the roles of prophet and martyr were complementary: a good death lent support to the predictions and criticisms that martyr had made in life."[9]

This concept of martyrdom set Quakers apart from most of their Christian predecessors. Sixteenth-century Protestants, like the early Christians before them, defined martyrdom in terms of the believer's death for the faith. Brad Gregory describes this as a type of "fractal geometry" of martyrdom in English Protestantism. People with "mutually incompatible beliefs" believed themselves to be "the true heirs to the tradition of Christian martyrdom."[10] In contrast, Quakers saw any act committed in the pursuit of God's plan was a demonstration of a commitment to the covenant. This notion aligned with the theological premise of "serving God" as the death of the self upon entering the covenant. If being a true Quaker (as defined in this early period) meant a willingness to suffer, and suffering demonstrated putting the faith above oneself, then all true Quakers were martyrs. This in no way represents the more general seventeenth-century notion of martyrdom. Most contemporaries ascribed to the traditional view of martyrs being people who died for their faith. Contemporary Christians extended this definition to include those people who died in prison as having died for their faith. The Quakers, however, adopted an even broader definition of the traditional view that death was required for martyrdom that suggested that those who died within a few years of imprisonment were accepted into the pantheon of martyrs.

While Quaker scholarship does not explore early meanings of martyrdom in great detail, the faith's approach to equating all suffering with the "death of the self" is most akin to medieval monastic notions.[11] Dating back to nascent Christianity, church father Origen described the different forms of sacrifice; his ideas were taken up by Celtic monks of the fourth and fifth centuries during their missionary efforts. "As a model of Christian perfection shifted to monasticism in the centuries after Constantine's conversion, martyrdom was transformed rather than abandoned," according to Gregory. "Prior to this, Western church leaders such as Cyprian had already broached the subject of Christian suffering in the absence of active persecution."[12] Accordingly, martyrdom was classified by three colors: red, blue (or green), and white. Red martyrdom constituted the most severe form of sacrifice where the witness or martyr died for the sake of his or her faith. Blue or green martyrdom refers to the sacrifices of the missionary who gave up his pre-proselytizing life for his faith. Finally, white martyrdom was the most passive variety in which the martyr "spiritually" suffered with little or no physical harm or sacrifice. It is this form that appears closest to "witness" as synonymous with martyr. Gregory notes that in the fifteenth century, ascetics like Margery Kempe participated "in a sublimation of martyrdom that stretched back a millennium."[13]

Virtually no Quaker scholarship has addressed the meaning of these various levels or distinctions of martyrdom with the exception of Carole D. Spencer's "Holiness: The Quaker Way of Perfection," in which she states that the "blood martyrdom" of the early faith gave way to "white martyrdom" after "persecution ceased."[14] Certainly it is true that the more passive form of suffering came to dominate the faith in the decades and centuries following its inception. However, as early as the first moments of the movement, all three forms of martyrdom were apparent. The rare and few examples of "red" martyrdom define the deaths of the New England missionaries, and this description could potentially include those who died in prison, as well. However, both itinerants and home-based Quakers like Margaret Fell typified the other colors of martyrdom as have been described here. Just as the early Christians transformed their meaning of suffering based on the experiences of those living centuries following intense persecution, so did the Quakers.

As has been described in Chapter 4, inchoate Quakers evoked the early church when shaping and demonstrating their theology.[15] White and blue martyrdom had been downplayed in the later Middle Ages in favor of emphasizing examples of those who died in defense of the church. In both the structure of the letter network and the ideas it espoused, Quakers harkened back to the pre-Protestant church, which they believed they were reinstating. Once again Quaker letters and Fell's management of them give us insight into their views on martyrdom. Like all other theological matters, there was no single Quaker view that encapsulated all discussion of martyrdom; there were three approaches to defining who was and who was not a martyr. The most general example included all Quakers. By accepting the truth of the light within the individual (i.e., adhering to the Quaker theology), one was a martyr. A previously noted letter reiterates this point. Thomas Salthouse and Myles Halhead wrote to Margaret Fell that they would rather remain in prison and be members of the true church than be free and maintain "A Couenant with death and so bring our selves into inward bondage."[16] Death for Salthouse and Halhead would be experiencing what others would call life or freedom; however, for Quakers, life did not exist outside of the faith. There was a biblical precedent for this idea of the role of the faithful believer: "Jesus then said to his disciples, 'Anyone who wishes to be a follower of mine must renounce self; he must take up his cross and follow me. Whoever wants to save his life will lose it, but whoever loses his life for my sake will find it.'"[17] Thus, the movement subsumed the individual. One gave up individuality to be part of the church. Just as one could lead a comfortable life, one could also suffer with those beaten or jailed. Just as one could be imprisoned, one could be at liberty with the faith. This logic applied to life as well. Just as one could live, one's individual sense of self could die, thus making one a martyr. This may be the closest thing to a consistent train of thought among the competing ideas of the early Quaker movement.

This notion corresponds well with the sense that Quakers, like many of their contemporaries, were waging the Lamb's War. Their suffering was not merely to promote the Quaker cause, but to continue the Christian struggle against all foes. During the Interregnum in England, there was no shortage of foes, including secret Catholics, conformist priests and congregations, sects that discounted the Quaker message, secular or sacred forces that impeded the spread of Quakerism, or really anyone who looked sideways at one of the brethren. As described in Chapter 4, there were numerous scriptural examples in their letters that identified their sense of struggle with the serpent or devil, which was most commonly juxtaposed to the lamb, most notably in Fell's epistolary battles with Quaker opponents. In their correspondence, Fox, or any given individual Quaker, could represent the lamb, but the term could also be used to signify the greater struggle of the sect at large.

Finally, the third meaning of martyr correlates more directly with the common understanding of the term. Quakers evoked the word in reference to those who actually died while in service for the cause. The only formal executions of members of this sect during the Interregnum were conducted in New England. William Braithwaite places a particularly harsh spin on these events in describing the innocent endeavors of the first Quakers in New England and their brutal treatment at the hands of Puritan authorities. In 1658, Massachusetts enacted a law against "the cursed sect," banning Quakers from the colony, upon pain of death if they returned after expulsion. Itinerant ministers, unwilling to avoid such persecution but embracing it, continued to attempt to settle in the colony; as Braithwaite states a "crisis of persecution followed this enactment."[18] Several Quakers returned to Massachusetts after being expelled the first time, and two were executed. Braithwaite describes these martyrs: "On Thursday 27th October 1659 they walked with transfigured faces, hand in hand, to the gallows on Boston Common, a mile from the town, where the two men suffered martyrdom, but Mary Dyer, at the last moment, was reprieved."[19] Dyer, however, returned to the colony in 1660 and was put to death for repeatedly breaking the law banning Quakers. Anne Myles recounts the ways that Dyer chose to ignore the potential consequences of her actions: "Dyer returned a second time to visit another imprisoned Friend, and Robinson, Stephenson, and

Dyer were arrested, briefly tried, and this time, in the face of their incorrigible returns, sentenced to death."[20] She was followed by "a fourth martyr" in 1661.[21] Thus, while Quakers were keen to publicize examples of extreme mistreatment by authorities, they ultimately treated it as one of many sacrifices made for the greater benefit of the movement in service to God.

However, none of this discussion means that the term "martyr" was used evenly to describe all suffering brethren. Like all matters of the 1650s, theological or otherwise, there was no single perspective that determined the use of this term. This problem is illustrated in Joseph Besse's unpublished eighteenth-century paper entitled "The Memory of the Faithful Revived or An Alphabetical List of the Names of more than three Hundred of the people called Quakers, who laid down their Lives in Person or through cruel usage, for their constancy in Religion, together with a Summary Account of the Causes of their Imprisonment, and the Deaths of Each of them."[22] Note that the term martyr does not appear in the title. However, those "who laid down their lives," suggests death at the cause of "their constancy in religion."[23]

This tract lists the names and circumstances of the deaths of 301 Quakers who Besse claims died while unjustly imprisoned. The accounts of their deaths came from letters that Fell maintained and the Great Book of Sufferings, which was compiled for and stored by the London Meeting. Of the 301 people mentioned in this text, for 60 of them (amounting to 20 percent of the total martyred) it is unclear where and when they died given that they are described as being imprisoned and subsequently dying "soon" or "shortly" after the date of incarceration; however, in such cases it is not clear whether or not they were released or remained in prison at the time of their deaths. For example, "Thomas Rogers, a Young Man, imprison'd in Newgate, from a Religious Meeting in or about London, Fell sick in prison about the Month of December 1662, and died soon after."[24] In most of the aforementioned cases, their deaths generally are attributed to damp, dirty, crowded prison conditions. Besse states:

> Oliver Atherton of Ormskirt in Lancashire was imprisoned in Lancaster Castle at the Suit of the Countess of Derby for Tithes. He being of a weake Constitution after about two Years and a half Confinement in a cold, damp, unwholesome place, was brought so low and weake, that there seemed no hope of Life, unless he would be removed hence. His condition was a represented to the Countess, but she turned the deaf Ear to all the Intreatis on his behalf. Being told that the Countess denied him any Liberty, the Expiring Man faintly replied, This will be the heaviest Blood that ever she Spilt, and soon after died in the Year 1662. The Countess also herself died about 3 Weeks after.[25]

Here Besse seems to suggest that the Countess's death was retribution for her ill treatment of Atherton. His source in this instance and throughout his text is Fell's cache of letters.

Twenty-six of Besse's martyrs either died after being released from prison or were never incarcerated, but rather were violently accosted and died from wounds suffered from those attacks. Such was the case of Richard Hebson, who "for opposing one of the Priests of those times, in the Year 1652, was imprisoned at Appleby in Westmoreland, where he was cruelly beaten and abused by an Unmerciful Goaler, insomuch, that being put out of the prison, he died within a few days after through the barbarous usage and Hardships he had there undergone."[26] There can be no question as to the martyred status of those who died as the result of being beaten, but the post-incarceration cases are more problematic. Those with dates of release followed by date of death run the gamut from a few days to several years. Humphrey Brewster went into Newgate Prison "till his body was so weaken'd and corrupted by Sickness contracted there, that he died in a short time after his Discharge in the year 1662."[27] The duration of a "short time" is difficult to assess. In contrast is Christopher Bacon of Somerset who was said to have suffered greatly due to the extreme cold, which caused him to become "very sick, when it was thought he would have died there, they turned him out, but he never recovered his health, but died there about two Months time."[28] Besse suggests that Bacon was "turned out" because the jailer did not want to be responsible for his death, thus demonstrating the inhumane attitudes toward suffering Quakers; however, Besse's assessment may be unfair, and the jailer may have actually been demonstrating restraint and a humane attitude by not wanting Bacon to die as a result of the jailer's actions.

Yet the cases of both Brewster and Bacon show a relatively direct relationship between prison conditions and death. However, in the case of Nicholas Complin, the time lapse between his imprisonment and death suggests that Besse liberally applied the term "martyr" to his subjects:

> Nicholas Complin, with 12 other of his Friends, being some of them on the Road, others in an Orchard, and some in other places, near Ringwood in Hampshire, were taken by an Officious Constable, with an Officer and Soldiers, without any Warrant, on the Last day of the Month called May 1665, and being carried before two Justices, were by them committed to Prison, and Justices alledging, that though they had not met, there was reason to believe they intended to meet: Thus they stretched the Law to the Punishment of Men's supposed Intentions who had not actually transgressed: At the next Assizes they were fined $10 each, and continued under close confinement above half a Year after, when by the Goalers favour, they obtained some Liberty, but continued prisoners at Large several Years, in which State Nicholas Complin died, and others of them were discharged by King Charles the 2d his Letters Patent in the Year 1672.[29]

This entry provides insights into the Quakers' perspective on the legal system and what constituted imprisonment in this period. That Complin died sometime in the several years following his actual stint in jail shows that Besse assigned the cause of death to the imprisonment. Furthermore, Besse attributes the death to what appears to be some type of house imprisonment, which presumably would not have been an intolerable environment.

This discussion is in no way meant to diminish the significance of these deaths, but rather to examine what the word "martyr" meant to members of the Quaker faith. Besse believed he was describing the deaths of martyrs regardless of when and where they died. That would certainly be true in the case of the one proclaimed martyr, Edward Grant, whose advanced age and the circumstances of his death require consideration. As Besse described it: "Edward Grant of Colchester in Essex, about 70 Years of Age, was knockt down by the Soldiers who came to break up a Meeting there, and survived the fatal Stroke but a few Days, before he died a faithful Martyr, for In Constancy in attending Religious Meetings, even the hazard and Loss of his Life."[30] While this example is extreme, it is not unique—there are similar tales of people dying or being attacked for no reason other than attending a meeting or performing a similarly mundane expression of faith. Others died in Newgate Prison in 1662 after being "taken at a Religious Meeting," including Edward Baker, of the same year as Richard Audley in 1664.[31] The use of the term martyr in this example thus should not be taken as a dramatic description, but seen as interchangeable with many other instances in Besse's list, and therefore, all cases in this text were tantamount to martyrdom for Besse and the people who originally wrote about these cases.

The egalitarian nature of suffering is seen in the discussion of martyrdom as well. The vast majority of those who suffered in this period did not die as a result of their punishments. Indeed, the suffering record suggests that a larger number died at the hands of their punishers than may be accurate. Most people who suffered and attained the status of martyr experienced more mundane types of punishment such as prison or corporal punishment. Therefore, the meaning of martyrdom was more complex than simply dying for one's faith.

This points to the possibility that under Fell's direction the Quaker movement constructed a gradated system of martyrdom. Seeing all suffering as a form of sacrificing the individual for the good of the faith resulted in greater numbers of martyrs among Quakers than among other radical sects, and as a result they stood out as persecuted people in the early modern period. Furthermore, Quaker leaders gained fame within the group and society in general, which cultivated their position as leaders and brought attention to their condition. In so doing, Quakers made a clearer connection between their efforts and those of the Apostolic Christians who similarly suffered and often martyred themselves for their faith.

Ultimately, conflicts with the legal system resulted in some itinerants being written about and recorded most in the early years. This intensified fixation on martyrdom became the defining characteristic in determining who should lead and be most valued in the early years of this faith. The variety of suffering experiences is best highlighted by the role Fell assumed as quietly enduring sacrifice for the truth's sake while remaining essentially unscathed by her suffering. As a result, Quakers established a martyrology that did not require that martyrs die; this resulted in more members of the sect being willing to suffer for their faith, since it honored those who were persecuted without demanding loss of life for recognition of their sacrifices. This also set them apart from earlier dissenters and their contemporaries as they drew more attention to their persecution than others had. It also explains why martyrdom became a defining quality of the group. Quakers saw their suffering as greater than that of others. This is a key feature that they took through the ages: Quakers are people who suffer for their beliefs. While what it meant to be a Quaker changed over time, during the transition from sect to church and the change in medium from Fell's letter network to Besse's martyrology, they remained suffering people even after they were no longer officially persecuted by the state. They prolonged this self-definition by generating works that preserved their concept of martyrdom, which aided them in this transition.

Publication of sufferings

From an early moment in the movement, Quakers sought to record and publish their sufferings. Kate Peters's excellent work on print culture in the 1650s stresses the importance of publication of sufferings. Peters notes that as early as 1654, Thomas Willan asked Margaret Fell to gather information from her catalogue of letters "so that the 'book of sufferings' could be printed."[32] Subsequently, leading Quakers Gervase Benson and Anthony Pearson wrote to Fell stating that they were "endeavouringe to gett together the sufferings of friends in the North parts for tythes and the ends for which people did give them; and how they have from tyme to tyme diverted them from the end for which they were given."[33] Peters focuses on the emphasis Quakers placed on practical ends for the promotion of sufferings. By publishing accounts of sufferings, Quakers of the 1650s hoped to convince readers of their unjust persecution. Peters states: "Examples of trials were published in order to rehearse the key issues of state interference in religion and to enable readers to raise concrete objections to their own prosecution."[34] Thus, Quakers hoped that published sufferings would change their image. The Quakers' "own zealous and sustained use of the press" resulted in "a very purposeful and organized movement."[35] Subsequent Quaker success was therefore due to such diligent record keeping and publication.

In order to promote the Quakers' connection to older sectarian communities, certain books were published *en masse* so they could be evenly distributed among meetings. By determining what circulated throughout the network, Margaret Fell oversaw this effort in 1654, making sure that the relevant reading materials would be accessible to all. This practice was similar to the Anglican demand that the presence of the Book of Common

Prayer or Foxe's work be present in every parish.[36] This was the precedent already in place for Besse's *Collection* to be published specifically for the meetings throughout England as early Quakers demanded that certain books be available to all. Fell wrote to John Stubbs in 1656 asking that he oversee the publication of a treatise so "they may goe forth amongst frends as the Rest of Books doeth, the same Quantety to Euery place, & as the are Called for soe the may bee prented in Quantety."[37]

The letter demonstrates the perceived need for publication of sufferings, as well. As early as 1653, members of the Valiant Sixty called for circulation and publication of suffering records. That year, Fell wrote to her husband, "let [sufferings] be printed th[a]t may openly apeare to the world what we live in and be not ashamed of the truth for it will stand," suggesting that Fell and those who shared her ideas on suffering hoped to spread stories to bolster support for their movement.[38] This gave her considerable discretion and influence in the Quaker community. Furthermore, by publishing these records, they also promoted the Quakers' image as sufferers to a larger audience, including those who may have been hostile to the movement.

In the decades after the Restoration, a formally organized church emerged from the Quaker movement. I have argued above that this process occurred in the Interregnum, though, as Peters points out, the effects of formally organizing can best be seen in the years following Charles II's return to the throne. In 1661, George Bishope published *New England Judged, Not by Man's, but the Spirit of the Lord,* and in 1667, *New England Judged: The Second Part.* These works focused on the four Quakers who died in New England and highlighted what Pestana calls "the twin themes of martyrdom and prophecy."[39] Bishope's works came from the earliest suffering accounts found in letters and late Interregnum publications highlighting the sacrifices of martyred brethren. Meanwhile, local meetings in England kept records of membership, marriages, births, and deaths, as well as suffering. The Meeting for Sufferings, which served as the executive body of the national church hierarchy, was created in 1675. John Miller identifies a "sense of injustice" that can be found throughout the meeting's records, which focused on the unfairness of laws that were used against the Quakers. "The minutes of this meeting, together with the Great Book of Sufferings and the Original Records of Sufferings, all in Friends' House Library" were the basis of Besse's source materials, the "original records of sufferings" being the letters themselves along with reports generated by the meetings that were based on the archived letters.[40] This committee commissioned the first substantial collection of sufferings, which was compiled in the 1660s by Ellis Hookes, Recording Secretary of what would become the central administrative meeting in London, the Second Day Morning Meeting. This two-volume manuscript compilation was a catalogue of Swarthmore letters from the 1650s.[41]

In the early eighteenth century, there were rudimentary efforts to commemorate early sufferings, such as Daniel Gould's *A Brief Narration of the Sufferings of the People Called Quakers* in 1700; John Whiting's response to Cotton Mather's Puritan apology *Magnalia Christi Americana,* entitled *Truth and Innocency Defended against Falsehood and Envy* in 1702; and Joseph Grove's 1703 *New England Judged by the Spirit of the Lord,* which was a revised edition of George Bishope's 1660s tracts.[42] In 1727, in light of these publications and building on Fell's earlier organizational efforts in the previous century, this meeting along with the Second Day Morning Meeting sought to "undertake a more systematic record of their sufferings,"[43] as well as the collection and cataloguing of all Quaker books. The executive body determined that in order to understand the trials of their founding members, it would have to organize and publish the early suffering records. This also served the purpose of documenting the ill treatment that the founding Quakers endured by the governments that persecuted them in the past, which had been recorded in their letters of the 1650s. And as Miller states, the publications also had a "propagandist purpose."[44] The resulting publication was the *Collection of the Sufferings of the People Call'd Quakers,* published first in 1733, and in 1738 under the title *An Abstract of the Sufferings of the People Call'd Quakers.* These early works covered the period 1650–1666 and were published in three volumes. The committee published a more comprehensive version in 1753, which included more information.[45]

Quaker archivist Norman Penney states that Quaker James Dickinson proposed the idea of a book of sufferings at the Quarterly Meeting in York in 1726.[46] He goes on to say that the idea was adopted by the Lancaster, Cumberland, and Kendal meetings but does not state the cause for the sudden desire to publish the first generation of sufferings. The initial proposal was "for the meeting of sufferings to take upon them the care of Collecting and digesting by proper persons the sufferings and Imprisonments of Friends for Tythes and on all other accounts, into proper heads from the beginning of our being a People to this time."[47] However, over time it became clear (if only to the archivists involved) that the meeting's main use was for genealogical purposes.[48] Meeting minutes provide some insights into the concerns of early eighteenth-century Quakers. They believed that an account of sufferings of the first 75 years of the church would essentially tell the history of their "being a people."[49] Furthermore, the specific reference to prison and tithes suggests one of two things: Most sufferings (or at least those best preserved in the memory of the first few generations) were because the early Quakers were persecuted for refusing to pay tithes, and imprisonment was either the most frequently allotted punishment or seen as the most severe. Finally, Besse makes no distinction between the first few years of Quakerism and the first several decades, which suggests that he placed less emphasis on the inchoate period. However, the question remains why these were his and the leadership's concerns.

Besse was a schoolmaster in Colchester and in 1716 worked as the transcribing clerk of the Essex Quarterly Meeting. This job included the responsibility of recording sufferings and maintaining Yearly Meeting Epistles.

In 1720, Besse moved to London where he engaged in the "literary life of Quaker London" and edited major Quaker biographies, including those of George Whitehead and William Penn.[50] By 1730 Besse was hired by the Yearly Meeting to organize and transcribe loose manuscripts and use them to create tables (i.e., indexes) of the materials contained therein. At this point Besse began the process of creating volumes of lists of sufferings that focused on the period up to 1720.[51] Also in 1730, noting the work Besse had done for the preservation of the memory of Quaker persecution, the Meeting for Sufferings appointed a committee to oversee the project of publishing the sufferings. This resulted in the committee's proclamation that, upon seeing Besse's work, "it may be of Great Service to be printed."[52] Thus the Quaker church began the process of publishing an abridged account of the first generations of Quaker sufferings.

The original publication, issued in 1734, received little response within the church as it did not contain all counties and regions. This, as well as the 1739 and 1750 versions, went into what became the definitive 1753 text, which was well received by English Quakers. So that each Monthly Meeting would have a copy, 1,000 were printed based on 719 initial subscriptions ordered at 22 shillings a piece.[53] Local meetings advertised the sale of the remaining copies to their members, and finally in 1755 more than 100 copies were distributed over 43 Quarterly Meetings, "expressly intended for the use of such Friends as are not of ability to purchase the Work, or to be lent occasionally to People of other Persuasions, where there is Prospect of Service."[54] An additional 50 copies were shipped to Philadelphia to "some great personages."[55]

The two-volume *Collection of the Sufferings of the People Call'd Quakers*, which listed sufferings chronologically according to alphabetical organization of counties and cities, was published in London. While working for the Yearly Meeting in the 1730s, Besse noted that some counties' records were incomplete and insufficiently transcribed, so he attempted to rectify this imbalance. However, an uneven account of the counties' suffering records remained, and the published work reflects the lack of complete sources.

Penney attempts to link the amorphous beginnings of the collection of sufferings to Fox, but as his and others' research demonstrate, Fell was central to this process. It seems likely that there was another reason for Penney's assertion—by the early twentieth century, any large undertaking for the Society needed to be linked back to Fox for validation because he was the undisputed founder of the church. Fell's part in elevating Fox was an implied, less significant aspect of the narrative that seemed unworthy of further discussion. Yet, the story as told in the records had very little to do with Fox's efforts, despite his benefiting from such recordkeeping. Therefore, once again, we can see the Quaker historical record making retrospective attempts to put Fox at the center of decision making, even after his place as head of the religion had been firmly established. It is again important to remember that while it is evident that she selected the documents to be preserved from the early years of Quakerism, thereby cultivating perceptions of Fox, we cannot know the exact methods she used in this effort.

In *Discourses of Martyrdom in English Literature, 1563–1694*, John Knott states, "no fact was too insignificant to note" for Besse's *Collection*.[56] Besse, like Protestant martyrologist John Foxe, seems to have used every resource at his disposal. This resulted in some unevenness in the description of particular sufferers, but that should not be interpreted as an indication that some suffering was of greater importance. Rather, some Quakers have longer entries in the *Collection* because more information was available to Besse concerning the circumstances of their suffering, such as mittimuses, warrants, letters, petitions to magistrates or parliament, reconstructions of trials, and individual accounts.[57] Besse's other major source was the "Original Book of Sufferings," which was the result of the Committee on Sufferings' collection of individual meetings' retrospective records of persecution as had been recounted in the letters written and circulated by Fell in the 1650s. The committee sought to persuade King Charles II's government that Quakers had been unjustly persecuted since the beginning of the faith. The "Original Book of Sufferings" was the compilation of those sufferings. This is not as useful a record as Besse's collection because he also consulted the letters of the major manuscript collections, thus providing a more complete account of suffering in the first few decades.[58]

Furthermore, Besse's *Collection* encapsulated Fell's goal of preserving and circulating accounts of suffering and more generally the early Quaker goal of publishing suffering records. The desire to make the early Quakers' suffering known to a wider audience was fulfilled by the mid-eighteenth century. However by 1753, the Quaker church sought to use this publication to help foster an institutionalized memory of the early years. Therefore, Besse's work helped shape not only how the Quakers were perceived by others, but also how they thought of themselves.

John Foxe: The model martyrologist

While collections of accounts of martyrdom were common during the centuries of Catholic authority in the Middle Ages, they became popular expressions of Protestant outcry against seemingly unjust power after the Reformation. Brad Gregory's work *Salvation at Stake* is a useful study of sixteenth-century martyrologies and highlights the similarities and differences among early approaches to the study of martyrdom after the break between Catholic and Protestant churches. Gregory states that "martyr" was a term that was "inextricable from one's religious commitment," meaning that the definition of the term was subjectively interpreted by those within a particular religious community.[59] In the preface to the *Collection*, Joseph Besse states: "A measure of this holy faith, and a sense of this divine support, bore up to the spirits of the people called Quakers, for near forty years, together, to stem the torrent of opposition, equally testifying against prophaneness and immorality."⁶⁰ Thus to understand what martyrdom meant to the Quakers, or any other religious group, one has to examine the ways that members of the faith used the term. It is therefore useful to trace the meaning of "martyr" back to those groups that the Quakers sought to emulate (overtly or otherwise): sixteenth-century Protestants and their model, the early Christians.

The benchmark of English Protestant martyrologies was John Foxe's *Acts and Monuments* or "The Book of Martyrs," initially published in 1563. Foxe fled to the continent like many Protestants of the era, where he participated in a community of Protestant martyrologists, or as Gregory calls it, "an international community of committed, educated Protestants and shared convictions about the Christian past, the plight of present Protestants, and the hope for the future of the Gospel that reached beyond martyrology per se."⁶¹ At this point, Foxe began the collection of material for his first martyrology that focused on the Lollards of the fifteenth century and the Henrician martyrs. When Queen Mary pursued the persecution of Protestants in 1555, Foxe expanded his work and shifted the focus to the Marian Martyrs. Four editions were published during Foxe's lifetime, in 1563, 1570, 1576, and 1583. Each subsequent edition included more material than the previous one. Foxe died in 1587, and five posthumous early modern editions were published, which included materials beyond the scope of his work on the early Protestants and included groups that were persecuted after his death. Those editions came out in 1596, 1610, 1631/32, 1641, and 1684.

As part of the Elizabethan Settlement, it was ordered that every parish in England was to have a copy of the *Book of Common Prayer* and of John Foxe's *Acts and Monuments*.⁶² While there are no accurate records of the application of this policy, by the mid-seventeenth century the vast majority of godly Englishmen would have been aware of, if not familiar with, Foxe's "Book of Martyrs." The majority of early Quakers belonged to such parishes. Anne Myles notes that the New England missionary Mary Dyer would have been well versed in Foxe's martyrology: "Like any English Protestant, Dyer would have had Foxe's Book of Martyrs and similar works deeply ingrained as a pattern for understanding both her own and Friends' collective experience."⁶³ Margaret Spufford notes that several Quaker meeting houses in Buckinghamshire were former locations of Lollard meetings "five generations before" the Quakers met there in 1689.⁶⁴ As described in Chapter 1, many future Quaker meetings corresponded with earlier dissenting communities. Furthermore, David Como points out the prevalence of radical ideas in the areas where Quakerism first developed, noting the overlap between Grindletonian and Quaker communities in the Midlands and northern England.⁶⁵

John Foxe's influence resurged at times of heightened anti-Catholicism. Gregory names seventeenth-century editions of *Acts and Monuments* in relation to the anti-papist sentiments of the time: In 1605 there was the "Deliverance from Gunpowder Plot" edition, in 1632 the "Look out for

Laud" edition, in 1641 the "Puritans Ascendant" edition, and the "No Popish Princes!" edition of 1684.[66] The existence of so many reprintings of the text demonstrates the revival of Protestant desires for a more purified church throughout the seventeenth century. The widespread acceptance of Foxe's ideas shows anti-Roman sentiments, but also indicates an array of Protestant perspectives throughout this era. Foxe's pro-Protestant agenda was supported by what Brett Usher states was the unique circumstance of Foxe's living under a Protestant regime.[67] Foxe's purpose was to show how "the martyrs' words and deeds were brilliant flashes of triumph in the flesh-and-blood spiritual battle that God and Satan waged in every age, and in every human being."[68] His martyrology was meant to bring all Protestants together in order to present a united front against their Catholic persecutors. However, as Gregory notes, Protestant sects that fought with their fellow reformers "chagrined" Foxe because he was incorporated into the dissenters' histories who "repudiated the English church," specifically mentioning George Fox and the Quakers among those who used Foxe's work.[69] Knott states that Besse seems more exhaustive than Foxe because he organized his text chronologically, covering each county and country where Quakers traveled.[70] It was also due to the fact that Besse benefited from Fell's organizational efforts, while Foxe did not have a similar resource.

Quakers and sixteenth-century martyrologists alike looked to the early Christian martyrs for their inspiration. This transformed their narratives into Christian histories and not exclusively accounts of martyrdom. Therefore, the model of Quaker suffering accounts and subsequent martyrologies was essentially narrative history punctuated with primary documents. Seventeenth-century Quakers, as well as Besse in the eighteenth century, attempted to achieve the same end: They sought legitimacy through suffering and superiority by demonstrating how corrupt their persecutors were.

Quakers living a century after the first appearance of John Foxe's *Acts and Monuments* similarly sought to vilify all religious and state authorities who disagreed with the Friends' agenda and punished them for their perceived indiscretions. A key distinction, however, between Foxe and the Quakers of the seventeenth century was that the basis of the *Acts and Monuments* was anti-Catholicism, whereas the Quakers were standing in opposition to a Protestant religious institution. They were reviled by virtually all of their contemporaries and were seen as outside of the Protestant milieu. Furthermore, while Foxe sought to unite all Protestants in their stance against Catholicism, Quakers sought to distance themselves from their Protestant predecessors and neighbors.[71] Despite this difference, Foxe's work on the Marian martyrs became the model for Joseph Besse's work on Quaker martyrs.

The recognition by Quakers of their place in the Protestant tradition in England is directly related to Foxe's martyrology. Early Quakers understood that they came from a tradition of dissent, which further suggests that they believed they were continuing a process of reform. Their almost certain familiarity with Foxe's work on Protestant martyrs supports this point because it is this aspect of their predecessors' behavior that Quakers emulated most exactly. Quaker scholars have largely ignored this point. One exception is Rosemary Moore who states that Quakers did not believe they were in any way connected to their dissenting ancestors. She claims that because they did not specifically reference early modern Protestant martyrs in their records, one cannot assume that they saw themselves as part of a Protestant martyrdom tradition. However, she does concede that "it is quite likely that the style of Sufferings tracts was influenced by memories of the *Book of Martyrs*."[72] She argues that Foxe's *Acts and Monuments* was not a model for Quakers when they started collecting sufferings because they were "forward thinking."

This seems counterintuitive because familiarity with the format of Foxe's work would have made them aware of the stories of early modern martyrs. Whether Quakers set their sights forward or backward seems a moot point when assessing the likely source of their focus on recording perceived persecution. Outside of the excitement of the Interregnum and creation of the church, subsequent Quakers would have been able to see the similarities between their suffering records and the martyrologies on which they were based. This is especially true given that the martyrs described in Foxe's work thought of themselves as imitating the early Christian martyrs, not their contemporaries or medieval martyrs. Moore says that for the Quakers, "examples they referred to were invariably biblical."[73] But in the cases of both sixteenth-century martyrs and the Quakers, they saw their immediate predecessors as having misrepresented the true church, hence the need for further reformation. If the Marian martyrs were theologically correct, the Quakers would not have needed to suffer a century later. Thus, Besse, working in the mid-eighteenth century, would have been comfortable copying Foxe's format once the flush of excitement about creating something new had worn off. Therefore whether the Quakers or their subsequent apologists acknowledged the connection, one did in fact exist between Foxe's *Acts and Monuments* and Besse's *Collection*.

In contrast to Rosemary Moore's claim, John Knott argues that the Quakers, specifically Besse, were not only aware of *Acts and Monuments* but also deliberately intended to emulate Foxe's work. Knott states: "Besse's two folio volumes constitute what amounts to a Quaker version of Foxe's *Acts and Monuments* ... [Besse] clearly saw himself as presenting a drama akin to Foxe's saga of protestant martyrdom." He goes on to acknowledge that Quakers emulated Foxe even before the publication of Besse's work as "part of the effort of Quaker leaders to justify their resistance to persecution by placing themselves in a tradition of martyrdom whose origins they found in the Bible."[74] Whereas Foxe's "periodization scheme ... synthesized themes from the Book of Revelations, English history and church history, patterns of persecution and martyrdom, and Protestant theology," Besse built upon this accepted knowledge of Christian martyrdom and added

Quaker experiences to this tradition.[75] Knott states that "Besse, like Foxe, albeit for a much shorter time period, relies on the accumulation of detail to convey the enormity of the persecution suffered by the faithful and the magnitude of their spiritual victory."[76] Foxe's *Acts and Monuments* "was a mirror in which the early Quakers saw what they looked for, among other things a faith denied by the refusal to swear oaths."[77]

Ultimately, Besse successfully emulated Foxe's martyrology. Reading the *Collection*, one determines that there were innumerable instances of suffering in the first decade of Quakerism. While the equation of suffering with martyrdom may be less convincing to some, it was an idea that was well received by those sympathetic to this notion. Thus, this Quaker martyrology should be considered along with other early modern texts that celebrate the sacrifices of religiously persecuted people of the era. Furthermore, Fell's contribution to this process requires further examination, too. Besse's tome would not have been possible without Fell's Interregnum efforts, a consideration that has been largely ignored heretofore.

Besse and Quaker memory of suffering

The success of Besse's work solidified the theory of egalitarian suffering and martyrdom, which was fully developed by the mid-eighteenth century. In the period between the inchoate movement and Besse's publication, Quakers ceased to be perceived as a threat to their English neighbors or the state. They were no longer seen as subversive once it became clear that they did not intend to overthrow the government and were clearly not capable of destroying the Restoration church. By the time the Act of Toleration became law in 1689, Quakers had been around for more than 30 years, and both they and their neighbors had adapted to their presence. As a result, Quakers no longer needed to highlight the suffering of a few individuals who were persecuted the most during the early years. Instead, the memory of early suffering shifted away from the few to a remembrance of the entire first generation. When Besse was commissioned to work on the *Collection*, it was not so eighteenth-century Quakers would remember Fox and Fell, but rather so they could see them as part of a moment of intense suffering that allowed the contemporary church to thrive.[78] By this time it was no longer necessary to persuade themselves and others of Quaker legitimacy through their suffering. Therefore, what started in the Interregnum was completed within the first century of growth from a movement into a church.

The overwhelming majority of people discussed in Besse's *Collection* were not leaders of the early Quaker movement. Instead, the majority of entries are similar to the following, which describes the mundane suffering of Quakers outside of the inner circle: "Eight for refusing to take the Oath of Allegiance, when tendered them by three officous Justices, who had come to a Meeting on purpose to apprehend them, vix. John Whitehead, Richard Hunt, John Cunningham, Robert Ball, Edward Andrews, Stephen Marshall,

Josias Bringham, and James Brierly."[79] This type of entry is repeated throughout Besse's work. For example, "John Evans of Englescomb, a Man of a considerable Estate, was taken up as a Vagrant at Wells, but eleven Miles from Home, and carried before a Justice of the Peace, who, because he appeared before him with his Hat on, committed him to Prison, where he lay about four Months."[80]

Persecution for hat honors was another mundane reason for imprisonment or suffering, like the above example of refusing to take an oath:

> The first instance of Persecution in this County was that of John Porter, a Man liscensed to sell Wares up and down the Country. He being, on a First-day of the Week, at the House of Richard White in Wickhamslyth, as he sat reading in a Book published by one of his Friends, Edward Harvey, a Justice of the Peace, came in with a Constable, and snatcht the Book out of his Hand, saying, You Rougue, what will you not pull off your Hat to the Protector? You are senducing Fellow, and read seducing Books: You shall be bound to appear at the Sessions, or go to Prison. Accordingly he gave Bond, and did appear at the Sessions, where the Majority of the Justices, at the Persuasion of the said Justice Harvey, seemed determined against him. Harvy, an embitter'd Man, on this Occasion turned Informer, and took his Oath, that the said John Porter did carry a Pack at his Back, and sold Quaker Books. Porter produced his License for traveling in the Way of his Trade, signed by five or six Justices and Officers, but the Court would take no Notice of it: They sentenced him to be whipt: which Sentence was most barbarously executed on the Market-day at Mendlesham, where the poor Man, tied by his Hands, was hung up on a Butcher's Spirket, till the cruel Execution gave him above twenty Stripes with a three-corded Whip, so that the Flesh and Skin hung in Flakes torn in piece on his Back, a miserable Sight, exciting Compassion even in the Hard-hearted among the Spectators.[81]

This is a rather lengthy description of a minor offense. From this we gather that seemingly insignificant acts could result in severe punishments. Furthermore, this example demonstrates that Besse included all of the information available to him, largely preserved in letters and local meeting records, to illustrate how prevalent suffering was for early Quakers.

Examples such as this are the most common sort of entry in Besse's text. Knott states that Besse plays up the "tragic scene" of dramatic examples of suffering such as the four "indisputable martyrs" who were hanged in New England.[82] Yet a thorough reading of Besse's *Collection* contradicts this statement. Based on the sources that Besse used, it is inaccurate to imply that Besse gave more attention to high profile suffers like the New England martyrs than he did to those who did not die from suffering. Knott notes that Besse used all available materials in his collection. While the passages concerning the New England martyrs are quite lengthy in comparison to many other entries, it is safe to assume that this spectacular event generated more materials for Besse to use. It was therefore not because Besse hoped to make a greater case for these Quakers' martyrdom, but rather that he had more material to write about their experiences. If someone lost a cow due to tithes, as in the case of Quaker John Bristow, and many documents were generated from that event, all evidence suggests that Besse would have devoted several pages to the pain and suffering experienced due to losing livestock. Furthermore, as Knott notes, Besse pays the same respects to leading itinerant Frances Howgill who died in prison as he did to Bristow's loss of cattle, hence denying the claim that the New England martyrs garnered more attention because of the severity of their suffering.[83] Therefore Besse remained fairly consistent about egalitarian reporting of suffering. Knott calls this Besse's "inclusiveness" which had a "democratizing effect" because his work included more than leaders of the movement.[84] The reason for this is that he used the sources available—those letters that Fell archived and preserved.

While it does not appear that there was any greater favor given to any Quakers in Besse's work, there is one exception to this rule: George Fox. Writing in the mid-eighteenth century, Besse viewed Fox as the undisputed founder of the group by the time that Besse published his work. This preferential status was apparent in two significant ways. First, there are far more references to Fox than to any other early Quaker. This is not because Fox was imprisoned or suffered so much more than other itinerant ministers; rather, entries concerning Fox were generally longer, including a petition or mittimus, which makes sense given that Besse's sources came from Fox's wife's home, Swarthmoor Hall. Fell's handiwork as Fox's champion is most apparent in this instance.

Second, Fox was always listed first in each section. This applies to larger entries in which he is the focus and in smaller examples where he is listed first among a group of people persecuted. In one of the earliest examples of Fox's suffering, Besse describes an episode in Cumberland in 1653: "George Fox, for preaching the Truth in the great Worship-house at Carlisle, after the Priest had ended his Sermon, and for witnessing a good Confession before the Magistrates and People there, was imprisoned seven Weeks, sometimes among Thieves and Murderers."[85]

Besse describes another instance of Fox's suffering when he was imprisoned in Lancashire in 1652. He states: "George Fox, preaching in this County, met with a Multitude of Abuses from the ignorant People, animated by designing Priests, whose Interest his Doctrine opposed. He endured the Insults, Beatings, Stonings, Kickings, Railings, Revilings, and Contradictions of Sinners with Christian Patience and Magnanimity."[86] Again, in Cornwall in 1655, Besse lists Fox's group suffering first: "The earliest Prosecution of the People called Quakers in this County appears to be that of George Fox, Edward Pyott, and William Salt, who traveled together, and preaching the Gospel, were taken into Custody, and, under Guard of House, sent to Prison."[87] It seems unlikely that all of Fox's sufferings occurred earlier than any other for each given county and year. Rather, it is clear that Besse followed Fell's lead when he made the slight adjustment of his egalitarian rule to mention Fox before all others in order to show a gesture of deference to the man who had become the established leader of Quakerism, or rather the sufferer before all other sufferers.

While there are not many examples of leaders receiving fewer references in Besse than the letter record would indicate were due, the case of James Nayler is a stark contrast to George Fox. Nayler is mentioned three times to Fox's 23 mentions. Instead of many descriptions of the numerous sufferings listed in the letters, Besse's work describes Nayler only in the context of group suffering. In 1656 in Devonshire, Nayler is listed among many Friends who suffered imprisonment:

> The Imprisonment of several in this County, and others in Cornwall, included many of their Brethren from several Parts of the Nation to visit them, and it was usual with some as they passed, to declare their own Experience of the Virtue of true Religion to the People: This alarmed the Justices, who made an Order of Sessions to apprehend, as Vagrants, all Quakers traveling without a Pass, in Consequence of which, above twenty Persons in the Months called July and August this Year, were sent to Exeter Goal, namely Elizabeth Cutland, Jane Bland, John James, James Naylor, Samuel Carter, John Brown.[88]

There is no description of Nayler's suffering following the affair in Bristol in 1656; rather, those who suffered because of Nayler's actions are given attention. The narrative recorded in the letters that Fell preserved is reflected when Besse describes imprisonments following mob attacks, and public beatings are described as: "Thomas Robinson and Josiah Cole, having first been grievously abused by the Populace, and dragged bareheaded under the Spouts in Time of Rain. John Smith, after he had been sorely beaten, and his Clothes torn by the Rabble. John Waring, Henry Waring, Margaret Thomas, and Elizabeth Marshall, after having been miserably misused by the Mob."[89] This is not surprising, given those writing after the Nayler Affair wrote at length about the persecution they experienced because of the negative attention that Nayler brought on the Quakers. Furthermore, given the friction that existed between Fox and Nayler, it should be expected that any subsequent memories would favor the former at the detriment of the latter.

Besse's description of Margaret Fell demonstrates how this work is more than a collection of sufferings. It is also a history of early Quakerism. While Fell did suffer imprisonment and personal sufferings in the later part of the seventeenth century, she did not "suffer" in the conventional sense during the Interregnum. Besse discusses Fell in terms of her intervention for suffering Quakers or her relationship to those who suffered. Fell's name appears on seven pages in all of Besse's work, and four of those are part of an extensive description of events in Lancashire in the 1660s. Another reference concerns events in Devonshire in 1661, which are beyond the parameters of this study. The two remaining descriptions, both technically within the Restoration as well, occurred in 1660. The first concerns her intervention on the behalf of those suffering in Bristol: "This was the Consequence of representing to the King the Grievous Sufferings sustained by them, from the Soldiers; which was repeatedly done by Margaret Fell, who with unwearied Application procured a second Proclamation as a Supersedes to the former, prohibiting the Officers and Soldiers from entering Houses without a legal Warrant."[90] The second time Besse mentions Fell in the context of the Interregnum reads: "In the Month called June of this Year, four Constables came with a Warrant to the House of Margaret Fell at Swarthmore, where they apprehended George Fox, and carried him before Henry Porter, Mayor of Lancaster, who examined him as follows."[91] Obviously this is not actually about Fell's suffering experience. Thus in these examples, Margaret Fell is mentioned in order to set the stage for subsequent suffering, as she did not personally suffer at this time. The most likely explanation for this is that her suffering was not recorded and later used in communal collections. This does not mean that her contemporaries saw her experiences as invalid, but that the experiences were not recorded as such.

Unlike the exceptional examples of Fell, Fox, and Nayler, Besse's work focuses on average suffering experiences. It provides the best, concise collection of average Interregnum Quaker sufferings because it includes such a wide array of causes and punishments meted out. Two such examples occurred one after the other in Essex in 1659: "John Pollard was also imprisoned in Colchester Castle fourteen Months, in the Upper Bench five Months, and in the Fleet some Years After. Sarah Cadney of Much-Braxsted had taken from her, for Tithes, by Distress, two Cows worth 11 [pounds]."[92] Again, one sees the egalitarian approach to suffering, and no punishment was too insignificant to be noted.

The preface demonstrates this approach, as well. Besse does not introduce each phase of suffering with lengthy descriptions of historical context; rather, he limited the background to a preface to the entire two-volume work:

> A Measure of this holy Faith, and a Sense of this divine Support, bore up the Spirits of the People called Quakers, for near forty Years together, to stem the Torrent of Opposition, equally testifying against Prophaneness and Immorality, on the one hand, and Superstition and Will-worship on the other. ... The Messengers of it were entertained with Scorn and Derision, with Beatings, Buffetings, Stonings, Pinchings, Kickings, Dirtings, Pumpings, and all Manner of Abuses from the rude and ungoverned Rabble: And from the Magistrates, who should have been their Defenders, they met with Spoiling of Goods, Stockings, Whippings, Imprisonments, Banishments, and even Death Itself.[93]

This passage demonstrates how each type of suffering and all of the people who suffered in the initial period of the movement received a group introduction that addresses a wide array of types of persecution, instead of singling out any individual martyrs.

However, there are examples of formatting that are similar between Foxe and Besse. At times, Foxe listed brief information on several individuals under a single section heading, such as, "W. Coker, W. Hopper, H. Laurence, R. Colliar, R. Wright and W. Stere."[94] It is clear here that Foxe's work was organized around specific individuals, but presumably he did not have enough information on any of these people to sustain an entire section for each person. Again, there is a brief introduction to all of these individuals in which Foxe states that he groups them together because they were all from Kent and were subjected to the same sufferings and form of martyrdom. After that broad general statement he singles out some other individuals:

> Elizabeth Warne, widow of John Warne, upholsterer, martyr, was burnt at Stratford-le-bow, near London, at the end of August 1555. ... George Tankerfield, of London, cook, born at York, aged twenty-seven, in the reign of Edward VI had been a papist; but the cruelty of the bloody Mary made him suspect the truth of those doctrines which were enforced by fire and torture. Tankerfield was imprisoned in Newgate about the end of February, 1555, and on August 26, at St. Alban's, he braved the excruciating fire, and joyfully died for the glory of his Redeemer.[95]

The result is that while John Foxe focused on the sacrifices made by individual Protestants, Besse's literary organization is more compelling because his work is punctuated with dramatic examples of execution or death in prison. In contrast, everyone in Foxe's work was a martyr in the traditional sense.

The key difference between Foxe's and Besse's works is that while the Marian martyrs suffered at the hands of the state more often than from angry townsmen, Quakers experienced abuse from "hostile crowds" more often than from legal authorities.[96] This is apparent in the above examples in which Foxe criticizes the royal authority, namely Mary I, whereas Besse first accuses "rude ungoverned rabble." This demonstrates the change that occurred between the mid-sixteenth and eighteenth centuries from the oppressed standing in opposition to the state in Foxe to Besse's case against unsympathetic neighbors.

The later editions of *The Acts and Monuments* included sects that were persecuted subsequent to Foxe's death. The last seventeenth-century edition included radicals of the Interregnum and highlighted Quaker sufferings. While the description of the early Quakers is full of inaccuracies, it does reflect the consensus around George Fox that was undisputed by the time of its publication in 1684. In it, Fox's suffering is singled out. Certainly while Fox disputed any connection to Protestant persecution, he would have appreciated Quakers being included in the most important martyrology of the early modern period.

Besse's *Collection* is the realization of the Quaker ideal of egalitarianism because it treated all sufferers, with the notable exception of George Fox, as equally valuable to the church. During the Interregnum, Margaret Fell highlighted some individuals in the letter network in order to promote stability and Fox's vision of Quakerism. However, by the mid-eighteenth century, the religion was stable, the "age of prophets" was over, and everyone's sacrifices through suffering could be remembered and celebrated. Besse's text thus shows the shift away from an elite inner circle to the memorial of everyone who lived through the inchoate period. It signals the Quakers' success of surpassing the time in which they had to rally behind a few individuals for their survival. By the eighteenth century, Quakers had become just another Protestant group that could trace its lineage back to the Marian martyrs and Apostles before them. They no longer had to isolate themselves, but rather could see themselves as part of the Protestant tradition.

Notes

1. Richard T. Vann, "Friends Sufferings: Collected and Recollected," *Quaker History* 61.1 (Spring 1972): 25.
2. Knott, *Discourses of Martyrdom in English Literature*, 223.
3. Ibid.
4. J. R. Collins, "The Church Settlement of Oliver Cromwell," *History* 87 (2002): 18–40.
5. Pestana, "The Quaker Executions as Myth and History," 447.
6. MSS vol. S81/44. Thomas Salthouse and Myles Halhead to Margaret Fell: Exeter, February 9, 1656.
7. See Chapter 4 for discussion of biblical usage of life and death.
8. MSS vol. S81/47. Myles Halhead to Margaret Fell: No date or location provided.
9. Pestana, "The Quaker Executions as Myth and History," 447.
10. Brad Gregory, *Salvation at Stake: Christian Martyrdom in Early Modern Europe* (Cambridge, MA: Harvard University Press, 1999), 195.
11. Carole D. Spencer, "Holiness: he Quaker Way of Perfection," *Quaker History* 92–93 (2003): 125.
12. Gregory, *Salvation at Stake*, 50.
13. Ibid.
14. Spencer, "Holiness: the Quaker Way of Perfection," 125.
15. The various ways that early Quakers evoked comparison to Christians of late antiquity can be found in Chapter 4.
16. MSS vol. S81/44. Thomas Salthouse and Myles Halhead to Margaret Fell: Exeter, February 9, 1655.
17. Matt. 16:24–26.
18. Braithwaite, *The Beginnings of Quakerism*, 404.
19. Ibid.
20. Myles, "From Monster to Martyr: Re-Presenting Mary Dyer," 6.
21. Braithwaite, *The Beginnings of Quakerism*, 404.

22. Joseph Besse, "The Memory of the Faithful Revived or An Alphabetical List of the Names of more than three Hundred of the people called Quakers, who laid down their Lives in Person or through cruel usage, for their constancy in Religion, together with A Summary Account of the Causes of their Imprisonment, and of the Deaths of Each of them." Unpublished manuscript, Friends House Library, London.
23. The basis of this manuscript was the letters exchanged amongst the early Quakers, which were subsequently housed in the Quaker library.
24. MSS 301/224.
25. MSS 301/13.
26. MSS 301/155.
27. MSS 301/31.
28. MSS 301/18.
29. MSS 301/65.
30. MSS 301/118.
31. MSS 301/7, 15, and 19.
32. Kate Peters, *Print Culture and the Early Quakers* (Cambridge: Cambridge University Press, 2005), 203. She does not provide a manuscript reference for this quotation, and it is not in the letters I have transcribed. I have yet to find the specific reference for this.
33. Ibid.
34. Ibid.
35. Peters, *Print Culture and the Early Quakers*, 9.
36. Penry Williams, *The Later Tudors: England 1547–1603* (Oxford: Clarendon Press, 1995), 468.
37. MSS vol. 378/40, and Peters, *Print Culture and the Early Quakers*, 68.
38. MSS vol. 364/1. Margaret Fell to Thomas Fell: Location unknown, February 18, 1653.
39. Pestana, "The Quaker Executions as Myth and History," 448.
40. Miller, "A Suffering People," 74.
41. Norman Penny, "Ellis Hookes," *Journal of the Friends' Historical Society* 1 (1903–1904): 15. For historiography on Fell's role in creating meetings and importance of meetings to early church, see: Su Fang Ng, "Marriage and Discipline: The Place of Women in Early Quaker Controversies," and Bonnelyn Young Kunze, "'Poore and in Necessity': Margaret Fell and Quaker Female Philanthropy in Northwest England in the Late Seventeenth Century," 559.
42. Pestana, "The Quaker Executions as Myth and History," 448–56. Richard Vann states, "After 1710 there were only three publications of any importance, and by now the era of retrospective compilations had begun." "Friends Sufferings: Collected and Recollected," 24. Vann omits most of those discussed above in favor of John Whiting's *Persecution Expos'd* from 1715 and Besse's 1730 *Abstract of the Sufferings of the People Call'd Quakers*, along with his final 1753 comprehensive *Collection*.
43. *ONDB*, "Joseph Besse."
44. Miller, "A Suffering People," 74.
45. Norman Penney, "The Story of a Great Literary Venture," *Journal of the Friends' Historical Society* 23.1–2 (1926): 1. Very little has been written on the systematic collecting and publishing of early Quaker sufferings in the eighteenth century. The only work that explicitly deals with this topic is a 1926 article from

The Journal of the Friends' Historical Society, written by the journal's editor and the Society of Friends' head archivist, Norman Penney. While the archival work is certainly accurate, this article was written for a Quaker audience; Penney makes unsubstantiated assertions like "George Fox constantly urged Friends to record the occasions of sufferings" without any explanation of why these efforts were necessary or the basis for such a statement.

46. Penney, "The Story of a Great Literary Venture," 1–2.
47. *Yearly Meeting Minutes*, vol. vi, p. 399, from Penney, "The Story of a Great Literary Venture," 2.
48. Penney, "The Story of a Great Literary Venture," 8.
49. Ibid.
50. Ibid., 10.
51. Ibid., 2.
52. Ibid., 4.
53. Ibid., 9.
54. Ibid., 8.
55. Ibid.
56. Knott, *Discourses of Martyrdom in English Literature*, 219.
57. Ibid., 218.
58. Vann demonstrates that the Great Book of Sufferings was not Besse's main source by pointing out discrepancies between the two sources. See "Friends Sufferings: Collected and Recollected" for a fuller discussion.
59. Gregory, *Salvation at Stake*, 5.
60. Besse, *A Collection of Sufferings of the People Call'd Quakers*, iii.
61. Gregory, *Salvation at Stake*, 168.
62. Williams, *The Later Tudors*, 468.
63. Myles, "From Monster to Martyr: Re-Presenting Mary Dyer," 14.
64. Spufford, *The World of Rural Dissenters*, 21.
65. Como, *Blown by the Spirit*, 268.
66. Gregory, *Salvation at Stake*, 194.
67. Brett Usher, "'In a Time of Persecution': New Light on the Secret Protestant Congregation in Marian London," in *John Foxe and the English Reformation*, ed. David Loades (Aldershot, UK: Scholar Press, 1997), 233.
68. Gregory, *Salvation at Stake*, 196.
69. Ibid., 195.
70. Knott, "Joseph Besse and the Quaker Culture of Suffering," in *The Emergence of Quaker Writing: Dissenting Literature in Seventeenth-Century England*, ed. Thomas N. Corns and David Loewenstein (London: Frank Cass and Company Ltd., 1995), 128.
71. David Loades, *John Foxe: An Historical Perspective* (Brookfield, VT: Ashgate, 1999), 9. It is important to note that Quakers were often accused of being Catholic. While this is mentioned earlier in this text, it is interesting that the book that they based their suffering records on was the essential sixteenth-century attack on Catholicism, and no one described by Foxe could have been misconstrued as a Catholic sympathizer.
72. Moore, *The Light in Their Consciences*, 161.
73. Ibid., 128.
74. Knott, "Joseph Besse and the Quaker Culture of Suffering," 218.

75. Donna B. Hamilton, "Theological Writings and Religious Polemic," in *A Companion to English Renaissance Literature and Culture*, ed. Michael Hattaway (London: Blackwell, 2002), 594.
76. Knott, "Joseph Besse and the Quaker Culture of Suffering," 127.
77. Ibid., 223.
78. Richard Vann, Carla Pestana, and others note that the shift also incorporated an eighteenth-century de-emphasis on prophecy and miraculous achievements. See Pestana, "The Quaker Executions as Myth and History," and Vann "Friends Sufferings"—the appendix in Vann's *The Social Development of English Quakerism* (Cambridge, MA: Harvard University Press, 1969) also includes a discussion of the censorship of Friends' journals (pp. 214–16).
79. Besse, *A Collection of the Sufferings of the People Call'd Quakers*, 76.
80. Ibid., 583.
81. Ibid., 657–58.
82. Knott, "Joseph Besse and the Quaker Culture of Suffering," 220.
83. Ibid., 219.
84. Ibid., 130.
85. Besse, *A Collection of the Sufferings of the People Call'd Quakers*, 127.
86. Ibid., 300.
87. Ibid., 113.
88. Ibid., 149.
89. Ibid., 41.
90. Ibid., 43.
91. Ibid., 305.
92. Ibid., 194.
93. Ibid., iii.
94. John Foxe, *The Acts and Monuments of the Church; Containing the History and Sufferings of The Martyrs: Wherein Is Set Forth at Large the Whole Race and Course of the Church, From the Primitive Ave to These Later Times. With a Preliminary Dissertation on the Difference between the Church of Rome that Now Is, and the Ancient Church of Rome That Then Was* (New York: Robert Carter and Brothers, 1856), xx.
95. Ibid., 292.
96. Knott, "Joseph Besse and the Quaker Culture of Suffering," 219.

Conclusion

The first generation of Quakers followed a path quite similar to those of many religious organizations, including the early Christians. The movement experienced something like a life-cycle: birth, growth, maturation, and the eventual demise of the sect as it transitioned into a stable church. In this particular case, Quakerism was born out of the godly environment of the early 1650s by providing a religious answer to Seekers' questions and alternatives to those dissatisfied with other sectarian options. While some individual congregations were content with the message of a charismatic itinerant minister, it was hardly a substantial movement prior to 1652. The nucleus of Quakerism was confined to the North Midlands and a handful of preachers with a simple message. What stimulated a change was the first meeting at Swarthmoor Hall and Margaret Fell's conversion. Early on, she was just like any convinced Seeker, but her contribution proved to be much more than any of her contemporaries. Further, what made this community different than other Interregnum sects was not simply its message, but the infrastructure that it developed in order to make sure the movement grew and evolved.

Once a Quaker entity was established, it defined itself and changed in a variety of ways, and Fell was conscientiously involved in all of them. In order to maintain the missionary efforts provided by an active itinerancy, Fell developed and maintained the extensive letter network. After the illustrious meeting in 1652, Swarthmoor Hall became the northern headquarters for the movement and a clearinghouse for letters. Itinerants traveled and wrote to Fell at her home, which was a base of operations and a respite from the weariness of the road. By deciding which letters to copy and send throughout the network, Fell helped promote George Fox to a position of authority; however, there were challenges to the authority that Fell and Fox worked to establish, most notably the Nayler Affair of 1656. Fox emerged from this conflict as the undisputed leader of the movement, which rapidly transitioned into a church. In terms of the sociology of religion, in the mid-1650s the Quakers experienced the transition from a religious group's itinerant phase, which was naturally followed by the more stable period of institutional development. Fell, as keeper of the records, was able to promote one version of the events that threatened to fracture the group, thus promoting Fox and allowing the once ill-defined movement to transition into a church.

Throughout this process the nascent Quakers were fully conscious of their intention to recreate the primitive, apostolic Christian church. Examining Fell's letters, along with those of others in the movement, and her use of scripture provides insights into Quaker theology, as well as the community's methods to emulate the early church fathers. The language used in letters demonstrated an intentional imitation of Christian forebears in how members described themselves, discussed their enemies, approached suffering, and even revealed their awareness of the existence of antecedent religious letter networks. The Apostle Paul stood out for both Fox and Fell as an example to follow when working to spread their message. While Fell and others often attributed beatific titles to Fox, it was Fell who served a similar function for the early modern Quakers that Paul did in the first century. Moreover, the Quaker ambition to live like the Apostles signaled to them, if no one else, that they had successfully returned to the primitive church.

Like the earliest Christians, Interregnum Quakers created an identity based on their experience of suffering for their faith. In addition to knowingly behaving in a manner that resulted in persecution, particularly imprisonment, leading members of the movement realized the benefit of recording their sufferings. Fell's maintenance of the letters sent throughout the network provided the source material for these sufferings. The Quaker approach to suffering echoed elements of their theology, particularly the idea that all suffering, no matter how small or seemingly insignificant, should be recorded and remembered. Yet, those who suffered the most deserved greater recognition and did receive it in the letters that Fell circulated in the Interregnum network. Thus, Quakers celebrated the enduring painful consequences their fellows experienced for spreading their truth.

The denouement of the early Quaker process came with the Restoration and the eventual cessation of persecution. It is difficult to see the subtlety of change from the end of the Interregnum to the return of the monarchy; however, by looking back from the eighteenth century and the ways that the early years of the movement were memorialized we see a clearer picture. The suffering that was celebrated in the 1650s and recorded by Fell became the basis of the greatest Quaker martyrology or hagiographic history. It also solidified the egalitarian spirit of Quaker approaches to suffering and extended that notion to martyrdom, as well. Any loss of the self for the greater good of the movement was revered and celebrated in Joseph Besse's *Collection of the Sufferings of the People Call'd Quakers,* which reverberated John Foxe's *Acts and Monuments* from a century before and placed the Quakers among a long history of suffering and martyrdom. Besse used the letters that Fell maintained as the basis of his suffering accounts, so the memory that she designed became institutionalized by the 1750s. It is clear that within a century, Fell's efforts to promote Fox to leadership had come to fruition and that Besse's work was the realization of Fell's objective.

Conclusion

In order to better understand the early Quakers and their role in early modern England, one must first reassess the people who played specific roles in its development. Margaret Fell has certainly been discussed in the past, but in a manner that diminishes certain aspects of her contribution to the faith while over-emphasizing other aspects. While she herself was flawed—particularly regarding her attitude toward women in the movement—as much as the historiography of her role has been flawed, her successful orchestration of a system that allowed the group's beliefs to flourish is due greater consideration. Neither Fox nor Quakerism could have survived the Interregnum, and certainly not the Restoration, without the stability and ingenuity that Margaret Fell provided.

As this book has argued, Fell's role in the creation of Quakerism, Quaker martyrology, and Quaker memory has been understated and often misinterpreted. In the beginning of the Quaker movement, Fell provided credibility through her station in society and personal connections with judges and magistrates. Furthermore, Fell's home gave itinerant ministers a base of operations and a spiritual center. They traveled and sent letters to her because they could trust that Fell—despite being based in remote Lancashire—would share news of successful conversions and persecutions endured for the faith. This gave her an immense amount of responsibility and power over how the movement grew and changed over time. She selected which letters to copy and circulate, resulting in Fell's exerting great influence over the content and tone of information that propelled the movement. She maintained the notion of Fox's being both a messianic and Pauline figure and, whether through censorship or careful promotion, prevented the rise of anyone else to the position of utmost authority.

Fell's control of the letter network resulted in the creation of an institutional memory. Prioritizing the experiences of suffering and martyrdom allowed Fell to focus the attention of the news circulating throughout the network on those who were imprisoned the most, Fox being one of those who spent a large portion of the Interregnum in jail. By the eighteenth century, Fell's vision of the community that she helped create was firmly established. Even beyond the narrative that Quakers created for themselves, they are now remembered how Fell envisioned them.

Bibliography

Adams, Beverly. "The Experience of Defeat Revisited: Suffering, Identity and the Politics of Obedience among Hertford Quakers, 1655–65." In *Religion in Revolutionary England*. Edited by Christopher Durston and Judith Maltby. Manchester: Manchester University Press, 2007.
Albrey, William. "The Persecutions of Sussex Quakers (1655–1690)." *Sussex County Magazine* 7 (1933).
Anderson, A.B. "A Study in the Sociology of Religious Persecution: The First Quakers." *Journal of Religious History* 9 (1977).
Anderson, Alan. "The Social Origins of the Early Quakers." *Quaker History* 68, no. 1 (1979).
Anderson, Benedict. *Imagined Communities: Reflections on the Origin and Spread of Nationalism*. London: Verso, 1991.
Bacon, Margaret Hope. *Mothers of Feminism: The Story of Quaker Women in America*. Philadelphia: Friends General Conference, U.S., 1997.
Barbour, Hugh. *The Quakers in Puritan England*. New Haven: Yale University Press, 1964.
——— . "Ranters, Diggers, and Quakers Reborn: A Review Essay." *Quaker History* 64, no. 1 (1975).
Barrow, Henry. "Writings of Henry Barrow." In *Elizabethan Non-Conformist Texts*, Vol. III, edited by Leland H. Carlson. London: Routledge, 2003.
Baxter, Richard. "Autobiography." In *Calendar of the Correspondence of Richard Baxter, Volume One: 1638–1660*, edited by Geoffrey Nuttall. Oxford: Oxford University Press, 1991.
Beaver, Daniel. *Parish Communities and Religious Conflict in the Vale of Gloucester, 1590–1690*. Cambridge, MA: Harvard University Press, 1998.
Bell, Mark. "Freedom to Form: The Development of Baptist Movements during the English Revolution." In *Religion in Revolutionary England*, edited by Christopher Durston and Judith Maltby. Manchester: Manchester University Press, 2007.
Besse, Joseph. *A Collection of the Sufferings of the People Call'd Quakers for the testimony of a good conscience, from the time of their being first distinguished by that name in the year 1650 to the time of the act commonly called the Act of Toleration granted to Protestant dissenters in the first year of the reign of King William the Third and Queen Mary in the year 1689*. London: Luke Hind, 1753.
——— . "The Memory of the Faithful Revived or An Alphabetical List of the Names of more than three Hundred of the people called Quakers, who laid down their Lives in Person or through cruel usage, for their constancy in Religion, together with A Summary Account of the Causes of their Imprisonment, and of the Deaths of Each of them." Unpublished manuscript, Friends House Library, London.

Bibliography

Bittle, William G. "Religious Toleration and the Trial of James Naylor." *Quaker History* 73, no. 1 (1984).
Blackwood, B.G. "Agrarian Unrest and the Early Lancashire Quakers." *Journal of the Friends' Historical Society* 51, no. 2 (1966).
Braithwaite, William C. *The Beginnings of Quakerism*. Cambridge: Cambridge University Press, 1912.
———. "Early Friends' Experience with Juries." *Journal of the Friends' Historical Society* 50, no. 4 (1964).
———. "Early Tithe Prosecutions: Friends as Outlaws." *Journal of the Friends' Historical Society* 49, no. 3 (1960).
———. *The Second Period of Quakerism*. London: Macmillan, 1919.
Bruyneel, Sally. "Margaret Fell: Historical Context and the Shape of Quaker Thought." *Quaker Religious Thought* 95, no. 4 (2000).
———. *Margaret Fell and the End of Time: The Theology of the Mother of Quakerism*. Waco, TX: Baylor University Press, 2010.
Bunyan, John. *The Pilgrim's Progress*. Edited by Roger Pooley. New York: Penguin Classics, 2009.
Butler, David M. "Friends' Sufferings 1650 to 1688: A Comparative Summary." *Journal of the Friends' Historical Society* 55 (1998).
———. "Untolerated Meeting Houses." *Journal of the Friends' Historical Society* 58, no. 3 (1999).
Cadbury, Henry J. "The Antiquity of the Quakers." *Friends' Quarterly* 7, no. 2 (1953).
———. "Friends and the Law." *Friends' Quarterly* 10, no. 1 (1956).
———. "A Quaker Approach to the Bible" (1953). Guilford College. Accessed on December 28, 2014. http://universalistfriends.org/printable/cadbury_printable.html.
Capp, Bernard S. "Godly Rule and English Millenarianism." *Past and Present* 52 (1971).
Carlson, Eric Josef. *Religion and the English People, 1500–1640*. Kirksville, MO: Thomas Jefferson University Press, 1998.
Carroll, Kenneth L. "Early Quakers and Going Naked as a Sign." *Quaker History* 67, no. 2 (1978).
Cherry, Charles L. "Enthusiasm and Madness: Anti-Quakerism in the Seventeenth Century." *Quaker History* 74, no. 2 (1984).
Clarke, Elizabeth. *Politics, Religion, and the Song of Songs in Seventeenth-Century England*. London: Palgrave, 2011.
———. "Religious Verse." In *A Companion to English Renaissance Literature and Culture,* edited by Michael Hattaway. London: Blackwell, 2002.
———. "Women in Church and in Devotional Spaces." In *The Cambridge Companion to Early Modern Women's Writing,* edited by Laura Lunger Knoppers. Cambridge: Cambridge University Press, 2009.
Clement, Olivier. "Martyrs and Confessors." *The Ecumenical Review* 52, no. 3 (July 2000).
Coggan, Donald. *The Revised English Bible with the Apocrypha*. Cambridge: Cambridge University Press, 1996.
Cole, Alan. "Quakers and the English Revolution." *Past and Present* 10 (1956).
———. "The Social Origins of the Early Friends." *Journal of the Friends' Historical Society* 48, no. 3 (1957).

Collins, J. R. "The Church Settlement of Oliver Cromwell." *History* 87 (2002).
Collinson, Patrick. *Godly People: Essays on English Protestantism and Puritanism.* London: Continuum, 1983.
Como, David. *Blown by the Spirit: Puritanism and the Emergence of an Antinomian Underground in Pre-Civil-War England.* Stanford, CA: Stanford University Press, 2004.
Corns, Thomas N., and David Loewenstein (Editors). *The Emergence of Quaker Writing: Dissenting Literature in Seventeenth-Century England.* London: Frank Cass and Company Ltd., 1995.
Couchman, Jane, and Ann Crabb. "Form and Persuasion in Women's Letters, 1400–1700." In *Women's Letters across Europe, 1400–1700: Form and Persuasion.* Edited by Jane Couchman and Ann Crabb. London: Ashgate, 2005.
Covington, Sarah. *The Trial of Martyrdom: Persecution and Resistance in Sixteenth-Century England.* South Bend: Notre Dame University Press, 2003.
Crawford, Patricia. "Historians, Women, and the Civil War Sects 1640–1660." *Parergon* 6 (1988).
———. *Women and Religion in England, 1500–1720.* London and New York: Routledge, 1993.
Cressy, David. *Coming over: Migration and Communication between England and New England in the Seventeenth Century.* Cambridge: Cambridge University Press, 1987.
Damrosch, Leopold. *The Sorrows of the Quaker Jesus: James Nayler and the Puritan Crackdown on the Free Spirit.* Cambridge: Harvard University Press, 1996.
Dandelion, Ben Pink. *The Creation of Quaker Theory.* Burlington, VT: Ashgate, 2004.
———. *A Sociological Analysis of the Theology of Quakers: The Silent Revolution.* Lewiston: Edwin Mellen Press, 1996.
Davies, Adrian. *The Quakers in English Society, 1655–1725.* Oxford: Clarendon Press, 2000.
Davis, J.C. *Fear, Myth, and History: The Ranters and their History, 1649–1984.* New York: Cambridge University Press, 1986.
———. "Fear, Myth, and Furor: Reappraising the Ranters." *Past and Present* 129 (1990).
———. "Living with the Living God: Radical Religion and the English Revolution." In *Religion in Revolutionary England.* Edited by Christopher Durston and Judith Maltby. Manchester: Manchester University Press, 2006.
Daybell, James. "'I wold wyshe my doings myght be ... secret': Privacy and the Social Practices of Reading Women's Letters in Sixteenth-Century England." In *Women's Letters across Europe, 1400–1700.* Edited by Jane Couchman and Ann Crabb. Aldershot and Burlington, VT: Ashgate, 2005.
———. "Letters." In *The Cambridge Companion to Early Modern Women's Writing.* Edited by Laura Lunger Knoppers. Cambridge: Cambridge University Press, 2009.
———. *The Material Letter in Early Modern England: Manuscript Letters and the Culture and Practices of Letter Writing, 1512–1635.* Basingstook, Hampshire: Palgrave Macmillan, 2012.
Disbrey, Claire. "George Fox and Some Theories of Innovation in Religion." *Religious Studies* 25, no. 1 (1989).
Durnbargh, Donald F. "Baptists and Quakers—Left Wing Puritans?" *Quaker History* 62, no. 2, (1973).

Durston, Christopher. *Cromwell's Major-Generals: Godly Government during the English Revolution*. Manchester and New York: Manchester University Press, 2001.

Durston, Christopher, and Judith Maltby. *Religion in Revolutionary England*. Manchester: Manchester University Press, 2006.

Eales, Jacqueline. "'So many sects and schisms': Religious Diversity in Revolutionary Kent, 1640–1660." In *Religion in Revolutionary England*. Edited by Christopher Durston and Judith Maltby. Manchester, England: Manchester University Press, 2007.

Edwards, Thomas. *Gangraena*. London: 1646.

Erbery, William. *Apocrypha*. London: 1652.

Ezell, Margaret. *The Patriarch's Wife: Literary Evidence and the History of the Family*. Chapel Hill and London: The University of North Carolina Press, 1987.

Farr, David. "John Hodgson: Soldier, Surgeon, Agitator, and Quaker?" *Journal of the Friends' Historical Society* 58, no. 3 (1999).

Fell, Margaret. "Women's Speaking Justified." London, 1666.

Feola, Maryann S. *George Bishop: A Seventeenth-Century Soldier Turned Quaker*. York: William Sessions Ltd., 1996.

Feola-Castelucci, Maryann S. "'Warringe with Ye Worlde': Fox's Relationship with Nayler." *Quaker History* 81, no. 2 (1992).

Foucault, Michel. *Discipline and Punish: The Birth of the Prison*. New York: Pantheon Books, 1977.

Fox, George. *The Journal of George Fox*. Edited by John L. Nickalls. Cambridge: Cambridge University Press, 1952.

Foxe, John. *The Acts and Monuments of The Church; Containing the History and Sufferings of The Martyrs: Wherein Is Set Forth at Large the Whole Race and Course of the Church, From the Primitive Ave to These Later Times. With a Preliminary Dissertation on the Difference between the Church of Rome that Now Is, and the Ancient Church of Rome That Then Was*. New York: Robert Carter and Brothers, 1856.

George, C.H. "Puritanism as History and Historiography." *Past and Present* 41 (1968).

Gibson, John. "Letters." In *A Companion to English Renaissance Literature and Culture*. Edited by Michael Hattaway, London: Blackwell, 2002.

Gill, Catie. *Women in the Seventeenth-Century Quaker Community: A Literary Study of Public Identities*. London: Ashgate, 2005.

Glines, Elsa F. *Undaunted Zeal: The Letters of Margaret Fell*. Richmond, IN: Friends United Press, 2003.

Greaves, Richard. *Deliver Us from Evil: The Radical Underground in Britain, 1660–1663*. New York: Oxford University Press, 1986.

———. *Dublin's Quaker Merchant: Anthony Sharp and the Community of Friends, 1643–1707*. Stanford: Stanford University Press, 1998.

———. *Enemies under His Feet: Radicals and Nonconformists in Britain, 1664–1677*. Stanford: Stanford University Press, 1990.

Greaves, Richard, and Robert Zaller. *Biographical Dictionary of British Radicalism in the Seventeenth Century*. Brighton: Harvester Press, 1983.

Greene, D.G. "Muggletonians and Quakers: A Study in the Interaction of Seventeenth-Century Dissent." *Albion: A Quarterly Journal Concerned with British Studies* 15, no. 2 (Summer 1983).

Gregory, Brad. *Salvation at Stake: Christian Martyrdom in Early Modern Europe*. Cambridge, MA: Harvard University Press, 1999.

Gwyn, Douglas. "Joseph Salmon: from Seeker to Ranter—and Almost to Quaker." *Journal of the Friends' Historical Society* 58, no. 2 (1998).

Habermas, Jurgen. *The Structural Transformation of the Public Sphere: An Inquiry into Bourgeois Society*. Cambridge, MA: MIT Press, 1989.

Hamilton, Donna B. "Theological Writings and Religious Polemic." In *A Companion to English Renaissance Literature and Culture*. Edited by Michael Hattaway. London: Blackwell, 2002.

Hammond, Gerald. "Translations of the Bible." In *A Companion to English Renaissance Literature and Culture*. Edited by Michael Hattaway. London: Blackwell, 2002.

Harwich, Judith J. "The Social Origins of the Early Quakers." *Past and Present* 48 (1970).

Hayden, Judith. *In Search of Margaret Fell*. London: Quaker Books, 2002.

Herrup, Cynthia. "Law and Morality in Seventeenth-Century England." *Past and Present* 106 (1985).

Hessayon, Ariel. *"Gold Tried in the Fire": The Prophet Theaurau John Tany and the English Revolution*. Aldershot, England: Ashgate, 2007.

Hibbert, G.K. "Quakerism: A Religion of the Spirit: A Study in Origins." *Friends' Quarterly* 1, no. 1 (1947).

Hill, Christopher. *Economic Problems of the Church, from Archbishop Whitgift to the Long Parliament*. Oxford: Clarendon Press, 1956.

———. *The Experience of Defeat: Milton and Some Contemporaries*. New York: Viking Penguin, 1984.

———. "Parliament and People in Seventeenth-Century England." *Past and Present* 92 (1981).

———. "Quakers and the English Revolution." *Journal of the Friends' Historical Society* 56, no. 3 (1992).

———. *The World Turned upside down: Radical Ideas during the English Revolution*. New York: Penguin Books, 1972.

Hinds, Hilary. *George Fox and Early Quaker Culture*. Manchester: Manchester University Press, 2011.

———. "Prophecy and Religious Polemic." In *The Cambridge Companion to Early Modern Women's Writing*. Edited by Laura Lunger Knoppers. Cambridge: Cambridge University Press, 2009.

Horle, C.W. "John Camm: Profile of a Quaker Minister during the Interregnum." *Quaker History* 71, no. 1 (1982).

———. "Quakers and Baptists 1647–1660." *Baptist Quarterly* 26 (1976).

———. *The Quakers and the English Legal System, 1660–1688*. Philadelphia: University of Pennsylvania Press, 1988.

Horrell, David. "Leadership Patterns and the Development of Ideology in Early Christianity." *Sociology of Religion* 58, no. 4 (Winter 1997).

Huntington, Frank C. "Quakerism during the Commonwealth: The Experience of the Light." *Quaker History* 71, no. 2 (1982).

Hurwich, Judith J. "The Social Origins of the Early Quakers." *Past and Present* 48 (1970).

Ingle, H. Larry. *First among Friends: George Fox and the Creation of Quakerism*. Oxford: Oxford University Press, 1994.

———. "The Future of Quaker History." *Journal of the Friends' Historical Society* 58, no. 1 (1997).

———. "From Mysticism to Radicalism: Recent Historiography of Quaker Beginnings." *Quaker History* 76, no. 2 (1987).
———. "Richard Hubberthorne and History: The Crisis of 1659." *Journal of the Friends' Historical Society* 56, no. 3 (1992).
James, Sydney V. "Review of *The Beginnings of Quakerism* by William C. Braithwaite." Revised and annotated by Henry J. Cadbury, *The William and Mary Quarterly* 19, no. 2 (April 1962).
Jones, R. Tudor. *Protestant Nonconformist Texts, Volume 1, 1550–1700*. Aldershot: Ashgate Publishing, 2007.
Jones, Rufus. *The Faith and Practice of the Quakers*. London: Metheun and Co., 1927.
———. *Mysticism and Democracy in the English Commonwealth*. New York: Octagon Books, 1965.
———. *Studies in Mystical Religion*. New York: Macmillan and Co., 1909.
Kent, S.A. "The 'Papist' Charges against the Interregnum Quakers." *Journal of Religious History* 12 (1982).
Kim, Chrysostom. "The Diggers, the Ranters, and the Early Quakers." *American Benedictine Review* 25 (1974).
King, John. *The Godly Women in Elizabethan Iconography*. New York: Renaissance Society of America, 1985.
Knott, John R. *Discourses of Martyrdom in English Literature, 1563–1694*. Cambridge: Cambridge University Press, 1993.
———. "Joseph Besse and the Quaker Culture of Suffering." In *The Emergence of Quaker Writing: Dissenting Literature in Seventeenth-Century England*. Edited by Thomas N. Corns and David Lowewenstein. London: Frank Cass and Company Ltd., 1995.
Kunze, Bonnelyn Young. *Margaret Fell and the Rise of Quakerism*. Basingstoke: Macmillan, 1993.
———. "'Poore and in Necessity': Margaret Fell and Quaker Female Philanthropy in Northwest England in the Late Seventeenth Century." *Albion* 21, no. 4 (1989).
———. "Religious Authority and Social Status in Seventeenth Century England: The Friendship of Margaret Fell, George Fox, and William Penn." *Church History* 57 (1988).
Lake, Peter, and Steven Pincus. "Rethinking the Public Sphere in Early Modern England." *Journal of British Studies* 45, no. 2 (2006).
Lamont, William. "The Muggletonians, 1652–1979." *Past and Present* 99 (May 1983).
Lewis, Enoch, and Samuel Rhoads. *Friends' Review: A Religion, Literary and Miscellaneous Journal* Vol. 20. Charleston, SC: Reprinted by Nabu Press, 2011.
Lister, Douglas G. "Shorthand as a Seventeenth Century Quaker Tool: Some Early Shorthand Systems and Their Use by Friends." *Journal of the Friends' Historical Society* 51, no. 3 (1967).
Loades, David. *John Foxe: An Historical Perspective*. Brookfield, VT: Ashgate, 1999.
———. *John Foxe and the English Reformation*. Aldershot: Scholar Press, 1997.
Loewenstein, David, and John Marshall (Editors). *Heresy, Literature, and Politics in Early Modern English Culture*. Cambridge: Cambridge University Press, 2006.
Loukes, Harold. *The Discovery of Quakerism*. London: G.G. Harrap, 1960.
Mack, Phyllis. *Visionary Women: Ecstatic Prophecy in Seventeenth-Century England*. Berkeley: University of California Press, 1992.

Marsh, Christopher. *The Family of Love in English Society, 1550–1630.* Cambridge: Cambridge University Press, 1994.
Marshall, John. "Defining and Redefining Heresy up to Locke's *Letters Concerning Toleration.*" In *Heresy, Literature, and Politics in Early Modern English Culture.* Edited by David Loewenstein and John Marshall. Cambridge: Cambridge University Press (2006).
Martin, W.J. "Elizabethan Familalists and English Separatism." *Journal of British Studies* no. 1 (1980).
Massey, Vera. *The Clouded Quaker Star: James Naylor, 1618–1660.* York, England: Sessions Book Trust, 1999.
McClendon, Muriel, Joseph P. Ward, and Michael MacDonald (Editors). *Protestant Identities: Religion, Society, and Self-Fashioning in Post-Reformation England.* Stanford: Stanford University, 1999.
Miller, John. "'A Suffering People': English Quakers and Their Neighbors c. 1650–1700." *Past and Present* no. 188 (August 2005).
Moore, Rosemary Anne. "Leaders of the Primitive Quaker Movement." *Quaker History* 85, no. 1 (1996).
———. *The Light in Their Consciences: The Early Quakers in Britain, 1646–1666.* University Park: Pennsylvania State University Press, 2000.
———. "Reactions to Persecutions in Primitive Quakerism." *Journal of the Friends' Historical Society* 57 (1995).
More, Henry. *Enthusiasmus Triumphatus.* London: 1656.
Morrill, John. *The Nature of the English Revolution.* London and New York: Longman, 1993.
Morris, Norval, and David J. Rothman (Eds). *The Oxford History of the Prison: The Practice of Punishment in Western Society.* New York: Oxford University Press, 2005.
Mortimer, Russell. "Bristol Quakers and the Oaths." *Journal of the Friends' Historical Society* 43, no. 2 (1951).
———. *Early Bristol Quakerism: The Society of Friends in the City, 1654–1700.* Bristol: Historical Association (Bristol Branch), 1967.
———. "Quakerism in Seventeenth Century Bristol." *Journal of the Friends' Historical Society* 38 (1946).
Mozley, J. F. *John Foxe and his Book.* New York: Octagon Books, 1970.
Mullett, Michael. "George Fox and the Origins of Quakerism." *History Today* 41, no. 5 (1991).
Myles, Anne G. "From Monster to Martyr: Re-Presenting Mary Dyer." *Early American Literature* 36, no. 1 (2001).
Ng, Su Fang. "Marriage and Discipline: The Place of Women in Early Quaker Controversies." *The Seventeenth Century* 18, no. 1 (2003).
Nuttall, Geoffrey. *The Beginnings of Nonconformity.* London: J. Clarke, 1964.
———. *Early Quaker Letters from the Swarthmore MSS to 1660: Calendared, Indexed and Annotated.* London: Friends' House Library, 1952.
———. *The Holy Spirit in Puritan Faith and Experience.* Chicago: University of Chicago Press, 1946.
———. *James Nayler: A Fresh Approach.* London: Friends' Historical Society, 1954.
———. "'Nothing Else Would Do': Early Friends and the Bible." *Friends Quarterly* 22, no. 10 (April 1982).
———. *The Puritan Spirit: Essays and Addresses.* London: Epworth, 1967.

———. *Richard Baxter*. London: Nelson, 1966.

———. *Studies in Christian Enthusiasm*. Wallingford, PA: Pendle Hill, 1948.

———. *To the Refreshing of the Children of Light*. Pendle Hill pamphlet no. 101 (1951).

Peek, Lori. "Becoming Muslim: The Development of a Religious Identity." *Sociology of Religion* 66, no. 3 (2005).

Penney, Norman. "Ellis Hookes." *Journal of the Friends' Historical Society* 1 (1903–1904).

———. "The Story of a Great Literary Venture." *Journal of the Friends' Historical Society* 23, no. 1–2 (1926).

Pestana, Carla Gardina. "The Quaker Executions as Myth and History." *The Journal of American History* 80, no. 2 (September 1993).

Peters, Kate. *Print Culture and the Early Quakers*. Cambridge: Cambridge University Press, 2005.

Reay, Barry. "Popular Hostility towards Quakers in the Mid-Seventeenth-Century England." *Social History* 5 (1980).

———. "Quaker Opposition to Tithes, 1652–1660." *Past and Present* 86 (1980).

———. "The Quakers, 1659, and the Restoration of the Monarchy." *History* 63 (1978).

———. *The Quakers and the English Revolution*. New York: St. Martin's Press, 1985.

———. "The Social Origins of Early Quakerism." *Journal of Interdisciplinary History* 11 (1980).

Rogers, R.M. "Quakerism and the Law in Revolutionary England." *Canadian Journal of History* 22 (1987).

Ross, Isabel. "Early Quakerism in Northern England." *Friends' Quarterly* 6, no. 3 (1952).

———. *Margaret Fell, Mother of Quakerism*. London: Longmans, 1949.

Rowntree, John. *Essays and Addresses*. London: Healdey Brothers, 1905.

Seaver, Paul. "The Puritan Work Ethic Revisited." *Journal of British Studies* XIX, no. 2 (1980).

Sewel, William. *The History of the Rise, Increase, and Progress, of the Christian People Called Quakers: Intermixed with Several Remarkable Occurrences. Written Originally in Low-Dutch, and Also Translated into English*. London: J. Sowle, 1725.

Shami, Jeanne. "Women and Sermons." In *The Oxford Handbook of Early Modern Sermons*. Edited by Peter McCullough and Hugh Adlington. Oxford: Oxford University Press, 2011.

Shideler, Emerson W. "The Concept of the Church in Seventeenth Century Quakerism." *Quaker History* 46, no. 1 (1957).

Shortland, Thomas. *The Lamb's Defense against Lies*. London: 1656.

Spencer, Carole D. "Holiness: The Quaker Way of Perfection." *Quaker History* 92–93 (2003).

Spufford, Margaret. *The World of Rural Dissenters: 1520–1725*. Cambridge: Cambridge University Press, 1995.

Taylor, Ernest E. *The Valiant Sixty*. London: The Bannisdale Press, 1947.

Thickstun, Margaret Olofson. "Writing the Spirit: Margaret Fell's Feminist Critique of Pauline Theology." *Journal of the American Academy of Religion* LXIII, no. 2 (1995).

Thomas, Keith. "Puritans and Adultery: The Act of 1650 Reconsidered." In *Puritans and Revolutionaries: Essays in Seventeenth-Century History presented to Christopher Hill*. Edited by Donald Pennington and Keith Thomas. Oxford: Clarendon Press, 1978.

Tolles, Frederick B. *Quakers and the Atlantic Culture*. New York: Macmillan, 1960.

Trevett, Christine. *Quaker Women Prophets in England and Wales, 1650–1700*. Lewiston, NY: Edwin Mellen Press, 2000.

Underdown, David. "The Independents Reconsidered." *Journal of British Studies* 3, no. 2 (1964).

Underwood, T.L. *Primitivism, Radicalism, and the Lamb's War: The Baptist-Quaker Conflict in Seventeenth-Century England*. Oxford and New York: Oxford University Press, 1997.

Usher, Brett. "'In a Time of Persecution': New Light on the Secret Protestant Congregation in Marian London." In *John Foxe and the English Reformation*. Edited by David Loades. Aldershot, UK: Scholar Press, 1997.

Vann, Richard T. "Friends Sufferings: Collected and Recollected." *Quaker History* 61, no. 1 (Spring 1972).

———. "From Radicalism to Quakerism: Gerrard Winstanley and Friends." *Journal of the Friends Historical Society* 49, no. 1 (1959).

———. "Quakerism and the Social Structure in the Interregnum." *Past and Present* 43 (1969).

———. *The Social Development of English Quakerism*. Cambridge, MA: Harvard University Press, 1969.

Warner, Michael. *Publics and Counterpublics*. New York: Zone Books, 2002.

Watts, Michael. *The Dissenters*. Oxford: Clarendon Press, 1978.

Webster, Tom. "Preaching and Parliament, 1640–1659." In *The Oxford Handbook of the Early Modern Sermon*. Edited by Peter McCullough, Hugh Adlington, and Emma Rhatigan. Oxford: Oxford University Press, 2011.

Williams, Penry. *The Later Tudors: England 1547–1603*. Oxford: Clarendon Press, 1995.

Worden, Blair. *The Rump Parliament, 1648–1653*. Cambridge: Cambridge University Press, 1974.

Index

Abraham, John 23
Act of Toleration 152, 168
Acts 5:19 111
Acts 9:5 97
Acts 9:22 114
Acts 13:50 113
Acts 16: 22–23 114
Acts 21:8 84
Acts 24:16 99
Acts and Monuments: model for Besse 151, 152, 166, 167, 168, 173, 179; most important English martyrology 165, 166
Adams, Elizabeth 34
Aldam, Thomas: prisoner at York Castle 12–13, 14, 57; as author of pamphlet 15, 59; as advocate of Fox's censorship 16, 45; as author of newsletter 17, 54; as intended recipient of letter 62; with concern about female preaching 87; using term "Friend" 116
Aldersgate London 20
Ames, William 25
Anabaptism 8, 44, 46
Andrews, Edward 168
Antinomianism 115
Apostolic Christianity: as model for Fell's letter network 6, 94, 98; as model for Baptists and/or Quakers 45, 95, 113, 151, 159; evoked with Quaker use of Scripture in letters 93, 137
Appleby Prison 13, 15
Archer, Judge John 111
Atherton, Oliver 56, 157
Atkinson, Christopher 18, 19, 20, 21, 22, 29
Audland, Ann 25, 109, 130, 141
Audland, John: as itinerant minister 17, 18, 19, 54; reporting on James Parnell's death 23; as author of newsletter 25, 55, 57; concerning James Nayler 26–28, 30, 32; regarding lost letters 60; calling Fell a maternal figure 74
Audley, Richard 159
Austin, Ann 22, 25
Ayray, Agnes 19

Bacon, Christopher 158
Baker, Edward 159
Ball, Robert 168
baptism, opposition to water 111, 112
Baptist Church: prior to convincement to Quakerism 10, 44, 79, 153; Quaker conflicts with 20, 21, 23, 96; Quaker cooperation with 32–33; comparison to Quakers 94–95, 102, 129
Barrow, Henry 43
Barton, Nathan 11
Bateman, Myles 25
Baxter, Richard 135
Behemenism 47
Bennett, Justice Philip 11
Benson, Francis 101
Benson, Gervase 57, 134, 160
Besse, Joseph 162, 163, 168, 169, 170, 171, 173
Bishop, George 28, 161
Blacklaine, Ann 133
Blackley, Justice 142
Bland, Jane 26, 87, 171
blasphemy 128, 130
Blasphemy Act of 1650 130
Bond, Christopher 58
Bond, Thomas 21, 51, 58
Book of Common Prayer 160
Braithwaite, John 26, 32, 56, 82, 111
Brewster, Humphrey 158
Bridewell Prison 18, 31, 32
A Brief Narration of the Sufferings of the People Called Quakers 161

Brierly, James 169
Bringham, Josias 169
Bristow, John 170
Brown, John 171
Brownism 33
Brunt, Timothy Westbie 13
Bull and Mouth Pub 20, 24, 31, 33, 52
Bunyan, John 141
Burden, Ann 32
Burden, Thomas 32
Burrough, Edward: as letter recipient 17, 58, 60–61, 145; deference to George Fox 18; as itinerant minister 19, 20, 22–24; coordinator of London Quakers 21; concerning James Nayler 25–28, 56–57; Bull and Mouth meeting 31; regarding Female Preaching 32, 86–87; giving regards to those at Swarthmoor Hall 50; regarding inward suffering 146
Buttery, Isabel 18, 86

Calvert, Giles 20
Camm, John 18, 19, 21, 57
Carter, Samuel 171
Caton Manuscripts 57
Caton, Will: hailing Fox's supremacy 19; itinerancy in Holland 20–21, 29; contradicting Fox's directives 30; concerning Seekers 21; as an itinerant minister 32; calling Quakers "Family of Love" 46; asking to be remembered by Friends 51; as author of typical newsletter 52; example of letter within letter 59; using term "nursing mother" 74; regarding unfair imprisonment 135–136; on meanings of sufferings 144
Cave, James 102
censorship 16, 17
Charles II 100, 152, 161
Children of Light 10, 11, 12, 24, 47, 115
Clarendon Code 152
Clayton, Ann 58, 74
Clayton, Richard 20, 21, 33, 57
Clement, Walter 23, 27, 28, 30, 53, 74, 81, 82
Coale, Josiah 171
Cock, Widow 24
Colchester Prison 23
Cole, Nicholas 51
A Collection of the Sufferings Of the People Call'd Quakers: realization of Margaret Fell's efforts 64, 88, 151; emulation of John Foxe's *Acts and Monuments* 64, 167–168, 179; source of egalitarian Quaker suffering 153, 169, 174; comparison to early Quaker martryologies 161; history of the text 163–164
Collinson, Robert 24
Colossians 1:24 108
Committee on Sufferings 63, 88
Complin, Nicholas 158
Concerning Persecution 152
"conscience sake" 98, 99, 112
Conventicle Act 152
convincement 47, 132, 139, 140
Conway, Lady of Ragley 46
1 Corinthians 1:12 114
1 Corinthians 11:23 106
1 Corinthians 12:13 112
1 Corinthians 14:34 84
2 Corinthians 1:12 95
2 Corinthians 12:5 84
2 Corinthians 13:11 97
Cotton, Arthur 19, 31, 54
Cotton, Priscilla 25
covenant 100, 109, 130, 137, 153, 154, 155
Coward, Elizabeth 33
Cromwell, Oliver 97, 98, 131, 133, 136
Cunningham, John 168
Cutland, Elizabeth 171

Daniel 2:45 97
Davis, Daniel 99, 103
Denham, Cornet's wife 15
Dewsbury, Ann 135
Dewsbury, William: favoring Fox as leader of Quakerism 14; as itinerant minister 15, 31; as prisoner in York 17–18; regarding translation of Fell's work into Hebrew 34; as author of newsletter 54; regarding copies of letters 57, 58; regarding Female Preaching 87; as letter recipient 99–100; on meaning of suffering 143
Dickinson, James 162
disturbing the peace 128
Duncan, Robert 54
Dyer, Mary 32, 156–157, 165

Edwards, Thomas 43
Elizabethan Settlement 165
Elletson, Jeffrey 99, 101, 112
endorsement system 45
Ephesians 2:2 97
Ephesians 4:1 106
Ephesians 5:8 10

Erbury, Dorcas 25, 28, 29, 80
Erbury, Mary 25
Erbury, William 43, 45
Essex Quarterly Meeting 162
Evans, Katherine 55
Exeter Prison 26

Familism/Family of Love 33, 46, 47, 153
Farnsworth, Richard 12, 14, 15, 18, 21, 26, 59
Fell, George 33
Fell, Henry 30–31, 33, 50–51, 53, 56, 61, 109, 129
Fell, Leonard 53
Fell, Margaret: as maternal figure 5, 24, 73, 76, 80, 82, 83, 85, 87; as proto-feminist 5, 73, 76, 85; nee Askew 11; as architect of letter network 42, 49, 84, 86, 89, 93, 94, 97, 105, 109, 117, 128, 140, 142, 152, 155, 156, 160, 170, 179, 180; creating Quaker Memory 43, 45, 63, 81, 82, 83, 86, 88, 89, 110, 113, 151, 168, 179
Fell, Margaret Jr. 51
Fell, Judge Thomas 11, 12, 63, 74, 83, 134, 161
female preaching 73, 77, 79, 80, 83, 85, 87, 88, 180
Fisher, Mary 13, 14, 22, 23, 25, 30, 54
Fisher, Samuel 23, 96, 115
First Publishers of Truth 1, 24, 87
Five Mile Act 152
Fletcher, Elizabeth 17, 88, 132
Fox, George: creating Quaker Memory 43, 45, 63, 81, 82, 83, 86, 88, 89, 110, 113, 151, 168, 179; background 1, 12, 42; image created by Fell 6, 17, 34, 75, 78, 93, 103, 151, 178, 180; as described by Braithwaite 8–9, 11; normal rules don't apply 10; as censor 16, 22–23, 26, 28, 31; concerning James Nayler 25, 27, 33, 83; conflicts with other sectarians 21; as sufferer 63; husband of Margaret Fell 73; regarding female preaching 88; as Pauline figure 109, 114; as martyr 154, 156; in Besse's martyrology 170–172, 174
Foxe, John 147, 164, 166, 168, 173
Friends House Library, London 8, 96

Galatians 5:22–23 110
Ganniclife, Nicholas 27
Gardner, Isabel 75, 80
Garnet, John 105

Geneva Bible 96
Goldborne, Richard 16
Golden, Thomas 53
Gould, Daniel 161
Grant, Edward 159
Great Book of Sufferings 88, 157, 161
Grindletonians 115, 165
Grove, Joseph 162

Halhead, Myles: as itinerant minister-pair with John Lancaster 18; as itinerant minister-pair with Thomas Salthouse 20–21, 55, 136–138; regarding Nayler Affair 30; requesting Fell write to him 56; showing mechanics of letter network 62–63; calling Fell "nursing mother" 74; regarding meaning of suffering 107–109, 143, 153; as prisoner 139–141, 145, 155
Hall, John 32
Harrison, James's wife 26, 87
Harrison, William 53
Harvey, Edward 169
Head, Peter 30
Hebrews 1:8 99
Hebson, Richard 158
Hebden, Roger 17
Henrietta Maria 97, 100, 101, 105
Hickcocke, Richard 31, 33
Hoiknell, William 54
"Hole in the Rock" Prison 135
Holme, Jane 13, 14
Holme, Thomas 17, 22, 23, 24, 25, 132, 137
Hookes, Ellis 152, 161
Hooton, Elizabeth 10, 13, 14, 15, 33, 57, 79, 80, 83
Horton, Humphrey 59
Howgill, Francis: as prisoner 15; as author of newsletter 18, 138; as itinerant minister 19–20; as itinerant minister-pair with Edward Burrough 21–25, 31, 146; regarding Nayler Affair 26–28, 56, 57, 82; explaining how news should be sent 50–51; regarding Female Preaching 86; as martyr 170
Howgill, Mary 26, 30, 87
Hubberthorne, Richard: as itinerant minister 15, 18, 19, 31, 33; regarding imprisonment 17, 20, 107, 130–131, 137, 139; regarding Christopher Atkinson's disgrace 21; regarding James Nayler 25,

27, 30, 81–82; asking Fell to write to him 51; concerning copying letters 56; as author of newsletter 58–59; regarding female preaching 87–88; using the term Friend 116; on meaning of suffering 143
Humble Petition and Advice 130
Hunt, Richard 168
Hunter, Richard 56, 116

Independent Church 21, 44, 46, 153
initials, use of in letters 61
inner light 101, 102, 111, 112, 132
interruption of church services 4, 128
Isaiah 2:21 98
Isaiah 20:3 111, 112
Isaiah 42:1 101
Isaiah 50:6 97
Isaiah 61 97, 110

James 1:17 97
James 2:23 116
James 5:12 112
James, John 171
Jeremiah 3:1 100
Jeremiah 17:9 105
Jessop, Edmund 43
Jesuits, Quakers accused of being 22, 25, 133
John 1:4 101, 102
John 1:5 97
John 1:9 97, 101
John 5:37–38 110
John 8:12 97
John 14:17 99
John 15:14–15 115
John-ap-John 16
Journal of George Fox 64, 74, 75, 77, 89, 113
Jude 1:8–9 104

Kempe, Margery 155
Kendal Fund 22, 32, 60, 61, 75, 56
Killam, Margaret 18
Knipe, William 104, 106, 111, 113

Lamb's War 95, 103, 105, 156
Lampitt, William 11, 12
Lancaster, John 18, 19
Lancaster, Thomas 21
Langstaffe, Joseph 143
Launceston Prison 27
Lawson, John 16, 53, 74
Lawson, Thomas 16, 21, 137

Lathom, George 53
Leavens, Elizabeth 17, 23, 24, 88
Legate Brothers 43
Lloyd, Morgan 15
Lollards 44, 45, 165
Lose, John 33
Luke 15:8–9 84

Magnalia Christia Americana 162
Malachai 3:1–2 97, 100
Manifestarians 21
Marian martyrs 152, 165, 166, 174
Marian statutes 129, 132, 133, 134
Marshall, Elizabeth 171
Marshall, Stephen 168
martyrdom: as detailed in Fell's letter records 128, 136; meanings of martyrdom 147, 151, 153–160, 164–165; Quaker martyrs modeled on John Foxe's *Acts and Monuments* 167–168; in Joseph Besse's martyrology 169–170
Mary I 165, 173
Mather, Cotton 161
Matthew 3:11 112
Matthew 5:18 106
Matthew 5:34 112
Matthew 5:48 97, 102
Matthew 6:22 97
Matthew 7:29 106
Matthew 10:16 104
Matthew 12:24 106
Matthew 15:14 97
Matthew 22:32 102
Matthew 23:34 106
Meeting for Sufferings 151, 161, 163
"The Memory of the Faithful Revived" 157, 158, 159
Micah 6:8 97
"Mildred and Judy" 24, 33
Mission of the 70 20
Moore, Christopher 132
Moore, Edward 53
More, Henry 46, 47
Morford, Thomas 53
Morgan, Elizabeth 33
Moser, Peter 75
Moses, Samuel 60
Muggletonians 20
Myers, James 25, 107

nakedness, as a sign of faith 4, 111, 112, 132
namesake 98, 153

Nayler Affair: as transformative moment in Quakerism 4, 34, 78; description 10; negative affects of 31, 54, 136, 152; generating numerous letters 56–57; criticism of female preaching 80–82; as recorded in Besse's martyrology 171–178
Nayler, James: power struggle with George Fox 1, 24–26, 45, 64, 88; at Swarthmoor Hall 12; as itinerant minister 13, 25; clashes with other sectarians 21; and Nayler Affair 27–33, 80–83; regarding circulation of news 57; aftermath of Nayler Affair 61, 171; meaning of suffering 63; regarding legal matters 134, 136; and martyrdom 154
New England Judged by the Spirit of the Lord 161, 162
Newby, Margaret 60
Newgate Prison 158, 159
newsletters 49, 55, 56
Nicholas, Henry 46
Nicholson, Ann 132
No Cross, No Crown 152
Norton, Humphrey 24
Norwich Castle Prison 19
"nursing mother" 73, 74, 75, 76

oath taking, refusal 111, 112, 113, 168, 169
Ollive, Thomas 54
"Original Records of Sufferings" 151, 161, 164

Parker, Alexander: hailing Fox's supremacy 19; conflicts with other sectarians 21, 33; concerning James Nayler 27; concerning female preaching 30, 88; giving directives in letters 51, 53; praising Fell 55, 145; regarding copies of letters 58
Parnell, James 18, 23, 132, 142, 154
Pattison, Barbara 19
Paul the Apostle: Fell as Pauline figure 6, 179; subjugation of women 84, 87; as example for Quaker letter writers 93, 95, 98, 106–110, 112–115
Pearson, Anthony: family obligations and itineracy 17; clashing with other sectarians 18; negative opinions of 20; contributions to Kendal Fund 22; concerning James Nayler 29; as an itinerant minister 30; complaining about lack of news 56; interception of letters 61; regarding female preaching 86–87; as letter recipient 99, 102; concerning legal matters 134; meanings of suffering 143, 145; recording sufferings 160
Pembroke, Earl of 18, 86
Penn, William 96, 163
Penney, Norman 162, 163
Perrot, John 33
1 Peter 3 112
2 Peter 2:3 97
Philemon 9–10 106
Philippians 1:7 108
Philippians 1:11 108
Philippians 1:28–29 108
piracy 25, 33
Porter, Henry 173
Porter, John 169
Presbyterianism 46, 95
Primitive Christianity Revived 152
Primitivism 43, 94, 146
Psalms 2:9 97
Psalms 7:9 105
puritanism 8, 10, 44, 129, 156
Pyott, Edward 170

Quaker Act 152
quaking 98

Ranterism 11, 20, 30, 33, 46, 47
Ravel, John 111
Rawlinson, Thomas 27, 50, 52, 58, 87, 109
Revelations 14:4 103
Revelations 14:10–11 103
Revelations 17:14 103
Revelations 20:8 105
Revelations 21:27 103
Rigge, Ambrose 21, 55
Righteousness 98, 100
Robertson, Thomas 21, 25, 26, 55, 136
Robinson, Thomas 171
Rogers, Thomas 157
Romans 1 114, 115
Romans 5:35 107
Romans 8:16–18 107
Romans 8:34 106
Romans 14:23 97
Romans 16:2–16 115
Roper, Richard 28, 32, 53
Rous, John 30, 32
Rous, Thomas 53
Rousson, Lt. Col. 50

Sale, Richard 132, 135
Salman, Joseph 30
Salt, William 170
Salthouse, Robert 32, 74
Salthouse, Thomas: member of Swarthmoor household 12; as itinerant minister 20–21, 25, 31, 33, 107; as itinerant minister-pair with Myles Halhead 55–56, 62–63, 108–109, 136–138, 140–141, 143–145, 153, 155; as author of newsletter 29; regarding sending news 53; referring to Fell as "nursing mother" 74; Quaker meaning of scripture 95; regarding God's law 130–131
Sawrey, John 12, 84, 99
Seacoke, Thomas 136
Second Day Morning Meeting 161, 162
Seekerism: as basis of Quakerism 10, 12, 15, 16, 48, 93; definition 43–44
Shattered Baptists 10
Shaw, Thomas 104
Simmonds, Martha 26–33, 80–83, 88
Simmonds, Thomas 21, 26, 30, 62
Slee, John 21, 31
Smith, John 171
Somers, W. 27
Song of Solomon 4:15 97
spirit: unmovable 98, 101, 102
Spooner, John 19
Story, John 20, 64, 78, 138
Stringer, Hannah 27, 29, 80, 81, 82
Stringer, John 31
Stubbs, Elizabeth 62
Stubbs, John: as itinerant minister-pair with Will Caton 20–21; traveling in Holland 21, 23, 30, 60; as author of newsletter 25; concerning James Nayler 27; concerning family matters 31; clashing with other sectarians 32; isolation without news 56; regarding publication of sufferings 161
sufferings: meanings of 6, 142, 143, 144, 145, 146, 151
Swarthmoor Hall: as sectarian meeting place 3, 11, 178; as Quaker headquarters and letter archive 5, 10, 14, 21, 50, 52–54, 57–58, 61–62, 86–88, 128, 151; location 9; household 13, 25, 52; Kendal Fund 75; Women's Monthly Meeting 77
Swarthmore Manuscript Collection 161

Taylor, George: as author of newsletter 19–20, 87; regarding transmission of news 22, 62; concerning James Parnell's death 23; concerning James Nayler 29, 31, 61; Kendal Fund 32, 45, 60; requesting ministers 54
Taylor, Thomas 134
Thee and thou 128
1 Thessalonians 5:5 10, 115
2 Thessalonians 1:4 107
Thomas, Margaret 171
tithes: refusal to pay 157, 162, 172
Tomlinson, Elizabeth 15
Travers, Rebecca 22
Truth and Innocency Defended Against Falsehood and Envy 162
truth: unchangeable 98, 99, 129, 137, 139
"Two Johns" 20, 25, 55, 64, 78

vagabonds/vagrancy 22, 128, 171
Vairy, Agnes 17, 87, 88
Valiant Sixty 1, 64, 76, 80, 161
Vallance, Jane 13, 15

Waller, Richard 23, 32, 53, 74
Wardell, Lancelot 30, 56, 143
Waring, Henry 171
Waring, John 171
Warne, Elizabeth 173
Warne, John 173
Waugh, Dorothy 19
Waugh, Jan 55
Weaver, Richard 16, 59
West, Col. William 110, 133, 134
White Hart Pub 28
White, Richard 169
Whitehall 20, 61
Whitehead, George 19, 21, 54, 163
Whitehead, John 168
Whiting, John 161
Widder, Robert 18, 60, 134
Wilkinson, Agnes 87
Wilkinson, John 20, 64, 78, 138
Willan, Thomas 24, 60, 61, 137, 160
Wilson, George 31
Wilson, Thomas 75
Women's Monthly Meeting 73, 77, 78
Women's Speaking Justified 80, 84, 85
Wooster House 33
Wyndham, Judge Hugh 101

Yearly Meeting Epistles 162
York Castle Prison 12, 15, 17, 132